NORTH PUGET SOUND

Afoot & Afloat

"...continues Marge and Ted Mueller's in-depth look at recreational opportunities in the greater Puget Sound area. With this book in hand, motorists, boaters, bicyclists and pedestrians will have enough information for a summer-full of exploration opportunities in one of the nation's most beautiful locales."
— Janet Ray, Editor, *Washington Motorist* (AAA)

"This most recent addition to the Muellers' *Afoot & Afloat* guides is the capstone for a resource now comprehensive for almost anywhere along Washington's inside waters. They have continued their high standard of thoroughness and accuracy, with plenty of local color and humor to make lively reading."
— Randel Washburne, author, *The Coastal Kayaker* and
Kayak Trips in Puget Sound and the San Juan Islands

"The *Afoot & Afloat* series has been valuable to me in planning my photography outings. This book follows in the footsteps of its predecessors with impeccable accuracy and thorough treatment."
— Pat O'Hara, photographer,
Washington: Images of the Landscape

"A sandy inviting beach, a quiet peaceful cove, quaint shops, good food, friendly people — all are found on North Puget Sound, Washington's treasure."
— Al Koetje, Mayor, City of Oak Harbor

"Our communities and natural environment on the Olympic Peninsula are diverse in their riches. *North Puget Sound* gives the visitor a local's point of view and aptly describes why I live here."
— Brent Shirley, Mayor, City of Port Townsend

"Visitors and residents alike will benefit from the accurate detail the Muellers present. This book is a must for Olympic Peninsula visitors."
— Frank McPhee, Mayor, City of Port Angeles

"Northwest Washington has an intriguing character — Victorian architecture, sparkling coves, and unhurried crossroads. This book captures the flavor of many nooks and crannies reached by car or boat."
— Tim Douglas, Mayor, City of Bellingham

NORTH
PUGET SOUND

Afoot & Afloat

MARGE & TED MUELLER
THE MOUNTAINEERS • SEATTLE

THE MOUNTAINEERS: Organized 1906
". . . to explore, study, preserve and enjoy
the natural beauty of the Northwest."

Published by The Mountaineers
1011 S.W. Klickitat Way, Suite 107, Seattle, Washington 98134

Published simultaneously in Canada by Douglas & McIntyre, Ltd.
1615 Venables Street, Vancouver, British Columbia V5L 2Hl

Edited by Toni Reineke
Cover and text designed by Judy Petry
Maps by Marge Mueller
Cover photos: Squalicum Harbor in Bellingham; inset: Digging for clams

Photo opposite title page: A sea stack on DNR Beach 429, along the Strait
of Juan de Fuca; title page photo: Limpets line a tidepool

Photos by the authors
Printed in the United States of America

Library of Congress Cataloging in Publication Data

Mueller, Marge.
    North Puget Sound, afoot & afloat / Marge & Ted Mueller.
        p.   cm.
    Bibliography: p.
    Includes index.
    ISBN 0-89886-149-7
        1. Outdoor recreation—Washington (State)—Puget Sound.
    2. Outdoor recreation—Washington (State)—Puget
Sound—Directories.
        3. Marinas—Washington (State)—Puget Sound—Guide-books. 4.
Puget
        Sound (Wash.)—Description and travel—Guide-books.   I. Mueller,
    Ted.   II. Title.   III. Title: North Puget Sound.
GV191.42.W2M83 1988
796.5'025'7977—dc 19   88-1808
This book is printed on 80% recycled paper.   CIP

CONTENTS

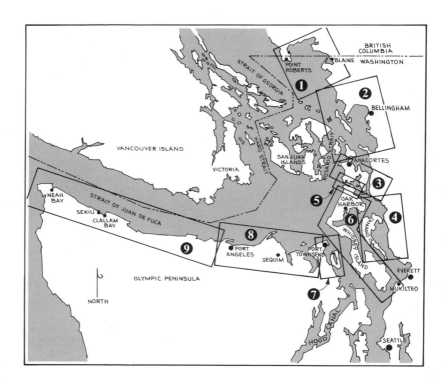

Afoot & Afloat

PREFACE

Many guidebooks are written with a specific activity in mind, telling
people such as bicyclists, paddlers, or clam diggers where to go to better
enjoy their favorite recreation. While the books of our *Afoot and Afloat*
series do cover some activities and areas strictly limited to boaters, we rec-
ognize that boaters frequently leave their vessels to walk beaches, dig
clams, or hike trails in nearby forests, and that some boaters even bring
bicycles with them to widen their explorations.

At the same time, many people who do not own boats love roaming
beaches or hiking bluff tops, enjoying the bite of salt air, the cries of
seabirds, and the rush of waves. The one common thread in this book is
shorelines, and all the activities associated with them, no matter how one
arrives there.

Descriptions of facilities are kept brief, since we feel that such things
as marinas and campgrounds are not ends in themselves, but merely places
that enable one to enjoy the shorelines and water.

Attractions are described in order to entice the visitor to out-of-the-
way spots they might otherwise pass by. Since exploration of any region is
more enjoyable if spiced with some of its history and ecology, information
is included on the historical background and natural life of some of the
areas.

DEFINING PUGET SOUND

The Indians who lived here before the arrival of the white man already
had a name for all of this inland sea: Whulge (loosely translated as "big
saltwater"). Since early explorers were not given to paying much attention
to the desires of the residents, this early name has largely been ignored.
That may be just as well; while the white man's tongue may have learned
to embrace such Indian names as Swinomish and Sequim, Whulge is more
than most English-speaking mouths can handle.

When British sea captain George Vancouver first visited the Pacific
Coast in 1792 and charted these inland waters, he gave the name of
"Puget's Sound" to the channels lying south of the Tacoma Narrows that
had been explored by his lieutenant, Peter Puget. Over the years usage of
that name has been creeping northward, and today most maps and charts

7

show Puget Sound as the waters running south from the entrance to Admiralty Inlet—or south of a line drawn from Port Townsend on the Olympic Peninsula to Admiralty Head on Whidbey Island.

Commonly, however, many local people (as well as some state agencies) today consider Puget Sound to be all of Washington's inland waters running north from Olympia to the Canadian border, and west to the Pacific Ocean. In time the name may be accepted for the entire area by the State Board of Geographical Names, and a long-running problem will be resolved.

In this book, the area that we are calling "North Puget Sound" might, by strict definition, not be considered to be part of Puget Sound at all. The problem is that there is no other tidy name for these waters lying at the entrance to what is "officially" known as Puget Sound. Yet, that's an awful lot of water to go nameless, so by virtue of common usage and by the necessity for this book to have a concise term for the area it covers, "North Puget Sound" it is.

THE NORTH SOUND IN A NUTSHELL

This area is, in many ways, the most interesting and varied of all the inland waters. It ranges from the harsh, wave-worn, rocky shoreline of the Strait of Juan de Fuca to the seeping saltwater marshes of the Skagit delta. Its attractions include beautiful turn-of-the-century towns, unique nature preserves, fascinating old army forts, parks for every possible taste, and the best stretches of boating waters to be found anywhere on the West Coast.

The areas in this book were surveyed over a period of several years and rechecked just prior to publication. Changes to facilities do occur, however. The authors and The Mountaineers Books would appreciate knowing of any changes to facilities so future editions can be updated. Please address comments to: The Mountaineers Books, 306 2nd Ave. W., Seattle, WA, 98119.

Marge and Ted Mueller
February 1988

INTRODUCTION

A recurrent theme throughout this book is the dominant presence of the military on North Puget Sound. We didn't set out to write it that way—it simply became obvious after reading countless bronze plaques and informational displays, browsing dozens of museums, and standing on scores of escarpments gazing out over vulnerable waterways.

The legacy of the military to the recreational public is far more than a few old cannons for delighted 8-year-olds to climb on, or a spate of concrete emplacements picturesquely surrendering to thickets of wild rose at several state parks along the sound. It is the precious land itself, uniquely preserved from early day claim-stakers and latter day developers and eventually delivered into the hands of government agencies for wildlife preservation and public use.

The History of Military Presence in North Puget Sound

At various times in history, military reservations, forts, and naval installations have occupied thousands of acres of prime Puget Sound shoreline, and as strange as the concept may be, many of these have become part of our recreational heritage. While this chain of events may not have been intentional, it is still cause for the beachcomber and birdlover to celebrate —and to look hungrily at other military lands we may yet claim.

But how did this come about?

THE FIRST FORTIFICATIONS

Early North Sound settlers, fearing raids by hostile Haida Indians from Vancouver Island, built strong, two-story blockhouses surrounded by log stockades. Some of these blockhouses dating from the 1850s are now in a National Historical Reserve on Whidbey Island. In 1855 the usually peaceful Puget Sound Indians, angered at being relegated to reservations and encouraged by uprisings east of the Cascades, took part in the short-lived Indian Wars. These hostilities brought the first federal troops to the North Sound the following year, and Fort Townsend, the first such fortification on the North Sound, was established. A second fortification was established at Fort Bellingham in 1856. The Fort Townsend contingent soon had a different adversary, however, when a company of these troops, as well as a detachment from Fort Bellingham, were hustled to San Juan Island in 1859 to counter the British threat during the Pig War boundary dispute. (This, too, eventually resulted in a magnificent park, but that's a different story.)

Fort Bellingham, which had been considered only temporary from the beginning, was abandoned in 1860. Fort Townsend was never a hit with the military, who found it poorly located and with precious little to defend along the sparsely settled shores of Puget Sound, and it was fitfully garrisoned until 1894 when the barracks were accidently destroyed by fire. It was decommissioned a year later, probably with great relief on the part of the Army, but remained a military reservation.

MILITARY LAND ACQUISITION

During the early 1850s, as our nation grew in size and importance, the government became concerned with the defense of its shores, and a Fortifications Board recommended the establishment of land reservations at key locations that might be used for future military defenses. In 1866 President Andrew Johnson set aside twenty-five such parcels of land scattered along the shores of Puget Sound. After the San Juan dispute was settled in 1872 and the islands officially became part of the U.S., seven additional tracts were reserved, commanding the entrances to Griffin Bay, which was to serve as a future harbor of refuge for the Navy.

Military apathy at building forts in such a remote corner of nowhere to defend a mere handful of citizens was further increased by the technical problems involved. The smooth-bore, muzzle-loading coast artillery pieces of the Civil War era had neither the range nor the accuracy to make effective fortifications possible—in short, at a distance they couldn't hit the broad side of a brigantine. To compensate for artillery deficiencies, proposals for lines of defense north of the Tacoma Narrows required one or more forts to be built in the middle of Admiralty Inlet. Needless to say, such expensive fortifications were never cost-justified. By the late 1880s larger, breach-loading, rifled guns improved the range and accuracy of artillery, and coastal defense of Puget Sound became feasible.

At this same time the major navies of the world shifted from sailing vessels to faster steam-powered battleships and cruisers with armor up to 18 inches thick and supporting as many as ten 12-inch guns. Rangefinding and fire control on the bobbing ships was still primitive, however. Land-based guns were technically superior and were now even more necessary to defend against the threat of these iron-clad leviathans.

In the government's view Puget Sound was still sparsely settled and of no ecomomic value, thus the Endicott Board, commissioned by Congress in 1885 to develop a comprehensive plan for coastal defense, recommended no fortifications for this unimportant corner of the country.

THE NAVAL PRESENCE ON PUGET SOUND

Shortly after the end of the Civil War a board of Army Engineers recommended the establishment of a naval station and drydock in the North Pacific. This may have resulted from the embarrassment of large naval and commercial vessels being forced to use the drydocks at Esquimalt, on Vancouver Island, a facility of the British, with whom relations were somewhat strained. Between 1878 and 1880 the Navy surveyed possible sites, and after ten years of commissions, studies, and pork-barrel infighting, finally confirmed a site on the southwestern reach of Port Orchard. Land was acquired in 1891, and the following year construction of the first drydock at Bremerton began.

Ultimately, the presence of the Navy shipyard, the arrival of a transcontinental railroad at Tacoma in 1883, and the recognition of the increasing economic importance of commercial shipping to the Orient and Alaska combined to lead to the approval in 1896 of the fortification of the first line of defense for Puget Sound at Point Wilson, Admiralty Head, and Marrowstone Island. By mid-1897 work had begun at Marrowstone Island, followed shortly by construction at the other locations. The Spanish-American War in 1898 gave added impetus to the need to protect the Pacific Coast.

Fortifications on Admiralty Inlet were completed by 1907, and were turned over to the Coast Artillery as Forts Worden, Flagler, and Casey. The three forts, poised at the entrance to the sound, became known as the "Triangle of Fire," which reputedly could blow to smithereens any enemy ship.

Even before the fortifications were completed the military began to realize that they had serious drawbacks. The guns on Marrowstone Island were poorly placed and had a limited sector of fire, and at the other forts visibility was often severely limited due to fog or smoke from frequent forest fires. Even under the best of conditions it took several minutes to load, aim, and fire each gun, and hitting a fast-moving ship ducking in and out of the fog was nearly impossible. The forts could prevent the enemy from anchoring offshore on a sunny day, but any ship that chose to slip up the sound in the fog could probably do so unchallenged.

An inner line of defense was planned to protect the sensitive Navy shipyard, and in 1898 land was acquired on Rich Passage at Beans Point, Middle Point, and Orchard Point. Mine fields, protected by smaller caliber rapid-fire guns, were to be laid here and at a planned location on Agate Passage in the event of enemy attack. Although the fortifications at Beans Point eventually became Fort Ward, the other sites reverted to caretaker maintenance and never saw the troops originally planned.

Battery Tolles at Fort Worden State Park

TECHNOLOGY MARCHES ON

In the twenty years following the work of the Endicott Board, technology and defensive requirements changed markedly, and in 1905 President Theodore Roosevelt appointed a successor, the Taft Board. This board classified Puget Sound among the ports of first importance and recommended both additional fortifications and heavier armaments at existing forts. Recognizing the visibility problems at Admiralty Inlet, a second line of defense was proposed at Foulweather Bluff and Double Bluff, where military reservations had existed since 1866.

The local artillery officers hotly debated these locations and suggested such alternatives as Old Fort Townsend, Nodule Point, Bush Point, Lagoon Point, and Partridge Point for additional armament. However, before the second line could be approved and implemented, the recommended fortifications became obsolete because of technology advancements during World War I, and they were never built.

The Taft Board also recommended arming Deception Pass to prevent enemy access to Saratoga Passage. Although the pass itself was never fortified in this period, a new fort, Fort Whitman, located on Goat Island, was built and commissioned in 1911 to defend Saratoga Passage.

WORLD WAR I ON PUGET SOUND

With the onset of the World War, Puget Sound military installations took on a new role as tens of thousands of young men were shipped here for training for the European front. Armament was removed from some of the batteries at the forts to be mounted on railway flatbed cars for use in Europe or as defensive guns aboard troop ships. The Navy shipyard tooled up for ship construction as well as repair and was also a training site for Navy recruits.

Battleships now carried 16-inch guns and displayed a dramatic improvement in fire-control techniques and high-angle firing capabilities. With these improvements and the introduction of precision aerial bombing, the coastal forts became not only ineffective, but also very vulnerable.

With the tightening of military funding following the "War to end all Wars," coastal forts reverted to a caretaker status. Only the naval facilities continued to grow as the Pacific Ocean gained an importance once reserved for Europe. The 1920s also saw the disposal of most of the unimproved military reservations in the area; some of these were turned over to local governments for public recreational use. A tract of over 1000 acres at Deception Pass was dedicated as a gorgeous new state park.

In the 1930s many of the older guns and mortars were removed from the Admiralty Inlet forts and melted down. The only additions were antiaircraft batteries, which were effective against both airplanes and torpedo boats. The inner defense lines on Rich Passage ceased to exist as Fort Ward was deactivated and turned over to the Navy in 1930 for their use as a recreation site. Only the Navy Yard at Bremerton continued to expand, partially because it was a convenient funnel for funds to address the critical unemployment conditions of the Depression.

THE SECOND WORLD WAR BRINGS MILITARY REVIVAL

The rumbles of impending war once again breathed life into the Puget Sound military bases in the early 1940s. Major maintenance took place at the remaining batteries at the Admiralty Inlet forts, and they were beefed up with additional searchlights and antiaircraft batteries. A new Harbor Entrance Control Post was activated at Fort Worden to coordinate harbor-defense activities and monitor new secret underwater detection and radar systems. Searchlights and guns were installed at Deception Pass on land requisitioned back from the state park, emplacements for mortars were dug at Cape George, and searchlights were placed at Middle (McCurdy) Point.

Long-debated plans for defenses at Point Partridge finally became a reality with the construction of Fort Ebey in 1942. The last in a series of fixed coastal guns was installed when 6-inch and 16-inch batteries encased in impregnable bunkers were built at Fort Hayden on Striped Peak.

At the Navy Yard a fourth drydock, large enough to accommodate any ship in the fleet, was completed in 1940. Old Fort Townsend was resurrected as a Naval Explosives Laboratory. A new mine and bomb storage facility was constructed at Indian Island in 1941, and in three years was supplemented by another ammunition depot at Bangor on Hood Canal. Dabob Bay became a torpedo test site. Whidbey Island saw the construction of a seaplane base at Oak Harbor and a Naval Air Station at nearby Ault Field.

As the Navy drove the conflict far into the Pacific, the waters of Puget Sound never saw an enemy vessel, and none of its protective guns were fired in anger. The only known damage inflicted occurred when guns at the forts were fired in practice, and the concussion caused local windows to break, plaster to crack, and pictures to fall from walls. At the conclusion of the war most of the military installations quickly reverted to peacetime caretaker status—many for the last time.

THE ERA OF THE PARK

A major benefactor of the demobilization was the Washington State Parks and Recreation Commission, as between the years 1949 and 1972 it acquired Middle Point (Manchester) and Forts Townsend, Casey, Flagler, Ward, Ebey, and Worden. Fort Whitman was acquired by the State Game Department, and Fort Hayden by the State Department of Natural Resources. Most of Fort Lawton became a Seattle city park. Other properties, or portions thereof, went to the management of other governmental agencies for public use.

The Navy presence is still felt in North Puget Sound, however, as the Navy shipyard has continued its growth at Keyport, Bangor, Indian Island, and Whidbey Island. The newest naval presence, the proposed Nimitz carrier group, is currently battling political and environmental barriers preparatory to establishing its base in Port Gardner at Everett. Who knows—if history is prologue to the future, we may now be witnessing the creation of a spectacular waterfront park for Everett citizens of the 21st century. One cannot help but wonder, wistfully, if it might not be wiser to skip the time and tax money involved in the military undertaking and go directly to a park.

Getting Around in North Puget Sound

To Puget Sound pioneers the network of waterways was a tremendous asset. The land was covered with forests so thick that even walking was difficult and road building was a Herculean task; however any of the homesteads and infant milltowns along the shore could be reached by boat with a minimum of effort.

In time, as communities were established, the rowboats and sailing ships of early settlers were joined by steamboats—reliable workhorses that churned through the waters of the sound transporting people, mail, and goods with little concern for the vagaries of weather. The number of little steamers grew to such a number, swarming hither and yon across wide channels and up narrow rivers and sloughs, that one observer referred to them as the mosquito fleet.

Although the automobile and the network of mainland roads it inspired brought to an end 70 years of activity by the steamers of the mosquito fleet, the sound still serves as a primary avenue of transportation for Puget Sound residents. A fleet of state superferries, assisted by a few county-run and privately operated boats, now carries goods and passengers to cross-sound destinations. Commercial ships fill the major channels, transporting goods to and from foreign markets. And every year hundreds of thousands of pleasure boaters use the sound to take them to fabled vacation destinations, such as those described in this book.

For boaters in large craft, most of the areas in the North Sound are within a day or two cruising distance from any other point on the sound, via protected waterways. Only the outer reaches of the Strait of Juan de Fuca present some difficulty in navigating and finding secure anchorages during bad weather.

Trailered or car-top boats are easily transported to any of a multitude of public or commercial launching facilities for quick access to recreation destinations. For those who want to enjoy the shorelines by foot or bicycle, most points on the North Sound are but a half day away from the major metropolitan areas via highway and ferry. Highway I-5 is the main north-south route along the east side of the sound. Most driving directions on the east side are keyed to exits from this thoroughfare.

The Olympic Peninsula—the westernmost point in this book—can be reached by driving south around the end of the sound then north on Highway 101, or by a shorter, but multi-step process of taking ferries from either Seattle or Edmonds, then driving across the Hood Canal bridge. The Olympic Peninsula can also be reached via the Keystone ferry from Whidbey Island.

Public Accesses

Public shorelines along Puget Sound rest in the hands of a variety of different agencies. Most parks are either city-, county-, or state-owned. Another major landholder is the Department of Natural Resources, which holds an extensive inventory of beaches lying below the mean high water level, although in a few cases the adjacent uplands are also included. The

U.S. Fish and Wildlife Service controls most wildlife refuges—in the area covered by this book the refuges at the mouth of the Skagit River and on Dungeness Spit are included in these lands. The State Department of Fisheries, which owns some boat-launch ramps, and the U.S. Bureau of Land Management, which maintains Coast Guard-operated lighthouses, are responsible for some of the smaller segments of public shore lands.

LAUNCHING FACILITIES

Public launching facilities are found at some state, county, and city parks, city marinas, and at sites owned by the State Department of Fisheries. If there are no public ramps nearby, many commercial resorts have either ramps or hoists. In nearly all cases a fee is charged for their use.

The quality and safety of launch facilities range from the sublime—with excellent surface, drop-off, and protection—to the ridiculously hazardous, where boaters risk getting stuck in mud at low tide or having boats reduced to splinters by ever-present winds.

Ramps are not always paved at the extreme tide levels; others are frequently choked by debris. Some ramps open out onto a long tideflat; some drop off very abruptly. Boaters should explore the surface of a ramp before launching to avoid miring the tow vehicle or launching it along with the boat. At times of wind or surges, extra care must be used to avoid damaging the boat or injuring boaters.

Launch facilities tend to change occasionally. Some are neglected due to lack of public funds and become unusable. Commercial ones close down for the season, or even go out of business. On the plus side, sometimes new ones are built or old ones improved. Any discovery of changes to boat-launch accesses should be referred to the authors or The Mountaineers Books so future editions can maintain accuracy.

MARINA FACILITIES

Boating facilities on Puget Sound run the gamut from meager wooden docks clinging to ancient piers to posh resorts complete with full dock hookups for boats and hot tubs for salt-encrusted crews. The information list at the beginning of the various areas includes those items that are of the most interest to captain and crew. "Complete boat and crew facilities" are considered to be: guest moorage with water and power, diesel, gas, marine supplies and repair, groceries, restaurant, restrooms, and showers. Marinas that have more or less than these amenities are noted.

Commercial marinas are operated by local port districts or private individuals. In either case a fee is usually charged for any use of the facilities, including launching. "Private marinas" that are mentioned in the text are open to members only and do not have facilities for visiting boaters.

DEPARTMENT OF NATURAL RESOURCES BEACHES

In the area covered by this book the Department of Natural Resources owns in excess of 80 miles of public shorelands at over 50 separate sites. The majority of these are accessible only by boat, and their usability varies. In some cases boat landing can be so difficult, or the beach drops off so steeply that it precludes any degree of public use. In a few cases, however, such as those lying east of Sequim Bay, the DNR beaches are exquisite tideflats offering extensive walking, beachcombing, and clamdigging opportunities.

When Washington was first established as a state, all tidelands were in the public domain, regardless of upland ownership. These tidelands were gradually sold off to private individuals, until the practice was discontinued in 1969. The remaining beaches that are suitable for public recreation have been inventoried by the DNR and are described in detail in booklets published by that agency. These booklets are listed in the reference section at the back of this text.

For most of the DNR beaches the public area is the tideflat below the mean high water line. On most beaches this would be just below the layer of driftwood or below the beginning of grass, trees, or other terrestrial vegetation. When the uplands are public, it is specifically mentioned in the text.

THE NATURE CONSERVANCY

The Nature Conservancy, a private conservation organization supported by membership and donation, has identified and purchased some environmentally important property on Puget Sound. Most of these areas are held by the organization as nature preserves. Occasionally land is acquired when it becomes available, with the intent to resell it, at cost, to an appropriate government agency when public funds become available. Through the efforts of this group some vital properties have been saved which might have been lost due to the slow turning of bureaucratic wheels. A portion of the Department of Natural Resources land at Eagle Cliff on Cypress Island was acquired by this means.

In general, lands owned by The Nature Conservancy are considered biological preserves and are open to the public for limited use—nature walks are fine, but camping and picnicking are not permitted. In some cases the area may be so sensitive that public visits are not permitted.

Recreation is Diverse

One of the most remarkable aspects of Puget Sound is the variety of activities the water and shoreline engender. It offers something for all ages, from tots experiencing the first squish of sand through toes, to senior citi-

Sailing in Oak Bay

zens enjoying retirement with leisurely beach strolls or boat cruises. Although boating in its various forms is one of the major considerations in this book, it is by no means the only one. Recreation also includes bicycling, beachcombing, hiking, scuba diving, sightseeing, wildlife watching, nature walks, photography, and the most delightful of all pastimes— harvesting and enjoying delectable fish and shellfish.

BOATING

On Puget Sound, boaters take to the water in everything from multi-million-dollar fiberglass "Ferraris" to lung-inflated plastic rafts from the neighborhood drugstore. The majority of local boaters, however, fall well between these two extremes. Along with a variety of craft comes a variety of points of view and areas of concern. The skipper of a high-powered cruiser is less interested in the strength of the tidal current then is a sailboater or a kayaker, but the cruiser captain breaks out in a sweat about water depths that kayakers breeze over.

Chartering. Renting a boat for a day of fishing or exploration, or chartering one for an extended cruise is common on Puget Sound. In the text, places are noted where such boats are available. No matter what size the boat, to attempt boating without somebody experienced on board is folly; many charter operators will check out clients before turning the boat keys over to them. If prospective boaters are obviously unqualified to operate a vessel safely, the charter operator may give them a quickie course, or may insist that an experienced skipper go along—for a fee.

Paddling. Particular mention is made of places that are appropriate for paddling—That is, muscle-powered boating in kayaks, canoes, dinghies, or inflatables. While this is the ideal way to reach many of the beaches along the sound, extreme care must be used, with an eye to tide rips and currents, the weather, and even larger boats. Kayaking recently has become extremely popular along Puget Sound; however crossing channels can be quite hazardous for the inexperienced. Many places offer classes, and guided trips are available to a number of destinations; this is an ideal introduction to the sport for newcomers, or for those with some experience who want the safety and comradeship of a group.

Boating Safety. A sailor's best ally in navigating Puget Sound waters safely is "sea savvy"—a generous helping of common sense augmented by boating safety courses and instruction in safely operating one's boat. The U.S. Power Squadron's classes in small boat handling are excellent; information regarding the course can be obtained through the U.S. Coast Guard.

This book attempts to address major boating concerns, but it is not possible to cover all navigational hazards that might affect all kinds of boaters. In some places water depths and particular current problems are noted, however this text cannot take the place of a *good navigational chart* and the knowledge to use it properly. The best chart for close-in navigating is the one with the largest scale—that is, showing the greatest detail. Charts for the areas covered in this book are listed in the back.

Rocks and Shoals. Most hazardous rocks and shoals lying in well-traveled areas are marked with lights, buoys, or similar navigational devices. In less frequented places these hazards may be unmarked, although they will be shown on large-scale charts. Local boaters will occasionally mark notorious keel-killers with a vertical pole; these aids are not always maintained and do not show on charts. Another warning of a rock or reef is long streamers of bull kelp floating on the surface—approach any bed of kelp cautiously.

The tidal range in Puget Sound is about 14 feet, except for extreme tides. The lowest of low tides run about −4 feet, the highest of high about +12. During extreme low tides, rocks and shoals that are normally well covered suddenly are close enough to the surface to cause grief to the unwary skipper. During times of minus tides use special care to consult navigational charts, and if mooring check tide tables to be sure the night will not find you mired on the bottom.

Tidal Current. Tidal current *is not the same as the tide*, although one does give rise to the other. Tides measure the vertical distance water rises and falls above the sea floor due to the gravitational attraction of the sun and moon as well as more obscure influences. Tidal currents represent the horizontal flow of water resulting from the rise and fall of the tide. Tidal currents in Puget Sound vary from one to ten knots, the most infamous being those through Deception Pass.

Tidal currents must be a concern for small boaters. Obviously a kayaker would rather be going in the direction of the current rather than struggling to make way headed into it. With long water passages such as found in Rosario Strait or the Strait of Georgia, a typical tidal current of two knots abeam can make as much as a 15° difference in the course to be steered—a difference that can be critical in conditions of fog and low visibility.

Tidal current tables (*not* tide tables), which are printed annually, are keyed to station points on the small craft portfolio charts. The approximate time of maximum velocity of the current can be computed by referencing the tidal current tables to the station point. Although many other factors enter into the actual surface velocity and even the direction of the current, general knowledge of the predicted velocity is invaluable to safe navigation.

Tide Rips. Small craft charts bear notations of "tide rips," typically off of points between channels. Tide rips are caused by either the impact of tidal currents meeting from differing directions or the upwelling of currents as they meet underwater cliffs. In either case the surface appearance is the same—the water appears to dance across an area in small to moderate choppy waves. A boat crossing a tide-rip area may find it difficult to maintain course as erratic currents spin the boat first one way and then another. Kayaks and small boats may find rips an uncomfortable experience, one that should be avoided. The positive aspect of tide rips is that the upwelling current also brings to the surface food-chain elements that attract game fish, so they are therefore considered ideal fishing spots.

Choppy Waters. A phenomenon peculiar to long open channels such as Rosario Strait or the Strait of Georgia is a very short, steep wave form that generally occurs when a strong breeze comes from the direction opposite to the tidal current. Long, relatively shallow channels with moderate to strong tidal currents build this wave form, in contrast to the broader swells built in the deep channel of the Strait of Juan de Fuca or the open ocean. These short, choppy waves chew away at forward boat speed and provide those persons prone to seasickness an excellent opportunity to head for the lee rail. Passage for small boats can be downright dangerous in choppy seas. A close watch on weather reports and tidal current predictions can help a skipper avoid these unpleasant experiences.

Fog. One of the prices often paid for warm sunny summer days is morning fog created by the temperature differential between the sun-warmed land masses and the perpetually chilly waters of Puget Sound. Fog generally lifts by mid-day, but early departure plans should also include a well-plotted compass course to destinations that may disappear in the sea-level morning mist.

WALKING AND HIKING

Very little of the footbound exercise described in this book is vigorous enough to be categorized as hiking. For the most part it involves easy strolls to viewpoints, short nature loops through forested glades, or walks along beaches. With time out for birdwatching, flower smelling, rock skipping, or any of the many other diversions, most of the walks described are ample enough to fill an afternoon.

For extended walks, many of the public areas can be linked by walking the beach at low tide, or at high tide following railroad tracks or city streets. Harvey Manning's book, *Footsore 3, Walks and Hikes around Puget Sound*, describes in detail lengthy shoreline walks for ambitious hikers.

The incoming tide, which laps benignly at tenny-runner toes, can pose a considerable hazard for persons lured into an extended beach walk beneath high vertical bluffs. Walkers may suddenly find themselves trapped between a rock and a wet place, and be forced to either climb up or wade out. Either can be very hazardous. The solution is prevention. Before undertaking beach walks, check a tide table to find out when the predicted high will occur and how high it will be, then plan your walk accordingly. Tide tables are published in small books that are available at boating supply shops as well as book stores. The daily tidal prediction is also published in newspapers along with the weather.

Some trails follow the shoreline along the top of vertical bluffs ranging up to 150 feet high. Typically such bluffs are of glacial till that is soft and frequently eroded and undercut. To compound the problem, the tops of many such bluffs are covered with a particular grass that is quite slippery, especially for smooth-soled shoes. Avoid walking near the edge of any bluff.

BICYCLING

Nearly all the area encompassed in this book is well-suited to bicycle exploration. Many of the roads are lightly traveled, yet are level and smoothly paved. Whidbey Island offers the best array of bicycle-to beaches, along with several fine campgrounds.

The most difficult bicycling route in the area described here is Highway 112 along the Strait of Juan de Fuca between Port Angeles and Neah Bay. Some venturesome bicyclists tackle this route as part of an Olympic Peninsula tour; however the road has numerous ups and downs, curves, narrow shoulders, and occasional logging trucks and hell-bent motorists. To compensate for this is some of the finest scenery on the face of the earth—if you survive.

On any public road in Washington, bicyclists must ride on the right side of the road (with automobile traffic), and travel in single file or no more than two abreast. If several cars become stacked up behind them, cyclists must pull over, but *not* at the crest of a hill or a bend in the road. Bicyclists need to stop where motorists can see them. Bicycles are welcome on any of the ferries. On state ferries they are loaded and unloaded ahead of vehicles; other ferries will give boarding instructions.

CAMPING

In addition to city, county, and state parks that have campgrounds, a number of resorts also have camping facilities. As of 1988 Birch Bay, Fort Flagler, and Fort Worden State Parks will accept reservations. At the other state parks campsites are on a first-come, first-served basis. At most state parks, campgrounds are gated at dusk, picnic areas are open only for day use, and parking lots cannot be used for overflow camping. If the campgrounds are full, the park ranger may be helpful in finding alternative space.

BEACH EXPLORATION

To many people a visit to the beach is like a visit to another planet, with alien landscapes and a menagerie of strange life forms to marvel at. Unfortunately some feel the need to cart buckets of these life forms home where they immediately die, create an ungodly stink, and in due time are thrown into the garbage.

All state parks and some county and city parks have regulations protecting nonfood forms of marine life such as starfish and sand dollars. Even in those areas that are unprotected by environmental regulations, beachcombers should avoid removing or destroying any of these animals. All play an important part in the food chain, and all add to the educational and esthetic richness of the beaches. Many tidelands in populated areas along the sound were once a bright tapestry of marine life, but are now virtually barren due to longtime abuse by beachcombers coupled with the effects of pollution.

Even nonliving beach objects such as driftwood and empty shells are an important part of the marine environment, forming homes for small creatures and helping to control erosion. If you must have a treasure from the sea as a souvenir of your trip, make it small, and check to be sure it is not harboring some tiny living marine creature.

HARVESTING SEAFOOD—BEACH FORAGING, FISHING, AND SCUBA DIVING

One of the greatest enticements of the seashore is the prospect of gathering food fresh from the water for a seaside feast or a quick trip home to the dinner table. In many areas on Puget Sound this is possible, but it is regulated, and regulations do change from time to time.

Licenses and Limits. The Washington State Department of Fisheries requires a license for salmon fishing. At this time licenses are not required for other types of saltwater fishing or for shellfish harvesting, except for Hood Canal shrimp. A freshwater fishing license is required at Pass and Cranberry Lakes in Deception Pass State Park and Lake Pondilla at Fort Ebey State Park.

It is the responsibility of the fisherman or seafood gatherer to be aware of all regulations. A saltwater sport-fishing pamphlet published by the Department of Fisheries and available in most sporting goods stores lists size and catch limits, seasons, and other restrictions for all types of shellfish as well as sport fish.

Digging Holes. State regulations dictate that holes dug in beaches in pursuit of clams *must always* be filled. Do not rely on the incoming tide to do the job; it may take several turns of the tide for displaced sand to be completely leveled. In the meantime small marine animals trapped in the pile may smother and others exposed to the sun may die of dehydration.

Oyster Shells. Removal of oyster shells from the beach is unlawful. Large shells frequently hold several oyster larvae that will die if the shells are discarded on land. Take a sharp, sturdy knife or oyster pick and plastic con-

Tongue Point Marine Life Sanctuary

tainers to the beach and shuck oysters where they are found.

Marine Sanctuaries. State and county parks generally permit the taking of those edible forms of marine life that are defined and regulated by the Department of Fisheries; however some parks have marine sanctuaries where it may be prohibited. Many underwater reefs are closed to spearfishing by scuba divers. At any park check the local regulations before gathering a meal.

Paralytic Shellfish Poisoning (Red Tide). When the State Department of Health periodically issues a "red tide warning" and closes particular beaches on Puget Sound, the public usually reacts with confusion or scepticism. A clearer understanding of the phenomenon of red tide will lead to a greater respect for its dangers.

The name "red tide" itself contributes to some of the public's confusion, for it is not always visibly red, it has nothing at all to do with the tide, and not all red algae are harmful. Paralytic shellfish poisoning (PSP) is a serious illness caused by *Gonyaulax catenella*, a toxic, single-celled, amber-colored alga that is always present in the water in small numbers. During spring, summer, and fall, certain environmental conditions may combine to permit a rapid multiplication or accumulation of these microscopic organisms. Most shellfish toxicity occurs when the concentrations of *G. catenella* are too sparse to discolor the water; however the free-floating plants sometimes become so numerous that the water appears to have a reddish cast—thus the name red tide.

Bivalve shellfish such as clams, oysters, mussels, and scallops, which feed by filtering sea water, may ingest millions of the organisms and concentrate the toxin in their bodies. The poison is retained by most of these shellfish for several weeks after the occurrence of the red tide; butter clams can be poisonous for much longer.

When the concentration of the toxin in mollusks reaches a certain level, it becomes hazardous to humans who eat them. The toxins cannot be destroyed by cooking, and cannot be reliably detected by any means other than laboratory analysis. Symptoms of PSP, beginning with the tingling of the lips and tongue, may occur within a half-hour of ingestion. The illness attacks the nervous system, causing loss of control of arms and legs, difficulty in breathing, paralysis and, in extreme cases, death.

Shellfish in all counties on Puget Sound are under regular surveillance by the State Department of Health. PSP (or red tide) warnings are issued and some beaches are posted when high levels of toxin are detected in tested mollusks. Warnings are usually publicized in the media; the state toll-free hotline listed in the back of this book has current information as to which beaches are closed to shellfish harvesting. Crabs, abalone, shrimp, and fin fish are not included in closures since there have been no recorded cases of PSP in the Northwest caused by eating any of these animals.

Safety Considerations

Many of the shores and waterways of North Puget Sound are the most exposed of any on the sound; conditions can vary widely. Storms can make the channels hazardous to small craft, and bad weather and incoming tides can make beaches impassable. Use care when storms are in the offing.

Not all walks described in this book are suitable at all times, or for all people. Do not approach too close to the edges of bluffs, as they may crumble. At no time should hikers attempt to climb or descend a bluff if there is no trail, and even when trails are present they can become treacherously slippery. The old army bunkers are especially enticing to children, but can be dangerous to the unwary. Do not allow youngsters to roam unsupervised; adults should use care where they step.

Emergency Assistance

Overall legal authority in all unincorporated areas of the state rests with the county sheriff. Emergencies or complaints should be referred to the local county sheriff's office at the number listed in the reference section in the back of this book.

Within state and county parks, the park manager assumes emergency assistance responsibilities. Not all parks have resident managers, however; the reference section indicates the locations of managers responsible for smaller parks.

The U.S. Coast Guard has primary responsibility for safety and law enforcement on Puget Sound waters. Marine VHF channel 16 is continuously monitored by the Coast Guard and should be the most reliable means of contact in case of emergencies on the water. The Coast Guard monitors Citizen's Band channel 9 at some locations and times, but it has no commitment to a full-time radio watch on this channel. Several volunteer groups do an excellent job of monitoring the CB emergency frequency and will assist as best they can with relaying emergency requests to the proper authorities.

Beach at Lighthouse Marine Park

1. THE STRAIT OF GEORGIA

The waters of the Strait of Georgia span the boundary between the United States and Canada. In summer this 10-mile-wide channel sees a steady flow of Canadian boaters headed south to fabled Washington islands and Yankee boaters headed north to island treasures in British Columbia—proving that even cruisers subscribe to the adage that the grass (or in this case, the water) is greener on the other side of the fence.

The several marine developments near the border on the U.S. side

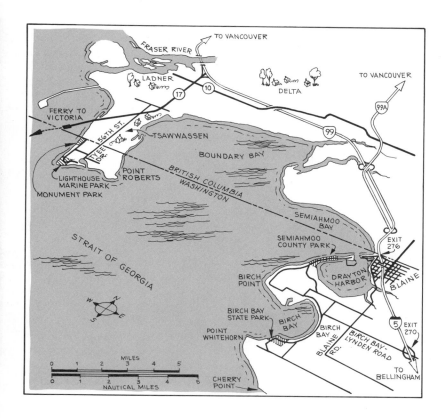

provide facilities and recreation to cruisers in transit, as well as permanent moorage for boaters who like to have their vessels within easy striking distance of vacation waters. Customs check-ins for boaters entering U.S. waters are at Point Roberts and Blaine marinas.

Three sets of range lights in Semiahmoo and Boundary bays mark the international boundary at the 49th parallel; the 60-foot-tall white-concrete Peace Arch that straddles the boundary on shore is also visible from the water during most weather. The Strait of Georgia is free of obstructions except for Alden Bank, a 3-mile-long shoal marked by buoys that lies northeast of Sucia Island. Tidal currents in the channel rarely exceed 3 knots; however a hull-jarring chop can occur when the direction of the current opposes that of the wind.

Point Roberts

Point Roberts is somewhat of a geographical curiosity—a political island created by a quirk in an early treaty. During the time of pioneer settlement both the U.S. and Great Britain vied for the territory between Oregon and Russia-owned Alaska. The Yankee cry in the 1840s of "54−40 or Fight" meant that the U.S. wanted to claim sovereignty over all the territory south of a latitude of 54 degrees, 40 minutes; the British insisted on an international boundary at the Columbia River. In 1846 a compromise was reached, with the 49th parallel established as the international boundary from the crest of the Rocky Mountains west to the Strait of Georgia where it dipped south, down the center of the Strait of Georgia, giving the Gulf Islands and all of Vancouver Island to the British.

The lawmakers back in Washington, D.C., due perhaps to inadequate maps, failed to note two geographical problems: The 5-square-mile tip of the Point Roberts peninsula that hung below the 49th parallel became isolated from the rest of the United States and the exact boundary through the San Juan Islands was not clearly defined. The oversight on the San Juan boundary brought the two nations to the brink of war in 1859 during the Pig War standoff. Point Roberts however, although a bit awkward, has created no major problems, and the U.S. citizens living there have learned to cope, and perhaps to enjoy their unique status.

Point Roberts is reached by land by crossing the border at Blaine and continuing north on Highway 99 for 12½ miles to the Highway 10 exit, which is signed to Tsawwassen and Point Roberts. In 5 miles turn left (south) onto B.C. 17, then in 3½ miles turn left again onto 56th St. All intersections are well signed. The customs check at Point Roberts is a total of 24 miles from the border at Blaine. Crossing the border at either location is usually a very quick process; slight delays may occur at Blaine when special events in B.C. or Washington create heavy traffic.

POINT ROBERTS MARINA

Facilities: Complete boat and crew facilities, laundry, U.S. Customs, boat pumpout station, boat rental and charter, restaurant, picnic tables, boat launch (hoist)

Convenience, both in facilities and location, is the byword at the Point Roberts Marina. The large comma-shaped yacht basin features the latest in moorage amenities as well as a wealth of fishing and cruising waters within a few miles of the entry breakwater. The basin, which holds over 1000 boats, is secreted slightly inland, giving it maximum protection during even the most severe weather. It is reached via a 200-yard-long dredged channel, which is in itself guarded by an angled jetty that also serves to prevent shoaling. Fuel and groceries are found on the dock just inside the entrance and guest moorage at the extreme end of the basin. By land, the marina is reached by driving south from the border on Tyee Drive.

Like many such recent commercial ventures, the marina hopes to succeed financially by virtue of the real estate development surrounding it, which offers condos and residential lots. It is planned that as the resort area grows, shoreline services such as cafes, theaters, and hotels will be added.

Orca in the Strait of Georgia off Point Roberts

MONUMENT PARK (WHATCOM COUNTY)

Park Area: 8 acres; 500 feet of waterfront
Access: Land, boat
Facilities: Hiking trail
Attractions: Historical marker, viewpoint, beachcombing

Although this tract of county-owned land is undeveloped, it offers some nice views of the strait from the uplands. Unfortunately English Bluff, the 150-foot-high cliff on which the park is perched, is so steep and treacherous that approaching the beach from above cannot be recommended. The park's extensive tideflats can be accessed by boat.

After crossing the border, continue south on Tyee Drive, and in 1¼ miles turn west on Gulf Road. At the water head north on Marine Drive to reach the park at the boundary. Next to a small parking area is a stone obelisk marking the boundary between Canada and the U.S.—the first, both historically and geographically, to be placed on the 49th parallel. Views through the trees are of the long causeway at the Tsawwassen ferry landing nearby and the green stretches of the Gulf Islands in the distance.

The public beach is easily identifiable from the water by a navigational marker on shore. The tideflat extends out for over ½ mile before plunging steeply downward.

Picnic area at Lighthouse Marine Park

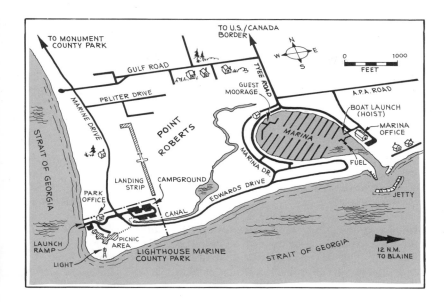

LIGHTHOUSE MARINE PARK (WHATCOM COUNTY)

Park Area: 22 acres; 4000 feet of shoreline
Access: Land or boat
Facilities: 25 campsites, picnic tables, fireplaces, kitchen, drinking water, restrooms, view tower, fire rings, informational display, concession stand, fishing dock, boat launch (ramp)
Attractions: Boating, fishing, beachcombing, clam digging

A spectacular site for a park: a gravelly cape of land thrusting into the surging waters of the Strait of Georgia, with views sweeping the length of the strait and out to emerald Gulf Islands. To the southeast looms Mt. Baker, queen of all. The lighthouse, after which the park is named, is not the traditional picturesque building but a metal framework tower with a rotating beacon.

The strong winds that sometimes buffet the point dictate a different approach to the usual assortment of park tables casually distributed along the beach, and the Whatcom County Parks Department has risen admirably to the challenge. Picnic sites are in angular wooden covered shelters on a long boardwalk; numerous fire rings near the beach are in the protection of shallow log-rimmed pits. When weather permits there is ample space on the beach to spread a blanket for lunching or sunbathing.

On one corner of the boardwalk a 30-foot viewing tower increases the sightseeing possibilities. Whales, which travel in the strait, can sometimes be spotted. An enclosed shelter midway along the boardwalk has a display showing photos of Orca whales (the ones most commonly seen) and describing fin characteristics, pod identification, behaviors, how they make sound, and other fascinating information.

The underwater shelf drops off sharply at the tip of the point, but to the north and east the tideflat flares out more gradually, providing opportunities for clamming and beachcombing at low water. At the north edge of the park is a two-lane boat-launch ramp; an adjacent line of floats, in place in summer, is used for boarding boats or fishing. Temporary anchorage can be found along the north side of the point in five fathoms of water, but wind and current conditions make this impractical for long-term stops.

By land, Lighthouse Marine Park is reached by continuing south on Tyee Drive after crossing the border at Point Roberts. At the marina, turn right, follow the road around the yacht basin, then turn west on Edwards Drive to the park. The day-use area is on the south and west sides of the road, campground to the east. A few low pines and a slight hill give the campsites some protection from winds off the strait. Owners of large RVs may prefer using one of the two commercial trailer parks located a few blocks inland since the campsites are a bit snug; they are ample, however, for tenters and small RVs. None have hookups.

A $2 fee is charged for day use by noncounty residents, as well as the customary fees for boat launching or overnight camping.

Blaine

Blaine is best known as a border town, offering a rest stop and refueling station to motorists going to and from Canada. Southbound boaters also sometimes stop here at the marina to check through customs, although several other ports near the border provide the same service. Town businesses are geared to persons passing through—heavy on restaurants, lodging, and north-bound duty-free shops.

Blaine lies on Drayton Harbor, a large shallow bay cut off from Semiahmoo Bay on the southwest by a 1½-mile-long sandspit and on the northeast by a man-made landfill jetty containing the town's marine industries. Only the dredged harbor by the jetty and a small portion of the bay near the entrance are navigable—the rest of it dries at the merest hint of low tide. The tideflats of Drayton Harbor, as well as those north of the marina jetty, are excellent for clam digging and oyster picking.

Shoals in Semiahmoo Bay spread outward for some distance on either side of the narrow entrance to the harbor. Boaters should give Semiahmoo Spit a wide berth and stay in the marked channel when entering.

During the Fraser River gold rush of 1858 Drayton Harbor was a staging site for prospectors headed to Canada. The gold boom was short-lived, however, and the town quickly dwindled away. At the turn of the century, fishing was the economic mainstay. The largest private salmon fishing

Blaine Marina

fleet in the U.S. was centered here, and some 30 fishtraps in Semiahmoo Bay and Drayton Harbor provided a steady supply of salmon to large processing plants on Semiahmoo Spit and Point Roberts. The enormous salmon runs became depleted, and after 30 years of operation the canneries closed. Today some fishing and crabbing boats still operate out of Blaine and there are processing plants here, but the industry is a shadow of its former glory.

BLAINE MARINA

Facilities: Complete boat and crew facilities, boat pumpout station, fuel, laundry, barbeque, restaurant, fishing pier, U.S. Customs, boat launch (ramp), tidal grid, shopping (nearby)

In recent years the Blaine boat harbor, which is operated by the Port of Bellingham, has been enlarged to 400 slips, and the rock breakwater extended to the east to completely enclose the dredged basin. To reach the boat facilities, turn west off Peace Portal Drive onto Marine Drive. The boat-launch ramp is on the east, at the end of Milhollin Drive. The two-lane concrete ramp has an excellent slope into the water. A loading pier separates the two ramps; a large parking lot is nearby.

A complex of small businesses, mostly marine related, occupy the landfill pier. Marina offices and accommodations for pleasure boaters are in the middle section, while commercial fishing facilities are at the far western end. The road terminates at a broad wooden pier where public fishing and crabbing are permitted. Downtown Blaine is about a ¾-mile walk from the visitors' floats.

An interesting feature of the marina is a tidal grid—a "poor man's drydock." It consists of a stable platform below the water level and some adjoining pilings where boaters tie their craft. As the tide goes out, the keel of the boat settles on the platform and the pilings support it for the duration of the low tide. The bottom of the boat is thus exposed for maintenance and repair. Numbers painted on the side of the pier or pilings (the "grid") indicate the depth of the water to the platform.

SEMIAHMOO MARINA

Facilities: Complete boat and crew facilities, laundry, boat pumpout station, propane, boat launch (hoist)

Much of the property on Semiahmoo Spit that was once owned by the fish packing plant, as well as a large portion of land on the Birch Point peninsula, is in the process of being developed as a resort community. One of the first facilities built by the resort was a fine yacht basin protected by a floating log breakwater on the eastern side of the spit, at Tongue Point.

Boating facilities here are new and nice, with concrete floats, power, water, and security gates. There is no designated guest float; check with the harbormaster for available slips. The marina store has some necessities.

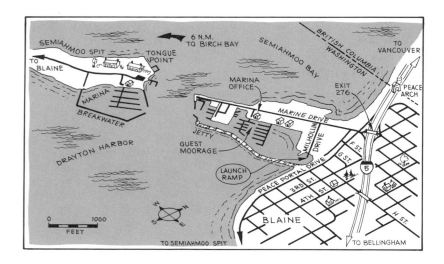

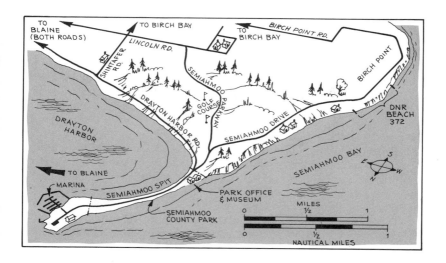

By land it is 9 miles around Drayton Harbor to Blaine; however the town can be reached by a short dinghy jaunt to the launch ramp at the east end of Blaine Boat Harbor. Enter the rock breakwater at its west end and follow it to the ramp. Downtown shopping is a short walk away.

By land, Semiahmoo Spit can be reached by following Peace Portal Drive south out of Blaine. Turn right onto Bell Road, which becomes Blaine Road. In 1 mile more turn right again onto Drayton Harbor Road. From here, signs pointing the way to Semiahmoo Resort can be followed inland, past the resort's golf course and residential area. For an alternate route stay on Drayton Harbor Road, which follows the shoreline to the spit. This latter road is narrow and winding, and most views of the the harbor are obscured by trees; however the light traffic and level road make it an ideal bicycle route.

The commercial marina shares the sandspit with Semiahmoo County Park, which is within walking distance of the boat basin.

SEMIAHMOO COUNTY PARK (WHATCOM COUNTY)

Park Area: 322 acres; 6700 feet of shoreline
Access: Land, boat
Facilities: Picnic tables, drinking water, restrooms, museum
Attractions: Clam digging, crabbing, beachcombing, swimming, bird-watching, fishing, paddling

This county park, which lies on the south end of Semiahmoo Spit between the residential and marine areas of the resort, offers a nice combination of the natural and the historical. The natural part is a pair of wonderful beaches—one a windswept, driftwood-laced strand facing west on Semiahmoo Bay, the other a more protected tidal flat that spreads into Drayton Harbor. Both beaches offer the opportunity to capture crabs in the eelgrass beds; clamming is best on the Drayton Harbor side.

The park's historical offering is in a group of buildings once used as bunkhouses for the salmon cannery. The museum in one of the buildings displays photographs, models, and artifacts that recall the era when the waters were filled with the graceful Bristol Bay sailboats used for gillnetting. A scale model of the bay shows how it looked in 1917 when it was filled with traps to snare the silvery deluge of salmon.

Boats can be hand launched at either of the beaches; use care in Drayton Harbor not to become mired when the tide recedes. Semiahmoo Bay also offers paddling possibilities, south around Birch Point to Birch Bay, 5 miles away. En route DNR Beach 372 can be explored. The gravelly beach lying beneath a steep bluff north of Birch Point is a likely spot to find some clams. There is no upland access; only the beach below the mean high water level is public. Strong winds off the Strait of Georgia can be a danger.

Birch Bay

Birch Bay is best known for the summer resort communities edging its shoreline. The cabins and condos at the towns of Cottonwood Beach and Birch Bay host families that come to revel in the sun and sand as well as enjoy the nearby golf course, waterslide, and other recreational offerings.

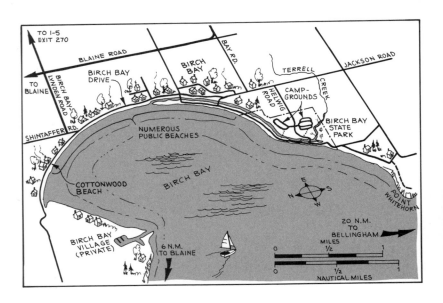

Canoeing on Birch Bay

Even the weather collaborates to make this a summer playland, as this section of Washington's inland waters receives far more sun than lower Puget Sound.

While entertainment at Birch Bay tends toward the upbeat rather than the sedate, the area has its placid side. Once the summer crowds are gone it becomes a quiet retreat, both for off-season guests and for flocks of migrating waterfowl that gather in the bay. Black brant, loons, oldsquaws, harlequin ducks are frequent visitors.

The bay itself is a shallow open bight, holding less than 2 fathoms of water throughout much of its extent—great for swimming, but offering little to deep-draft boats. A few spots to drop a hook can be found well out in the bay in 4–5 fathoms of water. Birch Bay Village, a private residential community on the north side of the bay, has a small dredged basin, but it is only for the use of residents. A marina south of the state park closed long ago, so there are no marine facilities for craft of any size. Car-top boats can be put in at numerous spots along the shore.

Birch Bay is reached by land by leaving I-5 at Exit 270 and following Birch Bay–Lynden Road west. By water, the bay is 7 nautical miles south of the marine facilities at Blaine, where the nearest boat launch is located.

COTTONWOOD BEACH AND BIRCH BAY PUBLIC ACCESSES

From Cottonwood Beach south to the state park, the beachfront is public, broken only by a few sections of privately owned (well-posted) property. The road paralleling the shoreline has numerous parking areas along the side. From a narrow band of driftwood, the tideflat recedes gradually into the water, remaining wading level out for nearly ½ mile. The beach is so wide and glorious that not one, but four, sandcastle competitions are held here every summer, with dozens of competitive teams shaping the fine sand into flamboyant architecture or bizarre creatures.

Kayakers or canoeists can enjoy some 7 miles of near-shore paddling within the protected arms of the bay. Strong winds that occasionally sweep in from the west off the Strait of Georgia can pose problems in open water.

BIRCH BAY STATE PARK

Park Area: 192 acres; 12,940 feet of shoreline
Access: Land, boat
Facilities: 167 campsites, RV hookups, picnic tables, fireplaces, drinking water, restrooms, trailer dump station, nature trail
Attractions: Boating, paddling, fishing, beachcombing, clam digging, crabbing, scuba diving, birdwatching

The climax of the Birch Bay shoreline is the state park at its southern end. Here the magnificent beach is complemented by grassy shores with picnic tables and ample space for playing volleyball, throwing Frisbees, flying kites, or for any of the other sports that go so well with sun and sand.

The state park can be reached from the town of Birch Bay by continuing south on Birch Bay Drive to the park boundary. The entrances are gated at sunset to discourage nighttime partying and the kind of recreation inspired by moon and sand. The east entrance is reached by turning off Birch Bay Drive onto Jackson Road. Drive south ¾ mile and turn west on Helwig Road, which leads directly to the park. The route is well signed.

The upland section, where the camping area is located, is in stately old-growth forest of cedar and Douglas fir. The loop road has trailer hookups. From here the road winds downhill past a large parking area to the beach.

Terrell Creek drains into a narrow estuary at the south edge of the preserve. The marshland here provides habitat for beaver, opossum, muskrat, and a variety of birds. A short trail follows the edge of the marsh.

Scuba divers entering the water at the park swim west to Point Whitehorn where the bottom drops off more rapidly and the rocky shoreline hosts a diversity of underwater life.

Reef net fishing in Legoe Bay

2. BELLINGHAM BAY

The several islands clustered around the edge of Bellingham Bay and Bellingham Channel suffer somewhat from an identity crisis. Although they are frequently referred to as part of the San Juans (which they strongly resemble geologically), they are not part of San Juan County, and therefore geographically are not "real" San Juan Islands.

In spite of the fact that they lie within a stone's throw of the major population centers of Bellingham and Anacortes, these half dozen large islands and their entourage of smaller islets have managed to escape industrialization, although real estate developments have made some minor inroads and the threat of major development is constantly present, especially on Cypress Island.

Boaters seeking to avoid the heavy crowds and hoopla of the San Juans will find this area makes a nice cruising destination, with enough channels and tucked-away coves to hold interest for a weekend. The city of Bellingham has full marine facilities.

Two of the islands, Lummi and Guemes, can be reached by car as well as boat, making them accessible for persons with car-top craft or those

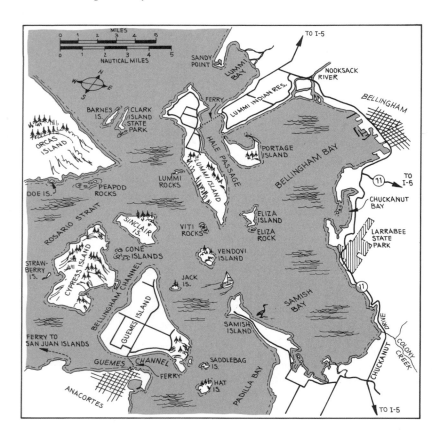

who want to explore the shores by foot or bicycle. Larrabee State Park, south of Bellingham, is largely inland, but it does have a campground and a short beachfront with a boat launch ramp.

Lummi Island and Hale Passage

Lummi is the most dramatic of the islands in the Bellingham vicinity—over 9 miles long and 1 mile narrow, with bluffs at its southern end rising precipitously for 1500 feet, while at the north end of the island the terrain abruptly flattens into rolling farmland. Its striking silhouette is visible from many of the northern islands and channels, further adding to the misconception that it is one of the San Juan group.

The island can be reached via a small Whatcom County-operated ferry. By car, leave Highway I-5 at Exit 260 and follow the signed route west on Haxton Way for 10½ miles to the ferry landing at Gooseberry

Point, on the Lummi Indian Reservation. The ferry runs half-hourly from 7 a.m. to midnight on weekdays, hourly on holidays and weekends; crossing time is about 10 minutes. A small combination grocery store-gas station on the island is ½ mile south of the ferry landing on Nugent Road. It has bicycles for rent to persons touring the island, and campsites.

Most of the island's beachfront homes and acreages are distributed on the flat northern half of the island. The road that follows this northern shoreline offers motorists and bicyclists temptingly scenic views of Lummi Bay and the Strait of Georgia; however there is no public access except at Legoe Bay, on the west side. Roads penetrate the south end for only a short distance before the steep and wild take over.

Hale Passage, a mile-wide channel, runs between Lummi Island and the mainland. The channel is unobstructed; however a bar that runs north from Lummi Point to Sandy Point, on the west side of Lummi Bay, is covered by only 2 fathoms of water at mean low water. Current in the channel runs up to 2 knots; canoeists and kayakers should time their ventures for a favorable tide.

GOOSEBERRY POINT

Facilities: Boat launch (hoist), gas and outboard mix (on shore), marine supplies and repairs, groceries, restaurant, gift shop

A commercial marina on the mainland, immediately north of the Lummi Island ferry landing, provides some boating amenities and a hoist for launching trailered boats. The marina has a short dock for loading and picking up fuel and supplies, but no overnight moorages. At minus tides the float sits on dry land. Boats launched here have ready access to the popular salmon fishing grounds along the end of Lummi Island and near Eliza and Vendovi Islands.

LUMMI MARINE PARK AND STOMMISH GROUNDS

A county-installed boat-launch ramp is available at Lummi Marine Park, farther south on Gooseberry Point. To reach it, continue south on Lummi View Drive for 1 mile from the ferry landing. The park is marked by fishing boats and nets on the beach, and a row of pilings in the water. Since the ramp is frequently covered with debris, trailered launching may be difficult. A large gravel parking lot is across the road.

Immediately to the south of the launch ramp, past a couple of homes, is the Stommish Grounds, a park where war canoe races are held a weekend in June during the annual Lummi Stommish (meaning "Old Warrior"). Members of nearly a dozen Northwest Indian tribes take part in the colorful event, which also includes a salmon barbeque, arts and crafts sale, and traditional Indian games. The event is open to the public.

The brightly painted racing boats, ranging up to 52 feet and holding

Gooseberry Point boat launch

from 2 to 11 people, are paddled on a round-trip course that begins at the park, runs south past Portage Point, and then ends back in front of the judge's stand at the park. The men's course is 5–6 miles long; women and youngsters paddle shorter distances.

Gooseberry Point and Portage Island are part of the Lummi Indian Reservation. An early Indian village was located at Gooseberry Point, and the natives portaged canoes from Hale Passage to Bellingham Bay across the sandbar that joins Portage Island to the mainland. Only members of the Lummi tribe are permitted to remove clams, crabs, or oysters from the tidelands of the reservation.

PORTAGE POINT AND PORTAGE ISLAND

Car-top boats can also be put in at the sandy beach at Portage Point, 1 mile south of Lummi Marine Park. At plus tides trailered boats are often launched at this beach, but care must be used as there is no surfaced ramp and the sand can be quite soft. Much of Portage Bay is dry at a minus tide; at extreme high tide even the sandbar is covered.

For very shallow draft boats, Portage Island is an interesting circumnavigation in protected waters. Beware of rocks that ring the south end of the island at Point Frances.

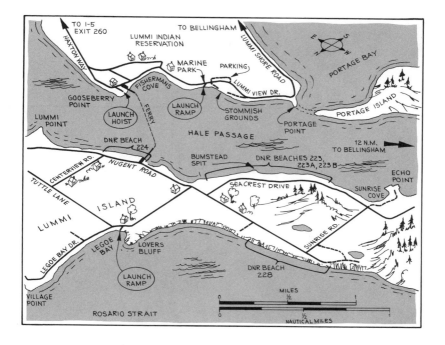

LUMMI ISLAND RECREATION SITE

Park Area: 42 acres, 2125 feet of shoreline
Access: Boat
Facilities: 5 campsites, buoy, fireplaces, latrines, hiking trail, *no water*

The eastern shore of Lummi Island, facing on Hale Passage, has a number of attractive little pocket coves offering some limited anchorages for large boats and some delightful exploring for paddlers of small ones. The shorelands are densely forested wildland, ensuring a quiet overnight stay interrupted only by the hooting of owls.

Three adjacent, unnamed coves 1¼ miles from the southern tip of the island are the site of a primitive DNR campground. The largest, most southerly of the little bays is just a few hundred feet across. A single mooring buoy placed in the cove is in ample water for most boats. The smaller pockets on the north side of the headland are oriented to the northwest and are shallower and more open.

The coves, which are bounded by rocky walls, are linked by wooden steps and a steep trail that climbs to the campground above. The DNR campsite is a favorite for kayakers, since the small coves do not attract many larger boats. A large sign onshore marking the campground is visible from the water.

Inati Bay

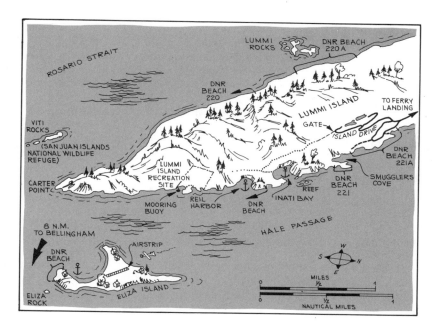

INATI BAY

Access: Boat, land (trail)
Facilities: Pit toilets, fireplaces, hiking trail

About ½ mile north of the DNR Recreation Site, the open bight of Reil Harbor provides space in calm weather for a couple of very scenic anchorages. The narrow gravel and rock beach quickly gives way to steep, wild bluffs.

The best anchorage on this side of Lummi Island lies ¼ mile around the rock knob to the north. Here at Inati Bay, the north-facing cove offers a pocket of protection for almost any weather, with ample space for a dozen or so boats. The bay has a rock shelf offshore about 500 yards marked on the south by a white can buoy and on the north by a black post. Enter south of the white buoy to avoid rocks and kelp in the entrance.

The Bellingham Yacht Club has leased land at the head of Inati Bay and has located pit toilets and fireplaces there for the use of boaters. A trail that widens into a primitive jeep road leads from the harbor north through dense timber, eventually joining the main road and civilization in 1¼ miles.

To hike to Inati Bay by land, drive south on Nugent Road from the ferry landing, and in ¾ mile turn left on Seacrest Drive, which eventually becomes Island Drive. About 5 miles from the ferry terminal the road passes two small ponds and makes its last hairpin turn—here an obvious primitive road heads south. Parking space nearby for 3–4 cars.

The last of the bays along the southeast shore, Smuggler's Cove, marks the end of the wilderness and the beginning of Lummi Island civilization. A gravel operation occupies part of this bay, but boaters may still find space to anchor.

Sunrise Cove, 1¾ nautical miles farther north along the shore, has space for some anchorages in the open, north-facing bay. The float and launch ramp on shore are owned by a private beach club.

LUMMI ISLAND DNR BEACHES

Large portions of the tidelands along the east side of Lummi Island are DNR beaches. Beach 224 has easy upland access; the others must be reached by boat. Only the tidelands below mean high water are open to the public, except for beach 220, which fronts the Lummi Island Recreation Site.

The northernmost of these tidelands, Beach 224 is a 2805-foot section running north from the ferry landing. It is possible to reach it by land by descending the bank on either side of the ferry landing. The shore immediately south of the ferry landing is private—do not trespass.

DNR Beach 223 (2574 feet long), Beach 223A (1188 feet long), and Beach 223B (1014 feet long), are all south of the ferry landing, in the vicinity of Bumstead Spit. These three beaches, along with beach 224, lie on

Fishing boats on the beach at Portage Point

sand and gravel flats that offer good opportunities at low tide for clam digging.

The rocky shores on the south end of the island also have extensive DNR beaches, but are much less hospitable. Beach 221A (4812 feet long) runs north from Smuggler's Cove, and beach 221 begins at the point east of the cove and runs south for 4481 feet. The longest section of public tidelands is Beach 220, a 23,533-foot strip that wraps around the end of the island and extends nearly to Lummi Rocks. All of these shorelands are rocky, with a scattering of gravel at the heads of occasional pocket coves.

Beach 220A, on the west side of the island, is a 3188-foot tideland opposite Lummi Rocks. Use extreme care approaching this beach by boat since there are submerged rocks in the vicinity and the tidal current is much stronger on this side of the island.

Beach 228, which is broken into several short sections, stretches for ¾ mile along the northwest shore of the island, south of Legoe Bay. Numerous homes are perched atop the steep 50-foot-high bank. The public shorelands, which lie below the mean high-water level, are not marked. Use care not to stray onto property that is signed as private.

LEGOE BAY

Facilities: Boat launch (ramp), fuel (service station), restaurant

Legoe Bay, on the northwest side of Lummi Island, offers the only marine facilities on this side of the island. The bay is open to winds from the south and west, making it poor for layovers in all but calm weather. The small marina at the head of the bay has a surfaced launch ramp, with fuel available from a pump on shore.

The bay is heavily used by commercial reefnetting fishermen who spread nets between skiffs in shallow water. Lookouts on ladder-like towers on the bow of the boat watch for salmon to swim into the net. When a school of fish is spotted, the corners of the net are drawn in and the fish are scooped up. This method was first devised centuries ago by early Indians. Modern technology has added outboard motors and synthetic nets, but the basic method remains the same.

Bellingham and Bellingham Bay

One of the first things a visitor will notice when wandering about Bellingham is its oddly mismatched sections of streets. This came about in pioneer times when early settlers along the shores of Bellingham Bay established four separate, rival communities. Whatcom, the first settlement (and the county seat when Whatcom County was established two years later), was the site of a sawmill in 1852. Shortly after the tiny mill on the shores of Whatcom Creek began churning out lumber, the discovery of a seam of

Sailing in Bellingham Bay; Mt. Baker beyond

coal brought the area a new industry and a new community — Sehome.

For some 25 years Whatcom and Sehome were the only towns on Bellingham Bay. The Fraser River gold rush and the coming of the transcontinental railroad, along with the supply and demand vagaries of the lumber, coal, and fishing industries, kept the area in a constant state of boom or bust. In 1858, at the height of the gold rush, the local population was 15,000, but within a year it had dropped to a few hundred and in 1878 when the Sehome mine was closed it was a mere 20 determined individuals.

When some 600 Kansans arrived in 1880, they established a third town on the bay — New Whatcom. Three years later the community of Fairhaven was founded. As the boundaries of the four burgeoning towns meshed, consolidation became inevitable, but selection of a name for this new metropolis was hotly disputed, with local residents all fervently pushing the name of their own town. In 1903 voters chose a name that pleased few, but offended none — Bellingham, after the bay named some 200 years earlier by Capt. George Vancouver to honor some now-obscure British nobleman.

Today Bellingham is the fourth-largest city on Puget Sound. Pride of the city is Western Washington University, at the base of Mt. Sehome. Established in 1899 as one of three state "normal schools" for the training of teachers, it has grown in scope and recognition over the years to become a fully accredited university.

Downtown Bellingham is dominated by the Victorian brick building at 121 Prospect St. that served as a city hall from 1892 to 1936 and that now houses the Whatcom Museum of History and Art. The first ordinance enacted in this building by the city council banned cows from walking the streets between 7:30 p.m. and 6 a.m.—the mayor's cow was the first to be incarcerated for violating the law.

A full range of goods and services is available in city stores and nearby malls. Old, ornate turn-of-the-century buildings in the Fairhaven business district recently have been restored and now house restaurants, craft shops, art galleries, and other interesting places to browse.

Since earliest times Bellingham has served as a portal for the San Juan Islands. Settlers routinely rowed the 30-plus miles from their island homesteads to Bellingham for supplies, mail, and even a Saturday-night date. With the advent of the steamboats of the mosquito fleet, a steady stream of goods and passengers flowed between the islands and their closest mainland point of commerce. Although many visitors now reach the San Juans via the ferry from Anacortes, Bellingham still maintains a strong tie through its marine businesses, with numerous boats chartered or berthed in Bellingham heading regularly for San Juan destinations.

Bellingham Bay is spacious and deep and has no navigational hazards. The extreme north end of the bay dwindles into mudflats, but anchorages can be found in 6–15 fathoms south of these flats.

BELLINGHAM MARINAS

Facilities: Complete boat and crew facilities, laundry, boat launch (ramp), boat rental and charter, restaurants, educational display, shopping

In recent years Bellingham has undertaken a revitalization program. The city's efforts are especially evident on its waterfront at Squalicum Harbor, where spiffy new facilities provide everything a visiting boater may desire. The Port of Bellingham marina is on the northwest side of the town, to the left of the industrial area as one enters the bay.

Squalicum Harbor consists of two large basins, separated by a landfill jetty, that provide moorage for pleasure craft and the local fishing fleet. The moorage to the east is a dredged basin behind a short rock breakwater. Port offices are in the building at the center of the bay, and guest moorages are on the two outer floats of the center dock; the first 24 hours are free. Floats by the adjacent boat-launch ramp may also be used for overflow moorage.

Squalicum Harbor is reached by land by leaving I-5 at Exit 253 and proceeding west on Holly St. On C St., at the downtown waterfront, turn left, then in 1 block turn right on Roeder Ave., which can be followed all the way to the boat basin. A 4-lane concrete launch ramp is adjacent the Coast Guard station, just off Roeder Ave. on Thomas J. Glenn Drive. Its protected location makes it excellent for launching in all weather; ample parking is nearby.

The boat basin to the west is protected by two overlapping rock jetties, with entry in the center. All of the commercial fleet is moored here, as

Squalicum Harbor in Bellingham

well as many permanently berthed pleasure craft. Some guest moorage may be available on the floats at the head of the bay, immediately below the two-story esplanade. The upper level of the elevated walkway affords a panoramic view of the harbor and the bustle of activity.

The attractive new shopping complex on shore has restaurants and a number of marine-related stores and services. City bus service provides transportation to downtown shopping. Harbor Center is fun even for non-boaters, who can view hard-working fishing boats and acres of pleasure boats from planked walkways and elevated decks. Restaurants offer fresh seafood, and shops have an array of goods ranging from anchors to artworks. A large open tank at the center of the mall displays local marine life for youngsters to squeal and giggle at.

CENTRAL FLOAT HAVEN

Downtown Bellingham fronts on several blocks of industrial wharfs. A city plan to develop this blighted area and attract new trade and industry is slated to be completed by 1990. At present a short float in the middle of the commercial wharfs, at the intersection of Chestnut St. and Central Ave., provides some public moorage to visiting boaters.

From the water it can be located by the three prominent stacks on the adjacent pier to the south. This float has neither water nor power hookups, but is within walking distance of the city center.

MARITIME HERITAGE CENTER

An interesting educational display near the mouth of Whatcom Creek tells all you may ever have wanted to know about salmon. The facility shows the complete life cycle of the fish, with rearing ponds, a fish ladder, adult holding pens, and a spawning channel arranged around an open concrete terrace. Eggs are fertilized and hatched in an adjacent building. Most activity is in the late fall when fish are spawning.

The center is located on C St., east of the intersection of Astor, 4 blocks from the downtown waterfront. During the rainy season Whatcom Creek pours into the Heritage Center in a dramatic waterfall. Children's play equipment nearby makes this a nice spot for a family outing.

BOULEVARD PARK

Park Area: 14 acres; 2800 feet of waterfront
Access: Land, boat
Facilities: Picnic tables, shelter, fireplaces, restrooms, drinking water, float, children's play equipment, viewpoint, hiking trail, craft studio
Attractions: Beachcombing, paddling, swimming, hiking, fishing, crabbing

Every city should be so fortunate as to have a park as gorgeous as this! Bellingham has made the most of a steep bluff and a swath of beach, having developed it into a two-level showpiece that seems even more spacious than its 14 acres. The upper section of the park lies along S. State St., on a

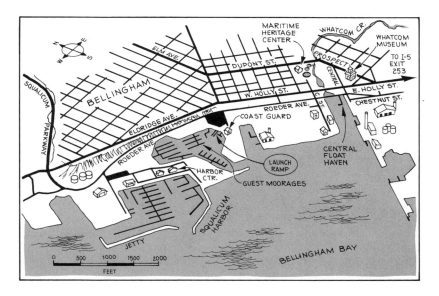

Kayaking near the pier of the Bellingham Cruise Center

bluff 75 feet above Bellingham Bay. A display at the overlook tells how the British explorer Capt. George Vancouver first sailed into the bay.

A path leads from the overlook past a gazebo, over a bridge, and then down to the lower park area. This lower section can also be reached by turning off S. State at its intersection with 11th St. onto Bayview Drive, which curves steeply downhill to the park.

At the north end of the park is a pier with a 40-foot float for visiting boaters. Since the moorage is not protected, it may be difficult to approach in rough water. The park closes at 10 p.m., and overnight moorage is not permitted.

Paths from here go north, paralleling the railroad tracks, all the way to downtown Bellingham. Headed south, the trail crosses an old railroad trestle that has been converted into a fishing pier and viewing site. Continuing along the shore for about two more blocks, it emerges at either Easton Ave. or ultimately a block farther at Bennett Ave.

HARRIS AVE. LAUNCH RAMP

A second boat-launch facility is maintained by the Port of Bellingham on the southwest side of the town. It is within a stone's throw of the Fairhaven business district, adjoining the facilities of the new Alaska Ferry Terminal.

If driving from I-5, turn off at Exit 250 and head west on the Valley Parkway. At 12th St. turn north, and in three blocks west again on Harris Ave. As the street approaches the waterfront, a sign points right to the Alaska Ferry auto loading and the public launch ramp. In a short distance the road turns right again, paralleling a chain-link fence, and finally arrives at the small launch area. The single-lane asphalt ramp is not as good as the facility at Squalicum Harbor, but it does provide quick access to this side of the bay. Rentals of canoes, kayaks, dories, sailboards, and small sailboats are available at an adjoining business.

BELLINGHAM CRUISE CENTER

Facilities: Ferry terminal, restaurant, viewing areas, historical display, gift
shop, restrooms

In 1989 the Alaska Ferry System pulled up stakes from Seattle's waterfront and moved its southern terminus to Bellingham, lured by the promise of a new terminal. The city made good on its promise with a stunning, $6.4 million facility covering 5.5 acres on the Fairhaven waterfront. Ferries arrive and depart from here every Friday throughout the year; during the last two weeks of May and first two weeks of June there are additional sailings on Tuesdays.

The activity on the huge ships can be watched from the adjacent pier or from the enclosed glass dome of the terminal. Even if the ferry is not in

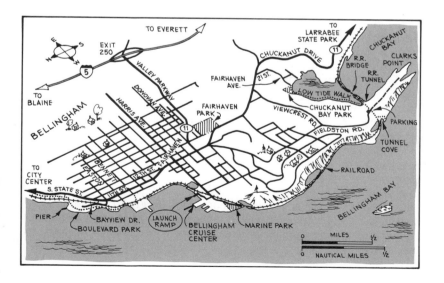

port, the terminal provides fine views of Bellingham Bay. Historical displays located around the edge of the pier give interesting vignettes of early exploration and development of Bellingham and Fairhaven. The terminal is reached by continuing west on Harris Ave. past the turnoff for the auto loading area and launch ramp.

MARINE PARK

Park Area: 3 acres; 730 feet of waterfront
Access: Land, boat
Facilities: Picnic tables, shelter, fireplaces, restrooms, drinking water

Harris Ave. continues west past the boat-launch turnoff and in about a block deadends at Marine Park—another example of Bellingham's dedication to fine parks. The beautifully landscaped park has facilities for picnicking and grassy lawns for afternoon siestas. Strategically placed benches look out to Bellingham Bay and passing marine traffic.

Although there are no boating facilities, small boats could be landed on the gravel beach at low tide, or hand-carried ones could easily be launched. From here the beach or railroad tracks can be walked south to Chuckanut Bay, or take to the streets for a brief stint and walk west and north to connect with trails to Boulevard Park.

CHUCKANUT BAY PARK

Although this city park has no facilities at present, it represents an important link in the system of trails interlacing Bellingham. For those planning a connecting walk, the section of path along the edge of Chuckanut Bay is accessible only at low tide, when it is possible to traverse the beach below a rocky cliff.

The park is reached by turning off Chuckanut Drive at 21st St. In 1 block turn right on Fairhaven Ave. and follow it for ½ mile to the park. When the water is in, car-top boats can be launched here, and paddlers can duck through an opening in the railroad bridge that crosses the bay to gain open water. At low tide the long mucky tideflat makes launching impossible.

Walking west from the park, inveterate hikers can skirt the edge of the bay, catch a trail across the wooded finger of Clarks Point, and then follow railroad tracks on to Bellingham. If high tide makes this section of the walk impossible, Clarks Point can be reached by turning off Chuckanut Drive onto Viewcrest Road, and then south onto Fieldston Road. The trailhead is well signed. Public access is limited to the vicinity of the trail only, but the surrounding lands are replete with nettles and heavy brush, so trespassing is not even a temptation.

CHUCKANUT BAY

Paddlers who gain access to Chuckanut Bay via the launch ramps at Chuckanut Bay Park or at Larrabee State Park, just around the corner to the south, can explore rocky shorelines and tiny islands that dot the long bay. Chuckanut Island, at the center of the bay, is a wildlife refuge of The Nature Conservancy.

Larger boats, too, will find the bay was made to order for gunkholing, with several little bays offering ample space for anchoring. Aptly named Pleasant Bay, at the extreme south end of Chuckanut Bay, is well protected from southerly winds. A rock ledge, 3 feet below the surface, has been reported just south of Chuckanut Island.

A "Chuckanut" is not some kind of local tree, as one might suspect, but an Indian word believed to mean "small cliffy bay next to big bay"—certainly an appropriate description for the site.

LARRABEE STATE PARK

Park Area: 1981 acres; 8100 feet of shoreline
Access: Land, boat
Facilities: 90 campsites, group camp, picnic tables, fireplaces, kitchens, picnic shelters, amphitheater, restrooms, showers, trailer dump station, boat launch (ramp), hiking trails
Attractions: Boating, paddling, fishing, swimming, tidepools, hiking, bicycling

Although most of Larrabee State Park lies inland, embracing the steep slopes of Chuckanut Mountain, a small corner of it touches the shoreline of

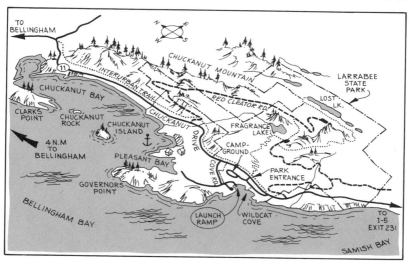

Canoeing off Larrabee State Park

Samish Bay. This corner contains most of the park's facilities, including the campground, picnic area, and amphitheater. The boat launch ramp is in an adjacent section of the park, reached by a separate road. The state park is 5 miles south of Bellingham on Chuckanut Drive, or it can be reached by leaving I-5 at Exit 231 (signed to Highway 11 and Chuckanut Drive) and driving north.

The camping and picnic area is in a narrow section between Chuckanut Drive and the railroad tracks. RV sites with hookups are spaced fairly closely together; tenting sites have a bit more privacy. Trails to the beach cross the railroad tracks or reach the shore via a tunnel.

At the intersection with Cove Road, ¾ mile north of the park entrance, a sign points west to the boat launch. The single-lane ramp is very steep but well-surfaced. Parking nearby is adequate for a dozen vehicles with trailers, but could get quite crowded on a busy day. Wildcat Cove, into which the ramp empties, is small and rock rimmed—unsuited for large boats. The cove has two sections separated by a rocky rib. At moderate to low tides enough sandy beach is revealed to permit beach towels to be spread for sunbathing or the waters to be tested for wading.

Another corner of the park touches the shore a mile to the south, but at this point the bluff is so steep that there is no upland access from the road. The beach can be reached by boat or by walking the railroad tracks or shore at low tide. Explore tidepools along the way, and marvel at the variety of wondrous creatures.

Larrabee State Park offers several miles of inland hiking trails on the slopes of Chuckanut Mountain. The trail up the mountainside is steep, gaining over 1500 feet, but the reward of crystal mountain lakes and lookout points with panoramic vistas makes the effort worthwhile. For low-level leg stretching, the Interurban Trail, which begins at the park, runs north for 7½ miles all the way to Bellingham with no appreciable elevation gain. The wide surfaced path is suitable for both hikers and bicyclists. The trailhead for both the trail up Chuckanut Mountain and the Interurban Trail is on the east side of Chuckanut Drive, across from the state park entrance.

The state park holds a distinctive spot in history—it was established on 20 acres of land donated by the Larrabee family, and was Washington's first state park. Additional donations and land purchases over the years have brought it to its present size. Steeply tilted layers of sandstone interbedded with lenses of shale are exposed along the shorelines of the park. Fossils of large palm leaves believed to be 60 million years old have been found in the shale deposits.

Eliza, Vendovi, and Sinclair Islands

Three moderate-sized islands lying at the front door to Bellingham Bay are privately owned and have little to attract tourists, although their bays and shorelines offer some interesting boat exploration.

ELIZA ISLAND

This island, which lies closest to Bellingham, is the most settled of the three. Small planes that land at an airstrip down the middle of the island bring landowners to their vacation retreats. Shoals and numerous rocks lie off the east and west sides of the triangular-shaped island—approach with care. A large open bight at the south end, facing the tip of Lummi Island, offers visiting boaters some anchorages, although the holding ground is poor and the bay is exposed to southerly blows.

The only public area on Eliza Island is a DNR beach at the extreme southern tip; however the shores are so rocky that few boaters would care to approach, even in small craft. Eliza Rock, which lies just off shore to the south, and Viti Rocks, ¾ mile southwest of the southern tip of Lummi Island, are both part of the San Juan Islands National Wildlife Refuge. Avoid approaching so close to either area that nesting birds are disturbed.

VENDOVI ISLAND

The most primitive of the three islands is Vendovi, lying 2 nautical miles southwest of Eliza. Its shorelines are smooth and rocky, except for a small bay on its northwest point. All of the island's shorelines, with the ex-

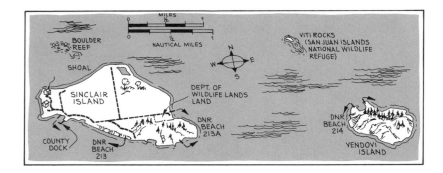

ception of those facing immediately on the bay, comprise DNR Beach 214; the public area lies below the mean high water level. The beaches are rocky, with some pretty little pocket coves. All the uplands are conspicuously posted with no trespassing signs—inland, snarling mastiffs presumably lie in wait.

SINCLAIR ISLAND

Sinclair Island, which at about 1½ square miles is the largest of the three, is the only one to have real roads. It lies at the north end of Bellingham Channel, 1½ miles west of Vendovi Island.

Although most of the island property is private, some limited access to the uplands is possible. A short county dock protected by a piling breakwater is on the southwest end of the island at the community of Urban. Overnight moorage is not permitted on the dock, but anchoring in the open coves to the north and south of the dock is possible. There are no commercial facilities on shore.

Rocks and a large shoal extend out from Sinclair Island on the north and west, reaching almost to Boulder Reef, ¾ nautical miles away. This dangerous reef, which bares at half tide, is marked by a lighted bell buoy. Kelp that surrounds the reef, giving further warning of danger, is often towed under by the current.

DNR Beach 213 extends east from the Sinclair Island dock for about a mile. It includes some tiny pocket coves and rocky beaches below a 60-foot bluff—when the uplands dip down and shorelines gentle, the public beach ends. Public beach is only that area below the mean high water level.

Beach 213A encompasses 2831 feet of shoreline at the southeastern tip of the island. The northern portion of this beach joins to Washington State Department of Wildlife lands, where visitors can extend their beach explorations with an upland nature walk through a small marshland. The Department of Wildlife lands can also be reached by walking east from the county dock for about 1½ miles. The public land lies south of the road near the east shore.

Cypress Island

The dream of saving this unspoiled island paradise from exploitation and development came within a hair's breadth of becoming, instead, a nightmare. The checkered history of attempts by the state to acquire the island for future generations finally ended in late 1989 when the DNR was able to purchase 4,408 acres of undeveloped property, giving the state title to more than 80 per cent of the island.

Land ownership on Cypress Island has had a controversial history. The island escaped early settlement due to its steep terrain and scarcity of water. Attempts at mining failed, and the land proved too harsh for agriculture. Over the years private individuals acquired some small sections, and a few residences were built, primarily on Strawberry Bay.

Between 1960 and 1978 a Seattle realtor, Sam Emmanuel, purchased property totaling about half of the island's 5500 acres. Although he considered developing it as a site for a nuclear plant or oil port, in the mid 1970s he began negotiations for sale of the land to the state DNR. Bert Cole, then land commissioner, set forth a grandiose plan, requiring a then-staggering $10 million, for purchase of the Emmanuel property and other holdings on Cypress Island.

Cypress Head

Negotiations stalled, and in September of 1978 Raymond Hanson, a Spokane industrialist, purchased Emmanuel's 2431 acres for $1.8 million. In the ensuing years Hanson set forth plans first for a 1000-unit exclusive residential development, then for a posh resort with a 200-room lodge, condominiums, a marina, and an 18-hole golf course. Both proposals, however, were met with fierce opposition but were eventually accepted by Skagit County commissioners.

State-owned property consisted of 800 acres of land and half of the tidelands. The only accessible sections were at Pelican Beach and Cypress Head, where primitive campgrounds had been developed. In 1987 the state legislature approved funds to purchase an additional 680 acres of the island—ironically at a higher price than they would have paid for half of the entire island in 1978. By the end of 1989 negotiations were concluded, and the bulk of Cypress Island was at last saved for the future.

The natural riches of Cypress Island include six small spring-fed lakes, several marshes, three excellent harbors, magnificent fortress-like cliffs, and forested mountains reaching to 1500 feet. More than 80 species of birds and a dozen kinds of mammals are known to live here, including bald eagles, hawks, deer, fox, river otter, raccoon, porcupine, muskrat, and weasel. The pristine environment of the island now appears to be safe from the potentially disastrous effects of development.

The unusual geological strata of the island support a great variety of flora; however one notable tree is missing—there are no cypress on Cypress Island. Captain George Vancouver erroneously named the island when he identified the local juniper trees as cypress.

Ferry travelers have an excellent view of the island as the boat leaves

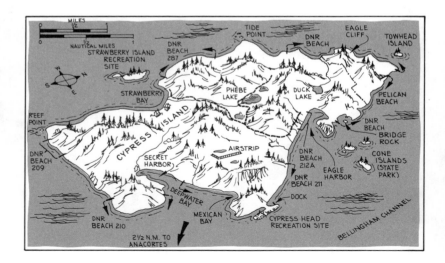

the Anacortes ferry terminal; the island's southern tip lies just 2½ nautical miles to the north, across Guemes Channel. The northwest shore is a popular salmon fishing ground, and cruising boaters sometimes drop anchor in Deepwater Bay or Eagle Harbor along the eastern shore, although beaches there are private.

STRAWBERRY (LOON) ISLAND RECREATION SITE

Park Area: 11 acres; 4000 feet of shoreline
Access: Boat
Facilities: 3 campsites, picnic tables, fireplaces, pit toilet, *no water*
Attractions: Boating, scuba diving

A ¼-mile-long narrow ridge of an island just off Strawberry Bay on the west side of Cypress Island is the site of a primitive DNR campground. Strawberry Island, like several of the other small park islands, has a familiar "dog bone" configuration, with two high, rounded shoulders of land joined by a low, narrow neck—in this case the northern shoulder is considerably larger and higher than the southern one, more like an exclamation point. The island offers a few picnic and camping sites along with pleasant shoreline scrambles and views of boats parading past in Rosario Strait.

The shores of the main section of the island are so steep that going ashore there is quite difficult. The only landing for small boats is at a sandy cove between the small southern knob and the rest of the island. Offshore waters are quite deep and have defied attempts to place buoys. Boaters in large craft should anchor in Strawberry Bay and dinghy across to the park.

Strawberry Bay was visited in 1792 by William Broughton of the Vancouver Expedition. Lieutenant Broughton, who first explored the inner channels of the San Juan Islands, anchored his brig *Chatham* here, and was delighted to find great numbers of wild strawberries on shore. Some days later, when Vancouver stopped over in the same spot at Broughton's recommendation, the strawberries were out of season, and his crew had to settle for wild onions. (Be grateful it's not named Onion Bay.)

CYPRESS HEAD RECREATION SITE

Park Area: 16.5 acres; 4800 feet of shoreline
Access: Boat
Facilities: 8 campsites, fireplaces, picnic tables, fire rings, mooring
    buoys, dock with float, pit toilets, *no water*
Attractions: Boating, paddling, fishing

The tiny peninsula of Cypress Head lies on the eastern-most bulge of Cypress Island. The wooded headland, which is joined to its parent island by a low grassy sandspit, has been developed by the DNR as a boat-in recreation area, with picnic facilities and overnight campsites.

Dock at Cypress Head Recreation Site

This pretty little spot is only 4 nautical miles from the boat launch ramp at Sunset Beach on Fidalgo Island, making it an ideal cruising destination. The long south-facing bay formed by the head is quite shallow and has a rock near the entrance; use care entering. The northern cove, which holds the dock and 5 mooring buoys, is somewhat deeper. The short float is for dinghys and loading only. Boats too large to be beached must tie to a buoy or drop a hook. Good anchorages can be found in 20–30 feet of water.

The rocky head has 5 campsites with tables and fireplaces, and 2 additional day-use sites that are too rocky for spreading a sleeping bag. On a grassy flat on the mainland are 3 additional campsites. A chain-link fence marks the western boundary of the park.

A rough trail circles the outer edge of Cypress Head, passing vistas gorgeously framed by twisted madrona and juniper. Beaches are rocky; in a few spots it is possible to scramble down the steep 10-foot bank to reach the shore.

The Cypress Head Recreation Area also leads to some 3 miles of public tidelands. DNR Beach 211, which is 15,652 feet in total length, including the Cypress Head tidelands, extends north from Cypress Head for about 1 mile and southwest to the middle of the north shore of Deepwater Bay. The western boundary is marked by a row of old pilings. At high tide the beach is almost nonexistent, but at low tide leads to some nice beach scrambles and a small pocket cove. All uplands, except for Cypress Head, are private.

PELICAN BEACH AND EAGLE CLIFF

Park Area: 220 acres; 7207 feet of shoreline
Access: Boat
Facilities: 4 campsites, fireplaces, fire rings, picnic tables, picnic shelter,
pit toilets, mooring buoys, hiking trails, *no water*
Attractions: Boating, paddling, fishing, swimming, scuba diving, hiking,
beachcombing

The finest parcel of DNR land on Cypress Island is a forested strip
spanning the far northern end of the island. On the eastern shore is Pelican
Beach, a beautiful little boat-in campground, on the west is the spectacular
rocky face of 750-foot-high Eagle Cliff, and between the two is a swath of
deep woods holding a few miles of hiking trails for exploration and en-
chantment.

Pelican Beach has 4 mooring buoys offshore and 4 formal campsites
just beyond the high-tide level. The gently sloping gravelly shore invites
wading (chilly) or sunbathing among the driftwood (warm). At its northern
boundary the beach becomes quite rocky. The shore, with its countless
little tidepools, can be followed for some distance around the point. Explorers need to be aware, however, that they can become trapped between
an incoming tide and the steep, high bank.

Public DNR beaches extend all the way around the north end of the island for 1½ miles to the south side of Foss Cove. South of Pelican Beach
public DNR tidelands continue south for ½ mile to Bridge Rock, opposite
the Cone Islands.

Leaving the campground, the trail that spans the park rises gradually
but steadily through open second-growth timber. In ½ mile a fork is

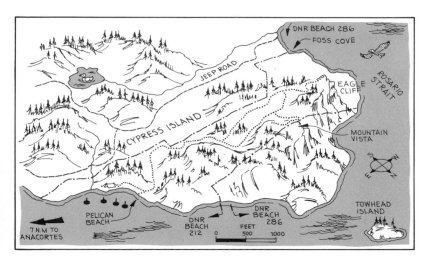

Eagle Cliff

reached—the left is signed to Eagle Cliff, 1.2 miles. Loop Trail, the unsigned right-hand branch, goes to Mountain Vista and eventually circles around to meet the Eagle Cliff trail.

If headed for Mountain Vista, be aware that as of 1987 the side trail that branches to the right from Loop Trail is not marked. Look for it in a tiny, open grassy area. If an open flat is reached (when hiking from the east) and the trail begins descending steeply into the forest, the side trail has been missed—go back.

The Mountain Vista side trail contours around an *extremely* steep, open side-hill—use care! Once around the side-hill the route ascends to the top of the mountain, with knee-weakening vistas west past Eagle Cliff to Obstruction Pass and Orcas Island. The trail ends at the 660-foot mountain top and more views—this time south and east to Anacortes, Guemes Island, the tiny dots of the Cone Islands, and Bellingham Channel.

The side trail to Eagle Cliff leaves the Loop Trail and follows a sparsely wooded ridge to the final rocky outcropping of the summit. Look down to Foss Cove on the west side of Cypress Island and out to toy-like boats bobbing in Rosario Strait. The masses of Orcas and Blakely Islands fill the view to the west. Neither viewpoint is a place for toddlers or persons afflicted with vertigo.

CYPRESS ISLAND DNR BEACHES

In addition to the public DNR beaches described above at Cypress Head and Pelican Beach, a few other stretches of Cypress Island tidelands are available to the public. Beach 212A begins at the south side of Eagle Harbor and extends south for 2118 feet. This very pretty beach has a row of driftwood at the high-tide level and gentles out into a sandy flat at low tide. Property above the mean high water level and tidelands at the head of the bay are private—do not trespass.

Beach 210 encircles the knob at the southeast end of the island, but forget it—the shore drops off so steeply that there is virtually no beach, even at low tide. Beach 209 more than makes up for it however. Located on the south side of the island, east of Reef Point, this latter beach, 1635 feet in length, includes a broad sand and gravel tideflat that extends out for some distance at extreme low water.

A final DNR beach, number 287, which is 8872 feet in length, lies due north of Strawberry Island. Several small caves caused by wave undercutting make this shoreline especially interesting.

CONE ISLANDS STATE PARK

Park Area: 10 acres; 2500 feet of shoreline
Access: Boat
Facilities: None (undeveloped)
Attractions: Scuba diving, paddling, birdwatching

Cone Islands, a cluster of miniature forested islands and low-tide rocks lying off the northeast shore of Cypress Island are undeveloped state park lands. With its steep rocky shores dropping into the water and surrounding kelp beds, most boaters are content to enjoy the islands from the distance as they cruise by, although scuba divers sometimes stop there and explore from anchored boats. The island walls are so abrupt that going ashore is nearly impossible.

The northernmost of the islands has especially interesting geology, displaying tilted beds of shale along its east side.

Guemes Island

Although separated only by mile-wide Bellingham Channel, neighboring Cypress and Guemes Islands are totally different in character. While Cypress Island is steep, rocky, and densely wooded, with deeply notched bays and a cliffy shoreline, Guemes has a rural atmosphere, with wide expanses of flatland and a long, smooth shoreline.

Guemes Island would be just another Anacortes suburb were it not for

the ½-mile-wide water barrier of Guemes Channel that serves to keep urban sprawl and industrial boom at arm's length. At one time the island was
eyed as a prospective site for an aluminum processing plant; however the
negative reaction of residents sent developers looking elsewhere. The island remains quietly pastoral, providing sanctuary for retirees, artists,
farmers, summer vacationers, and Fidalgo Island workers who commute
daily from their homes.

The little Skagit County-operated ferry scurries back and forth across
the channel like a busy water bug, carrying a few cars on its open deck
each trip. The voyage takes about 7 minutes; runs are made hourly
throughout the day. The ferry leaves from a terminal in downtown
Anacortes at 6th and I Streets.

A ferry has been serving the island since the early 1900s, first carrying horses, wagons, and farm produce. Some horses were so wary of the
watery crossing that they had to be blindfolded—not so the Model T's
however, when they began riding in the 1920s. The first fares were 50¢
for car and driver, 10¢ for milk cans, passengers free. One resident became so incensed when the ferry began charging 5¢ for foot passengers
that from then on he rowed across the channel.

Guemes is ideal bicycling country, with straight and level interior

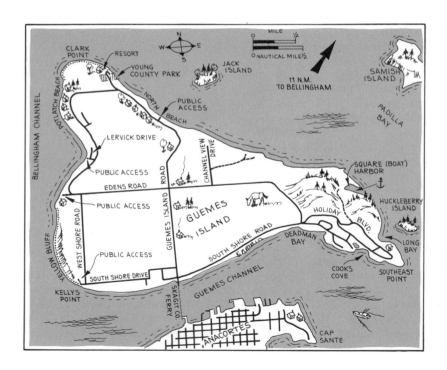

roads that pass by farmlands and orchards, while perimeter roads wind around the shores, with views out to cool sea and distant islands. The only commercial development is a small resort on the northern tip of the island, which has a few cabins, a campground, and boats for rent. There are no boat-launch ramps on the island, although hand-carried boats can be launched at several spots.

Guemes Island has a refreshing approach to public use of lands: here a few beaches are posted as "Open Space." Owners of such lands permit public recreational use as long as such use is compatible with its natural state—in other words, observe posted fire regulations, do not litter, and do not deface or destroy either personal property or natural features. The areas at Kellys Point and Clark Point are presently open space. If their status changes, do not trespass—look elsewhere for recreational land.

YOUNG COUNTY PARK AND CLARK POINT

Park Area: 11 acres; 500 feet of shoreline
Access: Land, boat
Facilities: Picnic tables, fireplaces, pit toilets
Attractions: Paddling, clam digging, swimming

A small county park at the north end is the island's only public recreation site. It faces on a nice driftwood-edged beach and a gradual tideflat. Tiny Jack Island, ¾ mile due east, is an enticing small boat destination. Even shallow-draft boats should approach the park with care at minus tide to avoid getting stuck on the flat.

Camping was once permitted in the park; however the sanitation facilities were inadequate, and the county was forced to limit it to day use. The adjacent resort has some campsites as well as cabins, rental boats, and a store that sells groceries and fuel.

Nearly 2 miles of beautiful clean gravel beach wrap around Clark Point to the north, providing terrific views first into Bellingham Bay, then north to Sinclair, Vendovi, and Lummi Islands, and finally swinging westward to lovely little Cone Islands and mountainous Cypress.

To reach the beach, walk north from the resort. Near the point the beach narrows, but should be passable at all but the highest tides or during heavy wave action. The bank above the beach is steep and heavily wooded, and there is no inland egress, so use care not to get trapped by high water. Open space ends at private property on Potlatch Beach on the eastern side of the point.

NORTH BEACH PUBLIC ACCESS

On the east side of Guemes Island, facing on a huge tideflat, is a densely settled area of beach-front homes and summer cottages, reminiscent of the south end of Hood Canal. A 40-foot-wide Department of Wild-

Square Harbor (Boat Harbor)

life public access to the beach is provided here for clam diggers. Watch carefully amid the cottages for a small sign on the east side of the road, near the south end of the beach. Hand-carried boats can be launched here, but nearby parking is limited.

SQUARE HARBOR (BOAT HARBOR)

Nearly all the shoreline of Guemes Island is smooth, with long tideflats. The one exception is at the southeast end where slightly mountainous terrain also signals steeper underwater walls. Two small bights are located along this shore. Long Bay, near Southeast Point, offers boaters some anchoring possibilities, although it is quite open.

An even better anchorage is at sublime little Square Harbor, a mile to the north. The 500-yard-wide rocky indentation has space for 2–3 boats with good protection from all weather except easterlies. It is a handy, secluded spot when nearby Saddlebag Island is filled to overflowing. The bay is easily located by the 100-foot sheer, barren cliff immediately to the north.

KELLYS POINT

On the southwest corner of Guemes Island, at the intersection of South Shore Drive and West Shore Drive, a short road spur continues west

Salamander found on Guemes Island

to a beautiful gravel and driftwood beach facing Bellingham Channel. The beach can be walked north for more than a mile, beneath the imposing 150-foot scarp of Yellow Bluff. Climbing on the bluff or digging caves can be hazardous as the bank is composed of soft glacial till and can collapse. Note the numerous holes that birds have burrowed in the hillside.

This is a good beach for finding agates—jasper, carnelian, and adventurine can be collected here as well as numerous other stones, some unique to the area. Many residents have extensive collections of agates gleaned from Guemes Island beaches.

The point is named after the notorious outlaw, Lawrence "Smuggler" Kelly, who had a hideout here in the late 1800s. Kelly brought illegal Chinese aliens into the country from Canada, as well as cargoes of opium and wool, which were heavily taxed at the time.

GUEMES ISLAND ROAD ENDS

Two road ends on the west side of Guemes Island provide spots to put in hand-launched boats. Property on either side of the road ends is private. Each has parking for a few cars.

Edens Road. From Kellys Point, West Shore Drive heads due north, and in 1½ miles T's into Edens Road. Turn west and in ⅛ mile, when the main road turns north and becomes West Shore Drive again, continue straight ahead to the dead end at the beach.

Great blue heron (Heidi Mueller photo)

Lervick Drive. About 1 mile north of the Edens Road/West Shore Drive intersection, a short side street heads left. A large log blocks the road end at the beach, but the street turns north and continues a short distance to some private homes.

Samish Bay and Samish Island

Samish Bay, the southern portion of Bellingham Bay, bares for nearly half its extent during low water. Most boaters avoid its shallow waters; however it does offer some fine paddling opportunities.

During migratory season Samish Bay is as good as Padilla Bay, to the south, for sighting a variety of waterfowl. Great blue herons from the rookery on Samish Island frequent the flats, and visitors are virtually assured of seeing these elegant birds. Flocks of black brant, canvasbacks, and Eurasian wigeons winter here; snowy owls, peregrines, and gyrfalcons may be spotted on shore.

The Samish Bay area was the site of an early utopian settlement. Equality Colony was established near Blanchard, on the north edge of the delta, and was active from 1898 to 1907. All that remains of the socialist group, now disbanded, is a small cemetery and a creek named Colony that flows into Samish Bay.

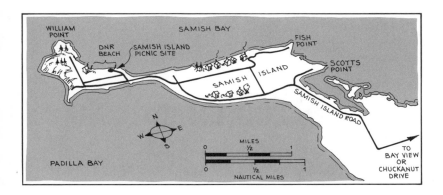

SAMISH ISLAND PICNIC SITE

Park Area: .5 acre; 1436 feet of shoreline
Access: Land, boat
Facilities: Picnic table, pit toilet, *no water*
Attractions: Beachcombing, paddling, clam digging, scuba diving

When the land-shaping glaciers withdrew from Puget Sound, Samish Island was two islands. Today it's a peninsula, joined by necks of sand to the mainland. The huge flat delta lands adjoining Samish Island were built up by the Skagit River, which now enters the sound several miles to the south.

To drive to Samish Island, leave I-5 at Exit 231, which is signed to Highway 11 and Chuckanut Drive. On the drive through the Samish Flats watch for the many birds that pause here in their migratory flights; hawks, falcons, eagles, and a variety of passerines frequently can be seen.

After leaving I-5, in 5 miles turn west on Sunset Road, in 1¾ mile at a T intersection north on Highway 237, and in ¾ mile west on Bay View–Edison Road. In 1 mile the road heads south and becomes Samish Island Road. Follow this main road through various turns to the north side of the island.

At road's end is a small park with picnic tables at the top of an 80-foot bank. A set of stairs descends steeply to the shore. The public beach extends west from the stairs. Low tide reveals a cobble shore and the massive tideflats of Samish Bay, but at high water there is no beach. Views are north to Hale Passage and Eliza and Lummi Islands, and across to the rocky cliffs of Chuckanut Drive.

3. FIDALGO ISLAND AND PADILLA BAY

Fidalgo seems barely an island at all, lying so close that bridges bind it to the mainland and provide easy access to civilization's conveniences. Yet it has an island's advantages of mile-upon-mile of shoreline, with beaches and bays to suit every purpose, and that sense of unique character that only true physical separation, and not political boundaries, can create.

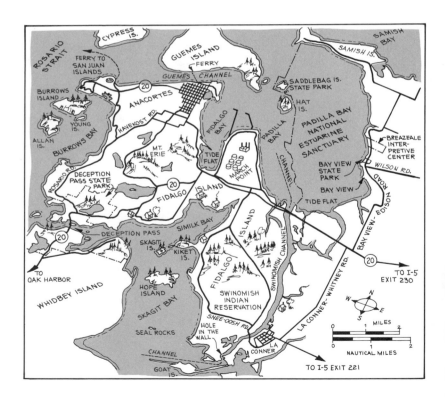

Padilla Bay and Mt. Baker at sunrise

The island is divided into three distinct sections, or "lobes." The eastern lobe, bordered on the east by the Swinomish Channel and on the west by Skagit and Similk Bays, almost entirely comprises the Swinomish Indian Reservation. Waterfront property on the west shore and at Shelter Bay on the southeastern tip is leased by the tribe to non-Indians for homes and vacation cottages. The heavily forested interior is selectively logged.

The long amoeba-like foot of March Point, extending into the tideflats of Fidalgo and Padilla Bays, comprises most of the middle section of the island. Huge storage tanks and refineries with billowing smoke stacks seem strange bedfellows to the small farms dotting the surrounding lands. Although the refineries with their pipelines and steady parade of oil tankers make environmentalists queasy, refinery jobs and the associated economic boom are generally welcome by Fidalgo Islanders, and the factories have thus far remained environmentally "clean." However there are those who fear that the refineries herald encroaching industrialism in the Skagit Delta and nearby islands.

The western lobe of the island, its largest section, displays the true "San Juan" character, with rugged shorelines, glacier-scrubbed granite domes, and pocket lakes nestled in green forest. Here, in its several public parks, visitors can explore beaches and bluffs to their heart's content and gaze out to the enticing shores of myriad more islands.

Fidalgo Island is reached by following Highway 20 west from I-5 Exit 230, just north of Mt. Vernon. In 8½ miles a soaring concrete bridge crosses the Swinomish Channel onto Fidalgo Island. In 3¼ miles more at Sharpes Corner at the end of Fidalgo Bay the highway splits into a Y. Both branches of the Y are still Highway 20. The right leg goes north for 2½ miles more to Anacortes, while the left branch heads southwest, reaching Deception Pass State Park in 4½ miles. A bridge over the Swinomish Channel at La Conner also crosses to Fidalgo Island, connecting with roads up the center and along the west shore of the Indian reservation.

The island can be reached from the south by taking the Mukilteo ferry to Clinton on Whidbey Island and driving north on Highway 525 (which midway becomes Highway 20) for a distance of 50 miles to the Deception Pass bridge. The Keystone ferry from Port Townsend to Whidbey Island provides access to the island from the Olympic Peninsula.

Fidalgo Island's two unique waterways, the Swinomish Channel and Deception Pass, serve as boating portals to the San Juan Islands and Canada's Gulf Islands for hordes of pleasure vessels traveling up Saratoga Passage from Puget Sound. The southern entrance to Swinomish Channel is about 50 nautical miles from Shilshole Bay in Seattle, and Deception Pass is 6 nautical miles farther.

Padilla Bay

SADDLEBAG ISLAND MARINE STATE PARK

Park area: 23 acres; 6750 feet of shoreline
Access: Boat
Facilities: Campsites, picnic tables, fireplaces, pit toilets, *no water*
Attractions: Fishing, crabbing, scuba diving, hiking

Conveniently located only 2 nautical miles northeast of Anacortes, near the mouth of Padilla Bay, Saddlebag Island Marine State Park is heavily used by boaters who drop by for the day to try their hand at crabbing and fishing, and by those on their way to somewhere else who use its coves as handy anchorages. For visitors who take the time to go ashore, the trails that circle the island's grassy bluffs give boaters a chance to steady their sea legs and enjoy bird's eye views of the activity below—sailboats with bright spinnakers looking like flowers blowing in the wind, fishing boats

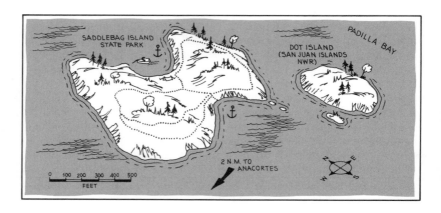

drifting offshore, and behemoth tankers heading for the oil refinery at March Point. Dot Island, just a stone's throw away from Saddlebag, is a bird nesting area and animal refuge of the San Juan Islands Wilderness.

Saddlebag Island is cast in the familiar San Juan pattern of two rocky, scrub-covered headlands joined by a low, narrow neck, creating the outline that inspired this island's name. The two coves formed on either side of the land mass face north and south, with the northern one slightly larger and more deeply indented.

The water east of the island is extremely shallow; approach from the west, especially during a minus tide. There are no mooring buoys at the park; however numerous good anchorages are available—the best are in the northern cove. The southern cove is shallower, with a thick growth of eelgrass, making it difficult for anchors to dig in.

A small camp area is at the head of the northern bay; pit toilets are along the trail that crosses the middle of the island. The southern bay has space for picnicking on the beach, but there is not enough room for tenting on the narrow driftwood-choked beach.

Saddlebag, Dot, and Hat Islands are perched on the edge of a huge submarine shelf; to the east is less than a fathom of water, while immediately west the shelf plummets to a depth of 30–40 fathoms. The rich variety of marine organisms living on the long flat and in niches of the steep walls of the shelf make this a feeding area for sea birds, fish, crabs, and even the local river otters.

PADILLA BAY NATIONAL ESTUARINE SANCTUARY

Park Area: 11,600 acres
Access: Land, boat
Facilities: (at Breazeale Padilla Bay Interpretive Center; see below)
Attractions: Paddling, fishing, crabbing, birdwatching

Until recently most boaters have looked on Padilla Bay as just a place to hurry through quickly—the huge shoal areas marked on marine charts were enough to give any sea captain nightmares. Now, thanks to the dedicated work of some Skagit County residents, the bay has received recognition as the ecological phenomenon that it is, and more and more people are pausing to learn about and enjoy the estuary.

Padilla Bay lies in a protected pocket between Fidalgo and Guemes Islands and the mainland. The north end of the Swinomish Channel is dredged along the western edge of the bay. In 1980 a large section of the bay was established as a National Estuarine Sanctuary, encompassing 11,600 acres of marsh and tidelands stretching along the east side of the bay from the Swinomish Channel to Samish Island. The vegetation, marine creatures, fish, birds, and mammals living in this area are all part of an important ecological system that has now been preserved in its natural state for study and for the benefit of future generations.

Twice yearly Padilla Bay hosts large populations of black brant. These small geese with a particular palate dine almost exclusively on eelgrass and sea lettuce found in huge beds in the brackish water of the bay. By late October they begin to arrive, pausing to feed on their way to wintering grounds in Baja California. A small number of the flock remain to winter in the bay. In early spring the large populations return, flying in long wavering lines, to again refuel on the bay's vegetation before the final leg of their trip to nesting grounds on the Alaska Peninsula.

To reach the sanctuary by land, leave I-5 at Exit 230, just north of Mt. Vernon, and follow Highway 20 west 5¼ miles to the intersection of Highway 237, which is signed to the Padilla Bay sanctuary. Follow Highway 237 north for 3 miles and turn west on Wilson Road. In 1½ miles is the small town of Bay View, on the edge of Padilla Bay.

Boat-launch ramps can be found at the town of Bay View, at March Point, and at the south end of Padilla Bay, where Highway 20 crosses the Swinomish Channel. Hand-carried boats can also be put in at Bay View State Park.

PADILLA BAY SHORE TRAIL

Facilities: Informational displays, picnic tables, benches
Attractions: Birdwatching, walking, jogging, bicycling

During the late 1800's (and before the days of Environmental Impact Statements), settlers in the Skagit Valley built a network of dikes to hold

Padilla Bay Shore Trail and farmlands

the saltwater at bay and claim the delta for farmland. A 2¼-mile-long section of these dikes is now officially open as a walking and bicycling path along the edge of Padilla Bay. The south end of the trail is on one of the branches of Indian Slough, on the Bay View-Edison Road, .8 mile north of its intersection with Highway 20. Here there is parking for a dozen cars on the shoulder. The north end of the Shore Trail is at the southern edge of the town of Bay View; parking is two blocks away on 2nd St. Handicapped parking is by the trailhead.

The wide path atop the dike, surfaced with fine crushed gravel, is ideal for jogging or family bicycling. Several interpretive signs along the route tell about the wetland habitat, and the effect of the dikes upon it. The Breazeale Interpretive Center provides a checklist of over 125 different species of birds that may be spotted here; take binoculars to scan the marshes and bay. Hunting is permitted from the dike, in season.

BAY VIEW LAUNCH RAMP

A short block north of the Wilson Road intersection in Bay View is a state Department of Wildlife boat-launch ramp. The one-lane concrete ramp is usable only at high tide, since it ends in a mucky tideflat at low tide. Parking space for half a dozen cars with trailers is adjacent the ramp.

BAY VIEW STATE PARK

Park Area: 24 acres; 1285 feet of shoreline
Access: Land, boat
Facilities: 99 campsites, picnic shelter, picnic tables, fireplaces, drinking
    water, restrooms, showers, children's play area
Attractions: Swimming, fishing, paddling

This state park is on the north edge of the town of Bay View. The overnight camping area lies on the east side of the road in stately old-growth timber, and RV sites with power and water hookups are in an open grassy area near the entrance. Some tenting campsites lie around the perimeter of a grassy field, but most are on shady forested loops.

A wooden staircase leads from the picnic area down an embankment to the park road where it ducks through a highway underpass and emerges on the west at a large parking lot and broad, sandy beach. This lower, day-use area of the park has picnic tables, fireplaces, and plenty of places to loll in the sun or test the water of the bay. Kayaks or inflatable boats can be carried the short distance from the parking lot and launched here for exploration of the vast waters of Padilla Bay.

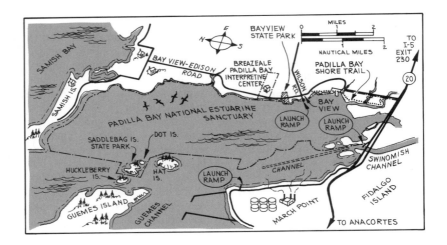

BREAZEALE PADILLA BAY INTERPRETIVE CENTER

Area: 64 acres
Access: Land, water (limited)
Facilities: Nature trail, view tower, restrooms
Attractions: Educational displays, hiking, birdwatching

To better appreciate the many forms of life in Padilla Bay, stop at the Breazeale Interpretive Center, which serves as headquarters of the sanctuary. The center is ½ mile north of Bay View on Bay View-Edison Road, within easy walking distance of the state park. While walking or driving the road to the center, watch for birds. Eagles nest near here, and there is a heron rookery on Samish Island. Hawks are commonly seen foraging along hedgerows.

At the interpretive center, models, illustrated displays, dioramas with preserved animals, a series of saltwater aquariums, and a "hands on" room for young visitors present a fascinating explanation of the marine environment. The center regularly offers programs and other environment-related activities for visitors; films are shown at 1 and 4 p.m. on Sundays. The center is open Wednesday through Sunday from 10 a.m. to 5 p.m., closed Monday and Tuesday.

North of the building a ¾-mile nature trail loops through the wildlife habitat area. Numbered posts along the route are keyed to a descriptive pamphlet that is available at the center. A second, short path leads west from the building to a beach overlook and a staircase that winds down to the beach. The beach access is open only from April to June and July to September; it is closed other times to avoid disturbing nesting and wintering birds. Visitors in small boats may land here to visit the interpretive center when the staircase access is open.

The ideal way to view the bay is by kayak or other small boat at high tide, when most of the bay is 6 feet deep or less. Boaters are likely to sight seals, herons, and a variety of waterfowl. At low tide the bay becomes a mucky flat where even kayaks may get stuck. Below, in the shallow water, is a teeming display of plant and animal life. The best place to launch hand-carried boats is from the beach at Bay View State Park. Be wary of strong winds that can cause problems for small boats.

The eelgrass beds offshore from Bay View State Park north to Joe Leary Slough are vital wintering areas for Black Brants. Avoid this area from September to November and February to May so they are not disturbed.

SWINOMISH CHANNEL BOAT LAUNCH

The easiest boat access to Padilla Bay is from a fine new launch ramp maintained by Skagit County Parks and Recreation at the north end of the Swinomish Channel. To reach it, leave I-5 at Exit 230 and follow Highway 20 west toward Anacortes. Just before the road crosses the Swinomish Channel bridge, turn right onto the old road that parallels the north side of the highway, then ends in a large parking lot under the bridge. Picnic tables and latrines are nearby. The two-lane concrete launch ramp has a finger pier for loading boats. A donation is requested for use of the ramp.

MARCH POINT BOAT LAUNCH

Access: Land, boat
Facilities: Boat launch (ramp), *no water*
Attractions: Boating, paddling, fishing, crabbing, birdwatching

Although the heart of March Point is given over to industry, timid shorebirds still skitter along its shores and rafts of migratory waterfowl still gather in the adjacent bays, providing good birdwatching in fall and winter from beach or boat.

To reach the shoreline road around March Point from Highway 20, turn right onto March Point Road ½ mile after crossing the Swinomish Channel bridge. The blacktopped road circles the point for about 7 miles, returning to Highway 20 at a junction at the head of Fidalgo Bay. Stopping places along the road are few.

A boat-launch ramp with a large parking lot is located near the tip of the point. The ramp is gravel and not well maintained; however it is generally usable at high tide. More parking is found a little farther along around the point. RV camping is permitted in both parking areas, but there are no toilet facilities or water. Boats launched here frequently head for Saddlebag Island State Park, 2½ nautical miles north or to the popular salmon fishing grounds just off nearby Hat Island.

Small boats such as kayaks or inflatable rafts can spend a pleasant afternoon along the shoreline and in the waters of huge Padilla Bay. Bay View State Park lies 3 nautical miles to the east on the far shore of the bay. Use caution, for the majority of the bay is less than 2 feet deep at mean lower low water. Watch water depth carefully, or explore on a rising tide so that incoming water can float off boats that become mired.

Anacortes

When Amos Bowman first arrived at Fidalgo Island in 1876, he came to the conclusion that Ship Harbor on the northern tip of the island, with its fine deep harbor and strategic location at the entrance to Puget Sound, was perfectly suited for a major seaport. He purchased 186 acres of land, convinced other settlers of the merits of the island, and founded a town, naming it Anacortes after his wife, Anna Curtis Bowman.

All that was needed to assure its future as "the New York of the Pacific Coast" was a railroad to provide connecting land transportation for the impending rush of people and goods. This was a time of feverish financial speculation—five different railway depots were built at locations around the island, each one expected to be the Northwest's connection to the Orient. When the Northern Pacific finally completed its first set of transcontinental rails to western Washington, its terminus, alas, was in Tacoma, not in Anacortes as Bowman had been led to expect. Instead of unloading at the wharf already constructed and awaiting cargoes at Ship Harbor, ships headed up the sound to Commencement Bay. The anticipated boom had fizzled.

The great westward expansion did benefit Anacortes, although in a more modest way than had been hoped. Railroad spurs eventually came down the sound, and canneries, sawmills, shipyards, and other industries brought steady growth to the area; however nothing inspired the boom that early entrepreneurs had prophesied. Perhaps the failure of those early city fathers eventually became a triumph; reflecting on the industrial sprawl and pollution attendant to Tacoma today, and imagining all of that transplanted to Anacortes, one can only shudder at what this fragile area might be if Amos Bowman had fully realized his dream.

Today the city serves as the portal to the San Juan Islands, with its ferry transporting over ¾ million tourists and residents to the islands annually, and its marinas chartering boats and offering marine services to thousands more. The Washington State ferry provides service from Anacortes to Lopez, Shaw, Orcas, and San Juan Islands and Sidney, B.C. A second ferry, operated by Skagit County, provides service to Guemes Island from its terminal in downtown Anacortes at 6th and I Streets.

Private airplanes can land at the municipal airport on the west side of town, ½ mile from the ferry terminal, or the local air service can be

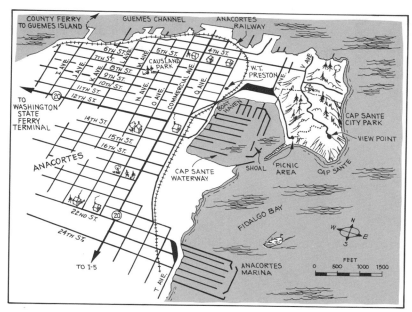

chartered for flights to the San Juan Islands.

Many tourists hurry through the city on their way to distant islands, not realizing that Anacortes itself has beaches, bays, viewpoints and natural treasures to rival those found on the more remote islands. The city has perhaps the finest parks of any city of similar size in the state, ranging from carefully groomed, pocket-sized Causland Park to Washington Park, with its rugged bluffs beautified by time and weather.

Anacortes has stores, restaurants, and services to meet every shopping need; most are on Commercial Ave. The old section of the town, at the north end of Commercial, is a mixture of a few new stores and a number of turn-of-the-century buildings that have been nicely renovated. One remarkable feature of a town of this vintage is the width of the streets. The men who platted the town were so sure of its future as a major city that they planned the streets accordingly. They even envisioned a grand avenue 200 feet wide that would run the entire length of Fidalgo Island.

ANACORTES MARINAS

Facilities: Complete boat and crew facilities, laundry, boat pumpout station, boat launch (hoist), U.S. Customs, boat rental and charters, restaurants and shopping (nearby)

For tourists arriving at Anacortes in their own boat, or planning to charter one, marinas are located around the saltwater perimeter of the city at Flounder Bay on the southwest, and on the east behind the protective headland of Cap Sante. Marinas on the north side of town, facing on Guemes Channel, have mostly permanent moorages but may have some space for transient boaters, and they do have some facilities such as fuel and boat rentals.

The Port of Anacortes provides moorages and amenities for transient boaters at its recently enlarged facilities at Cap Sante Boat Haven. A dredged channel leading into the waterway is marked with daybeacons and lights. Do not stray out of the channel as several submerged rocks lie near the headland. Guest slips and the harbormaster's office are on dock C, on the west shore.

The port has recently added several hundred moorages on the north side of the harbor; before tying up here, check in with the harbormaster. The service complex on the north shore has restrooms with showers and the marina laundry. To reach the old section of the marina, one must walk around the shore a couple of blocks on a blacktop path. The restaurants and stores of downtown Anacortes are within walking distance.

Anacortes Marina, a large new facility behind a piling breakwater on Fidalgo Bay, south of Cap Sante, has some transient slips when permanent moorages are vacant. It has power and water on the floats, and modern restrooms on shore.

For a description of the facilities at Skyline Marina, which is on the

Snagboat W. T. Preston

west side of Anacortes at Flounder Bay, see the write-up on Burrows Bay, below. Public ramps for trailered boats are located at Sunset Beach in Washington Park and at March Point.

W. T. *PRESTON* AND THE ANACORTES RAILWAY

An interesting addition to the Anacortes waterfront is the *W. T. Preston,* an historic sternwheeler built in 1929 that for many years worked as a snagboat on Puget Sound rivers and Lake Washington. It is now retired and is being restored as a museum. It is on shore, at the northwest corner of the Cap Sante boat basin, at 7th and R Ave. The boat is open for viewing on weekends in the summer, and other times as volunteer staff are available. A self-guided tour of the boat leads visitors through the engine room, crew quarters, galley, pilothouse, and decks, explaining the intricacies of the unique paddlewheeler.

The old Burlington Northern Railroad depot, which is just north of the *Preston,* has been restored and now serves as a community center. Here is also the terminal for a steam mini-locomotive, pulling three elegant brass- and velvet-decorated parlor cars, that offers rides along the Anacortes waterfront. It operates only in the summer.

CAUSLAND MEMORIAL PARK

If the boat crew is ready to mutiny after days of confinement aboard, an 8-block stroll and a picnic at Causland Memorial Park may be in order. From Cap Sante Waterway walk west to N Ave., then north to 8th. The 1-block park with its long walls and band shell of intricate stone mosaic is a small delight—and there are picnic tables to boot! Across the street to the west, at 8th and M, is the Museum of History, containing mementos of pioneer days on Fidalgo Island (hours 1-5 p.m., Thursday through Monday).

CAP SANTE CITY PARK

Park Area: 40 acres; 15,000 feet of shoreline
Access: Land
Facilities: Picnic tables, trail, *no water*
Attractions: Picnicking, hiking, viewpoint

An imposing rocky headland rising 200 feet above the marinas of Anacortes provides breathtaking views of Fidalgo Island, March Point, Hat and Saddlebag Islands, and Mt. Baker reigning over all. To reach the park from Anacortes, drive north on Commercial Ave. and turn right on 4th. Continue on 4th to its end and turn right on V Ave., following the winding road uphill to a parking lot atop the monolith.

A picnic area at the base of the rock can be reached by turning south

Mt. Baker and Hat Island from Cap Sante City Park

off 4th onto T Ave. and following it past private residences to a gated road. The rock jetty and views of the harbor are a short walk away. Several picnic tables are on grassy promontories overlooking the harbor. A crude trail leads through timber up the hillside to the top of the cape.

The viewpoint is a challenging hike from the Cap Sante marina. At the east side of the new section of the marina, follow a gravel road that runs south along the edge of the bay to the picnic area and the trail to the top of the headland. Total distance by foot to the top of Cap Sante is about ¾ mile, with an elevation gain of nearly 200 feet.

The rolling grassy hillsides on the west side of the cape can be descended with care, but they are certain to give mothers of small children cardiac arrest, for they seem to drop quite abruptly to the water. The south and east slopes are glacier-polished granite broken by patchy grass. Midway down, a row of iron posts marks the point where "rather steep" becomes "extremely steep" (and dangerous). End your exploration here.

WASHINGTON PARK

Park Area: 220 acres; 40,500 feet of shoreline
Access: Land, boat
Facilities: 48 campsites, picnic tables, fireplaces, drinking water (at Sunset Beach and in the campground only), restrooms, showers, shelters, playground, boat launch (ramp)
Attractions: Boating, hiking, viewpoints, scuba diving

Undoubtedly the crowning glory of the Anacortes city park system, Washington Park has 220 acres of forest and beach and panoramic viewpoints. In addition to the steady flow of auto-bound sightseers, many others wisely choose to use the park for road walking, jogging, or cycling, traveling slowly enough to fully soak in its beauty.

To reach the park from Anacortes, follow signs on Highway 20 west toward the San Juan ferry landing. When the highway turns downhill to the ferry terminal, bear left instead for ¾ mile to the park entrance. A bicycle lane is provided along the left side of the road much of the way.

Immediately to the right of the park entrance is Sunset Beach, where a large picnic area and a boat-launch ramp are located. For visitors arriving by boat, Sunset Bay is the only possible landing spot within the park. There is no overnight moorage; for long-term stays boats must be beached or anchored out in the bay. Boaters staying at the marina in Flounder Bay can reach the park by walking the road, a distance of about ¾ mile to the park entrance.

A few feet beyond the Sunset Beach road is the campground, with pleasant sites separated by timber and undergrowth. The campground is open year-round (fee).

From here the route and mode of transportation are up to the visitor. Pedestrians may choose to walk the road from sea-level forest upward to grassy knolls and glacier-scoured rocks 250 feet above the water, or hike the rocky beach from Sunset Bay westward until tide and the steep bluffs of Fidalgo Head force the route inland. The road can be avoided almost entirely by following forest paths near the edge of the bluff from West Beach all the way to the Havekost Memorial. Loop trip is about 3 miles, longer if enticing side trails are explored.

Whether traveling by trail or road, West Beach is an inviting wayside stop. At Green Point is a parking pullout by an interesting log shelter. Pic-

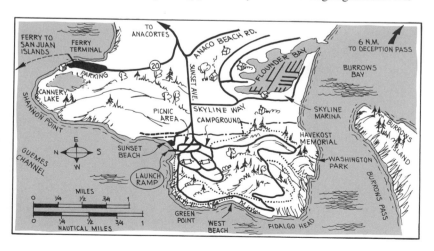

nic tables on the grassy point have balcony views of boating and ferry traffic in Guemes Channel, with backdrops of Cypress, Guemes, and distant islands. A wooden staircase leads from Green Point down to West Beach, where waves from Rosario Strait toss driftwood logs onto the narrow bedrock beach. South, beyond Fidalgo Head, can be seen a lighthouse situated high on a bluff on Burrows Island. This side of the park is a favorite with scuba divers experienced enough to handle the strong current and deep water.

Uprising cliffs of Fidalgo Head prevent a complete beach circuit of the park; however the shoreline on the south side can be reached by carefully descending the steep grassy slopes from the road viewpoints above. The bluffs drop off abruptly, so there are no beaches, but the tawny grass sprinkled with wildflowers, the weather-twisted trees, and the briny view more than compensate.

As the road makes its final loop before heading back down to the park entrance, a viewpoint features a small marble monument to T. H. Havekost, who bequeathed 8 acres of land to the city for this park. Havekost was a pioneer industrialist and land speculator on Fidalgo Island in the late 1800s. He purchased land expecting, like many others, that Burrows Bay would be the terminus of the new railroad. Following his initial donation, the city of Anacortes acquired additional lands over a period of time, until the park now exceeds 200 acres.

Burrows Bay

Lifting greenly forested shoulders from the waters of Burrows Bay, Burrows and Allan Islands may seem to be everyone's dream of an island hideaway; however the very rugged nature that gives the islands their beauty, coupled with the lack of water, has served to limit settlement.

Spanish explorers, viewing their fortress-like slopes, named them "Las Dos Islas Morrows" — Two Islands of the Forts. Mountainous Burrows Island, rising abruptly to a height of 650 feet, is often admired from promontories in Washington Park. Against the massive island backdrop, boats in the channel below seem almost to be toys.

Boaters attempting to run between Young and Burrows Islands should be wary of a large rock that lies in the middle of the channel. A rocky shelf extends out from the south side of Allan Island; use care approaching this shore. Small bays around the two islands serve as pleasant fair-weather lunch stops; however all shorelands are private, except for the western point of Burrows. Here, at the site of the lighthouse, Washington State Parks has acquired 40½ acres of surplus government property, unneeded now that the light is automated. The state also acquired 289 acres of waterfront property on the east side of the island in 1991; plans for a marine park on this more protected side of the island are under development.

Burrows Bay from Washington Park; Burrows Island on right

Heavy weather precludes placing mooring buoys in the slight cove just north of the lighthouse, but during calm weather small boats can be landed in the cove for onshore picnics or exploration. A stairway leads up the bluff. Overnight camping is permitted; however there is no water.

SKYLINE MARINA

Facilities: Complete boat and crew facilities, boat pumpout station, boat launch (hoist), boat charters, restaurant

This commercial marina on Flounder Bay, a dredged harbor on the north side of Burrows Bay, is a favorite stopover for pleasure boaters who are traveling through Deception Pass. It is 4 miles from the Anacortes city center; however the marina can meet most boating needs.

The entrance to the harbor is at the east end of the protective jetty. The channel is marked with lights and daybeacons on pilings. To secure overnight moorage, stop at the fuel dock and check in with the harbormaster. Hand-carried boats can be put in at the jetty for exploration of Burrows Bay and its islands.

Swinomish Channel

Fidalgo makes the grade to island status by virtue of the Swinomish Channel, a 10-mile-long waterway that separates it from the Skagit mainland. The slough, 100 yards wide throughout most of its length, is dredged throughout to a depth of 12 feet and both entrances are well marked with navigational devices for the use of commercial and recreational boaters seeking to avoid the turbulent waters of Deception Pass.

A trip on the channel is reminiscent of European canal boating, cruising slowly by farms, homes, and a village, waving cheerily to people on shore and fellow boaters. It is a unique experience for Northwesterners. When approaching the Swinomish Channel from either end even small boats should have on hand a navigational chart and follow it closely; only the marked channel is dredged and all the surrounding area is tideflat, where in places even a canoe can run aground. Do not be tempted to cut the corner into innocent-looking water, but follow the channel clear out to its end, or you may spend a tide change on the mudflat.

Travel at a no-wake speed in the canal—La Conner has a strict law

Swinomish Channel at La Conner

against boats throwing wakes. Stay on the starboard side; there is ample room for two good-sized boats to pass, unless one is a "road hog" and insists that his half is right down the middle. On rare occasions a raft of logs under tow may be encountered in the channel. Don't panic—there is room if you pass cautiously.

The southern entrance, known as Hole in the Wall, is a dog-leg run between the 100-foot vertical walls of two rock knobs. A lovely spot, but no fun in a fog. From here the canal straightens out to gently flow through Skagit flatland edged by levees.

Since the waterway connects two large bodies of saltwater (Skagit Bay on the south and Padilla Bay on the north), water flows inward at both ends of the channel during a flood tide and outward during the ebb. The precise location of the transition is hard to predict; however general knowledge of the forecasted tides can be useful to boaters in small craft. Tidal current in the channel can exceed two knots.

The rock jetty that stretches between Goat and McGlinn Islands and runs west from Goat Island for 1000 yards was built to divert the flow of the North Fork of the Skagit River and prevent it from filling the Swinomish Channel with silt. Near McGlinn Island a narrow break in the jetty was designed to allow migrating salmon that had mistakenly turned into the channel to get back to the Skagit River. The fishway is dry at low tide, but at mid to high tide the narrow slot can be used by kayakers to go between the two channels.

While the run through the channel is fun in a large boat, it can be enchanting in a small one, with side trips up narrow, meandering sloughs and eye-to-eye encounters with great blue herons, ducks, and other marsh birds. During the winter many of the birds common to the Skagit Game Range a few miles to the south—whistling swans, snow geese, black brant, gulls, ducks, and terns—may also be seen here from the water or from roads and trails along the levees.

LA CONNER

A mile north of Hole in the Wall, La Conner is the quintessential little seaside tourist village, with waterfront businesses built on pilings edging the canal. Founded in 1867, it was a center of commerce during the time of steamboat traffic on Puget Sound; many of the town's buildings are listed in the National Register of Historic Places. Today it is an artist's colony and tourist center with interesting shops, restaurants, museums, and historic sites. Favorite browsing places are antique stores, art galleries, and crafts shops. Town merchants can provide maps of the numerous tourist attractions.

The most elegant landmark in La Conner is the fully restored, 22-room Gaches Mansion. The historic home, built in 1891, is open for tours Friday through Sunday 1–5 p.m. from April through October, and Satur-

La Conner Marina

day and Sunday 1–4 p.m. in the winter. Young visitors will delight in the circa 1884 fire engine at the Fireman's Museum on First St. in downtown La Conner. The Tillinghast Seed House, at the corner of Morris and Maple on the east side of town, has a small garden-oriented museum, as well as fascinating shopping amid the tulip bulbs and turnip seeds.

The Skagit County Museum, perched on a small hill above the town, has one of the best viewpoints in town, with a vista of Mt. Baker and Skagit farmlands. It is located at 501 Fourth St.; to walk to the museum from downtown, look for a signed stairway on First St., next to the Rainier Bank. The museum's excellent displays cover a broad range of Skagit Valley life, including a moonshine still that operated there during the time of prohibition, a gas-operated light from an early lighthouse, a collection of Indian artifacts, and a wide array of household items from pioneer life. Don't miss the "calf weaner"—a muzzle with 2-inch metal spikes guaranteed to make any mama cow keep her offspring at a distance. Museum hours are Wednesday through Sunday, 1–5 p.m.

To reach La Conner by car, take Exit 221 from I-5. The route is clearly signed. The rich, flat delta land between I-5 and La Conner is favorite bicycling country, offering views of farms and, in spring, vast fields of brilliant tulips. A public restroom in the middle of town offers welcome relief to touring cyclists.

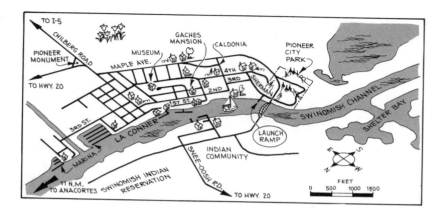

A number of floats along the La Conner waterfront offer temporary moorage to boaters stopping by to shop or dine in town. Some permit over-night moorage (for a fee). In late winter and early spring the docks along the Swinomish Channel are frequently lined with fishermen jigging for tasty little surf smelt. The sport is so popular here that the city annually schedules a smelt derby the first Saturday of February, with usually around 3000 people participating.

LA CONNER MARINA

Facilities: Complete boat and crew facilities, laundry, pumpout station, boat launch (hoist), boat charters, bait, ice, tackle, fishing pier, bicycle rentals

Just north of town the La Conner Marina, operated by the Port of Skagit Valley, has overnight berths with full facilities for boat and crew. The 500-slip marina occupies two large dredged yacht basins, with a boat yard on a section of land separating them. Guest moorages are on the two outside floats on the south basin of the marina and on the long outside float on the north basin. Tying up on the channel side of these floats can be diffi-cult due to current in the channel and boat traffic, and the moorages can also be uncomfortable at night due to excessive rocking.

Fishing is permitted from the outer docks of the marina. The angled floats that lead to the guest moorage on the north basin are a particularly popular spot.

Restrooms on shore are operated with a key card, available from the harbormaster. A number of businesses near the marina provide most boat-ing necessities, and downtown shopping is just a few blocks' walk away. Bicycles can be rented from a store at the head of the dock on the south marina basin.

A large commercial RV park east of the marina has nicely landscaped

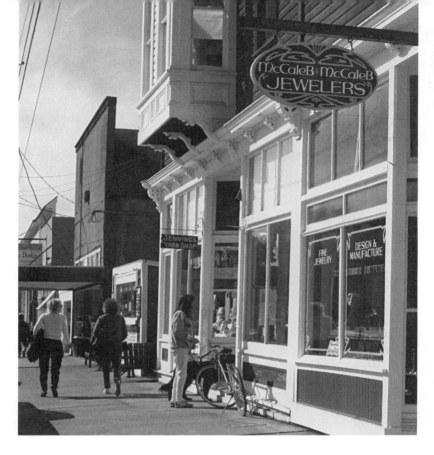

La Conner

level campsites with trailer hookups. The park's facilities include a grocery store and an indoor swimming pool.

PIONEER CITY PARK

Access: Land, boat
Facilities: Boat launch (ramp), campsites, picnic tables, picnic shelter, drinking water, restrooms
Attractions: Picnicking, viewpoint

At the eastern end of La Conner's orange-colored Rainbow Bridge is a combination city park and public boat ramp. To reach the launching ramp follow Chilberg Road into La Conner. Just past the Pioneer Monument turn left onto Maple, then right onto Caldonia, left on 2nd, and right on Sherman to the waterfront. An ample parking area adjoins the concrete-surfaced ramp.

The park section of the area lies on the embankment above the ramp. It can be reached by the trail that leaves from the edge of the parking lot, or by driving south past the boat-launch ramp on the road that curves uphill to the park. To drive to the park from La Conner, continue straight ahead on Caldonia and turn on a signed side road that branches to the left just before the road crosses the bridge.

Camping is permitted in the area at the top of the knoll. Below are picnic tables, a kitchen shelter, and a small bandstand. Through the trees can be seen boat traffic in the channel below. Trails lead to the bridge; walk across for wide-open views of the Swinomish Channel, La Conner, and Mt. Baker rising prettily to the north.

SWINOMISH INDIAN COMMUNITY

On the west shore of the canal, immediately across from La Conner, are the Indian boat docks, fish cannery, fresh fish market, and restaurant. Visitors' temporary boat moorage is provided at both the restaurant and fish market. From the La Conner waterfront it can be reached by walking or driving over the Rainbow Bridge. The restaurant offers authentic Indian barbequed salmon.

GOAT ISLAND

The old World War I forts of Casey, Flagler, and Worden are well known to anyone who's done a bit of traveling around Puget Sound, but what about Fort Whitman? It did exist, and right here on Goat Island on the south side of the Swinomish Channel. The fortification was built as part of the system protecting the Northwest's inland waters from enemy attack and was in service from 1911 until 1944.

The best access to the island is at the rock beach on the north side, next to the old dock. From here a trail climbs west to the old, overgrown battery emplacements on the western end of the island. The four 6-inch disappearing guns located at Battery Harrison guarded Deception Pass and Saratoga Passage. The fort also had a mine-control center similar to the one that can be seen at Middle Point in Manchester State Park, but there is no evidence that mines were ever planted in the passage.

Goat Island is now part of the Department of Wildlife's Skagit Wildlife Recreation Area. Hawks and eagles nest in the tall firs; use care when exploring, especially in spring. Camping is not permitted.

4. SKAGIT DELTA AND CAMANO ISLAND

Delta Flatlands

Not long ago, as such things are measured, when the last of the land-gouging ice sheets melted, Puget Sound lapped against the rugged Cascade foothills, and mountain streams tumbling down precipitous slopes emptied directly into tidal waters. After the last glaciation it took 13,000 years for the constant wearing down of streams and rivers to build up over 100,000 acres of rich Skagit flatland stretching from the base of the Cascades to its present boundary on Puget Sound. The growth continues at the rate of 100 million tons of sediment deposited each year, and in time, although certainly not for many generations to come, Fidalgo, Camano, and Whidbey Islands will be solidly bound to the mainland.

The two rivers that meander through this flatland, the Skagit and the Stillaguamish, terminate at an estuary that edges Skagit Bay and Port Susan. Boaters passing by wisely stay well to the west, in the channel that follows the Whidbey Island shoreline. Although it is not generally thought of as a cruising boat destination, it is possible to approach the tidelands from the west in a shallow draft boat at mid to high tide. A cautious approach from the water side can be the best way to observe the enormous flocks of snow geese and other waterfowl that winter in the estuary. Channels lead along the north edge of Camano Island into West Pass, and also north into Tom Moore and Boom Sloughs. Consult a navigation chart and proceed with care. The tidelands west of Browns Slough are good for clam digging.

SKAGIT WILDLIFE RECREATION AREA

Area: 12,700 acres
Access: Land, boat
Facilities: Hiking trails; (at headquarters): information center, restrooms, boat launch (ramp)
Attractions: Birdwatching, paddling, clam digging, hiking

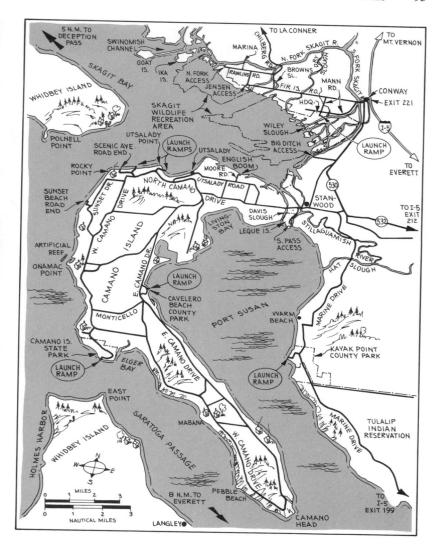

The Skagit WRA covers a major portion of the shoreline from Camano Island north to the Swinomish Channel. Here the State Department of Wildlife has preserved a natural habitat that supports a wide variety of birds, fish, and small mammals. The tidelands, sloughs, and adjoining fields of the estuary are a major stop on the Pacific Flyway for migratory birds. Hunting and fishing are permitted in season, but the area is also heavily used by observers who come to hike along the dikes or boat in the channels and simply to enjoy the wildlife and scenery.

English Boom and tideflats of the Skagit Wildlife Refuge Area

The most spectacular attraction of the area is the 25,000–30,000 snow geese and some 100 whistling swans that winter here. The best time for viewing the flocks is from the end of hunting season in December through April, when the snow geese depart for breeding grounds on Wrangell Island, north of Siberia. Any time of year one is assured of seeing birds: brightly feathered ducks bobbing placidly on coves and sloughs; regal herons on stilt-like legs standing in tideflats; hawks, and even bald eagles, soaring over fields; or meadowlarks, wrens, and other songbirds flitting in hedgerows. Over 175 species of birds have been observed here as well as river otter, rabbit, muskrat, beaver, skunk, and raccoon. Anglers land Dolly Varden, steelhead, and several species of salmon.

The inner edge of the Skagit WRA is bordered by private farmland. Sometimes birds feeding in pastures and fields can be seen from the roads, but for best viewing and for boat put-ins, drive to the area's road end access points. To reach the WRA headquarters, where a map showing roads, boundaries, and access points can be obtained, leave Highway I-5 at Exit 221 to Conway and drive west on Fir Island Road. Immediately after crossing the Skagit River, an intersection is marked Mann Road—do not take this turn, but continue west another mile to the second intersection with Mann Road (Mann Road is a loop). Turn left here and follow signs south to the headquarters.

A boat launch is at the left end of the T road, immediately east of park headquarters. Hand-carried boats can also be put in easily at Big Ditch access just north of Stanwood and at Leque Island west of Stanwood. The other recreation access points may entail a long carry to reach navigable water. At the north section of the WRA a commercial resort and marina on the North Fork of the Skagit River, just off Rawlins Road, has a launch ramp as well as boat rentals and supplies; canoes and kayaks can be put in for a fee.

Personnel at the WRA headquarters can give advice regarding boating in the estuary. Mid to high tide is necessary to navigate many of the channels. Improper planning can result in becoming stranded in the muck and having to get out and wade. In the river channels the current can be quite strong. It is possible to become disoriented in the reedy marshes if it is foggy or if low overcast covers the mountains; carry a map and compass.

Land-bound visitors can walk trails along the dikes or wander for miles on the tideflats. Rubber boots are a good idea.

LEQUE ISLAND AND SOUTH PASS ACCESS

A road that skirts the southeast shore of Leque Island, at the mouth of the Stillaguamish River, provides water access to marshes at the south end of the Skagit WRA. To reach it, drive west from Stanwood on Highway 532 onto Camano Island. Immediately after crossing the bridge over West Pass, a side road to the south, Eide Road, heads back toward the channel, paralleling the bridge abutments. At the channel a short road stub goes straight ahead to the water. The dirt ramp here is suitable for launching hand-carried boats—trailers may become mired in the mud. Parking space for a couple of cars is under the bridge.

Eide Road continues south, paralleling the dike, to a gate. During hunting season the Department of Wildlife releases pheasants here, and the area is used extensively by hunters. At other times wander freely on the south end of Leque Island and on to the tideflats at the end of Port Susan.

KAYAK POINT COUNTY PARK (SNOHOMISH COUNTY)

Park Area: 670 acres; 3300 feet of shoreline
Access: Land, boat
Facilities: 34 campsites, picnic tables, fireplaces, picnic shelter, restrooms, drinking water, boat launch (ramp), float, fishing pier, hiking trails, golf course
Attractions: Boating, paddling, fishing, crabbing, scuba diving, swimming, hiking, golf

In summer the sun-warmed waters of shallow Port Susan find the perfect complement in the wide beaches of Kayak Point, along its east shore.

Kayak Point County Park

On hot summer days the park becomes a northern version of Seattle's Golden Gardens, with mobs of swimmers, sun bathers, picnickers, and sand-encrusted kids. But even in chilly weather the park has a lot to offer visitors. Hiking trails lace the upland woods between the beach and Marine Drive. Immediately across the road from the entrance, 225 acres of park-land are dedicated to an 18-hole golf course.

Cod, perch, flounder, or (with luck) salmon can be caught from the 300-foot-long fishing pier that juts into Port Susan, and crab pots or star traps strategically lowered may result in Dungeness or red rock crab. At the end of the pier is a short float for loading boats; a single-lane launch ramp is immediately north of the pier. Boaters should leave or approach the area with caution, watching for swimmers and scuba divers in the water.

The weak current in the bay makes this a popular spot for beginning scuba divers who can find crab, nudibranchs, moon snails, and orange sea anemone on the smooth bottom. Divers should stay well away from the fishing lines and boat props by the pier and launch ramp.

By land the park can be reached by leaving I-5 at Exit 199, turning north in ¾ mile on a road signed to Tulalip and following this arterial, Marine Drive, all the way to the park—a total distance of 12½ miles. At one time the point was occupied by a resort that loaned kayaks to its guests, thus the name of the area. The resort is long gone, but the joy of paddling around the placid bay remains.

Camano Island

Although Whidbey and Camano join together politically to form Island County, the two islands are quite different in character. Unlike Whidbey, which is three times larger, Camano Island has no towns or major businesses—there are just a few grocery stores and gas stations near centers of population. Many of the homes concentrated along the shoreline are owned by retirees or summer residents.

The island was logged in the 1850s to supply local mills and ship builders. Second-growth forest now covers much of the island; relatively little of it has been cleared for farming or agriculture.

Since it lies in the protection of Whidbey Island, Camano has fewer wind-buffeted beaches, but the western shore does suffer some of the severe weather off Saratoga Passage and the shallow bights offer little shelter for boaters.

Camano and Whidbey Islands were more closely allied in early times when boats were the major mode of transportation and Saratoga Passage was seen as a water link, not a barrier between them. Today it is not possible to travel directly between the two islands except by private pleasure boat. By car Camano Island can only be reached via Highway 532, which crosses a low bridge over Davis Slough at the north end of the island.

UTSALADY COUNTY PARK (ISLAND COUNTY)

This park consists only of a boat launch and a 50-foot strip of beach on the west side of Utsalady Bay. To reach it, drive west on North Camano Drive, which climbs steeply as it rounds the bay. On the far side of the bay turn right at a sign "To Utsalady Point." In about a block the concrete ramp is reached. There is parking nearby for half a dozen cars with trailers; do not park along the road.

The lazy little bay with its swath of beach homes is a far cry from the industrial center it was during the 1860s. At that time Utsalady was a sizeable town, and the shores of the bay held a large sawmill and a major shipwright that operated for over 30 years and built a number of the steamers that plied Puget Sound.

SARATOGA PASSAGE BEACH ACCESSES

Maple Grove Launch Ramp. Just around Utsalady Point, 1 mile to the west, is a second public launch ramp. To reach it, turn off N. Camano Drive onto Brown Road, ¼ mile west of the Utsalady Point Road intersection. As it reaches the water at the community of Maple Grove, the road bends left and becomes Beach Drive. In ¼ mile a short side road leads to the unsigned, single-lane launch ramp, between two private residences. There is parking nearby for 8 or 10 cars. From the water the launch ramp is

Utsalady Bay

about halfway between Utsalady Point and Rocky Point. The adjacent beach is private.

Scenic Ave. Road End. From the Maple Grove launch ramp Beach Drive continues west and in ½ mile deadends at the intersection with Scenic Ave. The gravel road end of Scenic Ave. is also a public beach access between private lands. There is no launch ramp here, and very little parking space—only a place to reach the water and possibly put in a kayak.

Sunset Beach Road End. Driving from the north, turn off West Camano Drive onto Sunset Drive and follow it for 2¼ miles to Blackburn Road. To the right, at the end of the road stub, is a low-bank beach access.

ONAMAC POINT

Midway along the western shore of Camano Island, the meager sandspit of Onamac Point pokes outward into Saratoga Passage. Immediately north of the point a pair of lighted buoys mark an artificial reef placed by the state Department of Fisheries for the benefit of fish and fishermen. Crags and crannies of the broken concrete reef provide habitat for ling cod, rockfish, and other bottom species. The protected waters of Saratoga Passage are favored by small boat fishermen; many troll for winter blackmouth and spring Chinook salmon in the area between Polnell Point and Camano Island's Rocky Point.

Although it sounds quite exotic Onamac Point is not some ancient Indian word meaning something like "place where giant fish leap out of the water"—it is merely Camano spelled backwards.

CAMANO ISLAND STATE PARK

Park Area: 134 acres; 6700 feet of shoreline
Access: Land, boat
Facilities: 87 campsites, group camp, picnic tables, fireplaces, restrooms, drinking water, nature trail, hiking trails, boat launch (ramp)
Attractions: Boating, hiking, swimming

What is perhaps the finest beach on all of Saratoga Passage is, astonishingly, not in an exclusive real estate development, but in a magnificent state park where all can enjoy it. The park stretches for more than a mile along the Camano Island shoreline, incorporating both superb upland forests and gently flaring, wave-swept beach. The land route to the park is not well signed; however the island is small enough and major roads are few enough that it is difficult to miss the way. From Utsalady, drive south on West Camano Drive; about 10 miles south of Utsalady, at a major intersection where the road turns east, continue south on Park Drive to the park entrance in ½ mile.

Immediately inside the park entrance the road forks; the branch to the

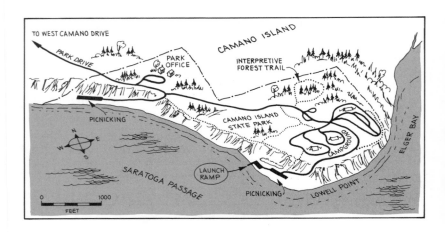

right swings downhill to the day-use area at North Beach. Picnic tables and fireplaces are stretched along the embankment 30 feet above the beach. Stairs lead down to the beach, and a ¾-mile bluff-top trail leads south to Lowel Point.

The left fork of the park road passes an interpretive forest trail, the group camp, and two campground loops. All park campsites are away from the bluff in timber; none have views of the water. The road loops steeply downhill to the beach and parking lot at Lowell Point. At the far north end of the area are a two-lane surfaced launch ramp and a large parking lot for vehicles with trailers. There is no loading float; a bit of wading may be necessary to launch and load boats.

Below a silvery collar of driftwood the beach slopes gently outward—fine swimming or wading for souls brave enough to test the chilly water of Saratoga Passage. A former salt lagoon between the beach and bluff is now filled with sediment and grass; by summer the marsh dries enough to host games of Frisbee or one o'cat. In late May buttercups and wild roses bloom here in profusion.

Hiking trails climb the steep 150-foot glacial-till bluff and wander along the bluff top. Rough-hewn benches along the way provide a spot to pause and enjoy eagle's-eye views down to boating traffic in Saratoga Passage, out to Whidbey Island, and far beyond to crystal Olympic peaks.

PORT SUSAN

Most boaters hurry by on the main highway of Saratoga Passage, rarely lingering to enjoy the detour into the quiet waters of Port Susan. The 11-mile-long inlet leads only to a long, shallow tideflat and limited shoreside marine facilities, but it is a pleasant out-of-the-way corner, well

Beach at Camano Island State Park

worth the time for a visit. The cove offers some anchorages along the northwest shore in 10 fathoms; beware of shoals that rise up abruptly two miles from the head of the bay and the extensive mudflat that lies along the northeast shore.

CAVELERO BEACH COUNTY PARK (ISLAND COUNTY)

Park Area: .6 acre; 300 feet of shoreline
Access: Land, boat
Facilities: Picnic tables, latrine, boat launch (ramp)
Attractions: Boating, swimming

The east shore access in this little park gives boaters and beach lovers a chance to sample Port Susan waters. To reach the park by land, turn onto East Camano Drive from Highway 532 and drive south for about 5 miles. Turn east onto Cavelero Drive, and in ½ mile turn left then right onto a narrow, steep, single-lane road that drops down to the park.

The boat-launch road is dirt leading down to a concrete ramp at the water level. The narrow access road, primitive condition of the ramp, and shallow outfall preclude launching large boats. At low tide launching of any boats but hand-carried may be impossible.

Enjoying the sun at Cavelero Beach County Park

Park facilities consist of a few picnic tables and a single latrine; however the pretty beach needs no embellishments. The park is a favorite in summer with families who bring toddlers to dabble in the shallow, sun-warmed water.

ENGLISH BOOM

A pretty spot at any time, but incredibly impressive during clear weather when the mountains emerge to add their splendor. To reach it, turn north off Utsalady Road onto Moore Road at the airstrip. If traveling from the east, turn off Highway 532 at Good Road, which curves and becomes Utsalady Road. Moore Road deadends in ½ mile at English Boom. The tideflat was once the booming ground of the English Logging Company. The sparse forest of old pilings was used for tying up rafts of logs.

So much to see—mountains and foothills, islands and delta, all blending in a misty gray-green mosaic. To the north and east lie the wandering estuaries of the Skagit Wildlife Recreation Area, but waterfowl who haven't read the maps often stray here.

Deception Pass from Hoypus Point

5. DECEPTION PASS STATE PARK

Park Area: 2474 acres, 77,000 feet of shoreline
Access: Land, boat
Facilities: Extensive camping, picnicking, and boating accommodations—
refer to specific areas
Attractions: Hiking, boating, bicycling, paddling, swimming (fresh- and
saltwater), scuba and free diving, beachcombing, sand dunes, tidepools, fishing (fresh-and saltwater), sightseeing, viewpoints

With its generous samplings of all the treasures created when land
meets sea, Deception Pass serves as a perfect introduction to the San Juan
Islands. Here are quiet virgin forests; coves, bays, and wave-tossed
beaches holding treasures from the sea, awesome rock escarpments, grassy
bluffs festooned with twisted "bonsai" trees and bright meadow flowers;

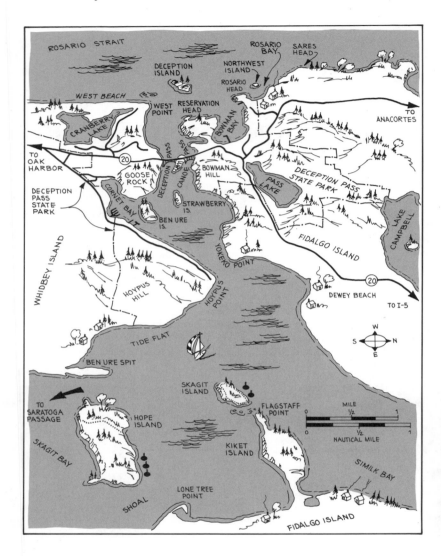

deer, seals, otters, eagles, and bizarre marine life; and lakes hosting trout and waterfowl--all to be enjoyed by motorist, bicyclist, pedestrian, or mariner.

Although Deception Pass is separated from the San Juan Islands by bureaucratic boundaries, it has a strong geologic and historic kinship with those islands. The same strata of Late Jurassic igneous rock that underlies

Turtleback Mountain on Orcas Island forms the enclosing granite walls of Deception Pass. The Pleistocene glacier that rasped its way across Orcas, San Juan, and Lopez Islands 15,000 years ago also gouged out the bays and channels of Deception Pass and smoothed the brows of Bowman Hill and Goose Rock. The first explorers that charted the islands noted the relationship of these islands and their network of waterways and designated the entire area as the "San Juan Archipelago."

So captivating are the physical beauties of the park that many visitors never realize that the area is equally interesting historically. Pioneer life of the Deception Pass area was colorful, sometimes even lurid—replete with tales of hardy pioneers who settled the land and of some equally hardy smugglers, cutthroats, and pirates who sought greater fortune, or perhaps just greater adventure.

During the late 1800s a portion of the land within the present park was designated as a military reservation for the coastal defense of the region. At the end of the First World War local residents began a movement to have the area, already a favorite picnicking, camping, and rhododendron-viewing spot, officially designated as a park. In 1921, 1746 acres were dedicated as Deception Pass State Park.

At the outbreak of WW II some of the land was temporarily requisitioned back from the park. Three 3-inch guns brought from Fort Casey on Whidbey Island were set up at North Beach and Reservation Head, and a searchlight was installed at West Point. Concrete pads from these emplacements are still to be seen at some spots in the park.

Since the dedication of the original tract of land, additional property has been purchased, donated, or transferred to the jurisdiction of the park from other state agencies and private citizens, until the present acreage is slightly in excess of 2300 acres, encompassing six entire islands, parts of Whidbey and Fidalgo Islands, two lakes, and one ocean (as the park brochure describes it).

Evening fireside talks and slide shows telling of the history of the park or describing the flora, fauna, and natural features are conducted during summer evenings near Cranberry Lake Campground, greatly enhancing understanding and enjoyment of the park.

Deception Pass State Park can be reached by ferry from Mukilteo to Columbia Beach on the southeast tip of Whidbey Island, then by car or bicycle along Highway 525 (which becomes Highway 20) the length of the island to its northern end, a distance of 50 miles. To approach Deception Pass from the north, avoiding the occasionally crowded, although always scenic, ferry ride, leave I-5 at Exit 230, just north of Mount Vernon and follow Highway 20 east. Signs direct the way to the park, 18 miles from the freeway.

Deception Pass lies just east of the confluence of the Strait of Juan de Fuca and Rosario Strait. Mariners approaching from the south often duck behind the shelter of Whidbey Island and run Saratoga Passage and Skagit Bay northward to reach the pass. Trailered boats can be launched at ramps at Cornet Bay and Bowman Bay within the park.

Deception Pass

One cannot fail to be impressed by the drama of Deception Pass, whether viewing it as a land-bound tourist from the heights of the 182-foot-high bridge or experiencing it as a skipper attempting a first white-knuckle run through the narrow passageway. Measured against the timelessness of granite and the power of the boiling tidal current, man's great structural achievement of concrete and steel seems fragile indeed.

The entrance to the waterway was charted by early Spaniards, but it was the British sea captain George Vancouver who first explored it in 1792, naming it to express his feeling of deception, for he originally thought the pass was the mouth of a large bay indenting the peninsula that is now known to be Whidbey Island. Before the days of engines, large sailing ships unable to maneuver in its confines, avoided the pass, choosing instead to sail southward along the outside shore of the island. Captain Thomas Coupe, who settled near Penn Cove in 1852, is said to be the only man to sail a fully rigged tall ship through the pass.

The rock-walled main channel of Deception Pass itself is scarcely 500 feet across, and Canoe Pass on the north is a claustrophobic 50 feet wide at its narrowest point, with a sharp bend along the way. It is, however, the current pouring through the channels and its associated churning eddies that are the concern of most skippers, for it reaches a velocity of up to eight knots as the granite spigot of the pass performs its twice-daily task of filling, then draining, then refilling Skagit Bay. Very experienced kayakers use the pass as an area to practice running strong currents.

Boat pilots are advised to consult local tidal current tables and run the pass during slack water, when the velocity of the current is at its minimum. Although fast boats do make the pass at other times, boating skill and knowledge of the local waters is advisable. High-powered boats should stay well away from other boats in the channel so their wake does not cause the less powerful vessels additional problems.

DECEPTION PASS BRIDGE

The Deception Pass bridge, which was begun in 1934 and completed the following year, spans the gulf between Fidalgo and Whidbey Islands, utilizing little Pass Island for its central pillars. Nearly 30 years of effort in state and national government was required to bring the bridge into being.

Deception Pass bridge

As early as 1907 the land link to Whidbey Island was urged in order to support the military garrison at Fort Casey and as an assistance to agricultural growth on Whidbey Island. Blueprints were prepared, but time and again hopes were dashed as funds for the project failed to be appropriated.

Finally in 1933 the bridge appeared about to receive approval in the state legislature; Skagit and Island counties earmarked $150,000 in local funds and work began on the approaches to the span. However once more the state legislature balked, and it was not until the following year, after some fast footwork by local politicians, that the money was finally approved, along with some matching funds from the federal Public Works Administration. In August the excavation of solid rock for the first pier of the bridge was begun.

A high-line with 4-ton capacity was rigged to Pass Island to transport the derrick for structural steel work, water lines were laid from Cranberry and Pass Lakes for mixing the concrete, and a month was spent building an aggregate bunker and a cement warehouse. Month after month the steel fretwork grew against the sky, until in July of 1935, slightly less than a year from the beginning of the first excavation, the cantilevered spans stretching outward from Fidalgo, Pass, and Whidbey Islands were ready to be joined. Steelworkers clambering on the bridge under the hot summer sun were unable to align the sections; however in the cool of the following morning when the metal had contracted enough to allow proper matching of the diagonals, the final joining was completed. Deception Pass was bridged!

PASS (CANOE) ISLAND

Parking areas at either end of the bridge and on Pass Island (which is sometimes known as Canoe Island) permit sightseers to leave their cars and walk along the span for a view of the pass that George Vancouver never enjoyed. Trails eastward from the middle parking area traverse the rocky meadowland of grass, sedges, wildflowers, and gnarled, weather-twisted trees. Use extreme care and keep a tight hand on small children as the bluffs drop off steeply into the churning water. At the far eastern tip the slope gentles enough to enable hikers to reach the water's edge.

A magnificent display of underwater life on the walls of Goose Rock and around Pass Island rewards venturesome scuba divers; however the treacherous tidal current makes this an area only for experts.

PRISON CAMP

Looking from the east end of Pass Island north to the cliff wall of Fidalgo Island a gaping cave and an outfall of rock debris can be seen. This is the remainder of a rock quarry that was operated in conjunction with a state prison camp, through Walla Walla State Penitentiary, from 1909 until

View east from the Deception Pass bridge; Strawberry Island on right

1914. A large wooden rock crusher was built below the quarry, stretching down the cliff to the water's edge. Rock dug from the quarry was put into the crusher, then mechanically sorted into bins, and eventually loaded via chutes onto barges that were brought into Canoe Pass.

The penal colony was located on a small bay due north of the eastern end of Pass Island. Up to forty prisoners at a time lived in the stockade; service buildings and homes of the prison guards were nearby. Only scant evidence of the colony remains—a round cistern, some bricks, and scattered tiles, all nearly covered by brush. Park rangers discourage hikers from climbing in the cliffs in the quarry's vicinity as they are extremely dangerous. Be content to view it from the water or Pass Island.

STRAWBERRY ISLAND

Perhaps Strawberry is the perfect island; its 3 acres are just enough to assure visitors a measure of solitude in the middle of a busy freeway, while its mossy granite slopes are an insular rock garden bedecked with wind-shredded junipers, sedums, and wild strawberries. To this add the crowning touch—a stupendous view into the jaws of Deception Pass.

Salmon fishermen sometimes anchor offshore, but the island itself is accessible only to kayaks and other boats small enough to be drawn up on the rocky beaches. Skill and experience in boat handling are necessary to reach the island. Landing is easiest on the south and east sides, where the slopes flare more gently into the water. Small boats should approach on a rising tide, when the flow will push the craft eastward into quieter water, rather than draw it into the pass, less than ½ mile away.

Although the island is part of the state park, there are no camping amenities on shore. Please take any trash back home with you and leave the island as pretty as when you arrived.

CORNET BAY

Access: Land, boat

Facilities [at the state park]: Dock with float, mooring buoys, boat launch (ramp), picnic tables, fireplaces, drinking water, restrooms; [at marina]: dock with floats, boat launch (hoist), diesel, gas, groceries, snack bar, laundry, restrooms, showers

Attractions: Fishing, boating, paddling, bicycling, scuba diving, hiking, beachcombing, clam digging

Just a watery mile east of Deception Pass, Cornet Bay is a placid refuge from the often-turbulent waters of the pass. For boaters heading east to cruise the quietude of Skagit Bay, or those waiting for slack tide to enable them to run the pass, Cornet Bay offers both launching facilities for trailered boats and mooring facilities for larger ones that arrive by water.

To reach Cornet Bay by land, drive south across the Deception Pass bridge onto Whidbey Island and past the park headquarters at the Cranberry Lake entrance. About 1 mile south of the bridge turn east onto Cornet Bay Road. The state park marine facilities are reached in 1¼ more miles.

Traffic is generally light on this road, making it an excellent bicycle detour. The blacktopped run is downhill or level all the way to road end at Hoypus Point, with a 100-foot climb back to the Highway 20 intersection on the return.

The state park dock has moorage space for six to ten boats on a float. Seven buoys in the bay provide additional tie-ups. Moorage is limited to 36 hours. Good anchorages can be found across the bay near Ben Ure Island; the head of the bay is too shallow. Immediately adjacent the dock are boat-launch ramps, finger piers for cargo loading, and a large parking area. A commercially operated marina that is slightly farther into the bay, has fuel, a float with overnight moorages, a launching lift, and supplies.

Privately owned Ben Ure Island, lying in the mouth of Cornet Bay, was named for an Anacortes businessman-turned-smuggler who lived there with his Indian wife during the late 1800s. The story goes that when planning to be away on a "business" trip, Ure would instruct his wife to build an evening campfire on the northern tip of the island. If Revenue agents were lying in wait in Cornet Bay, she would signal her husband by standing in front of the fire to block the light. If all was clear she sat to the side and its beacon would guide him home. Today a navigational light is loc-

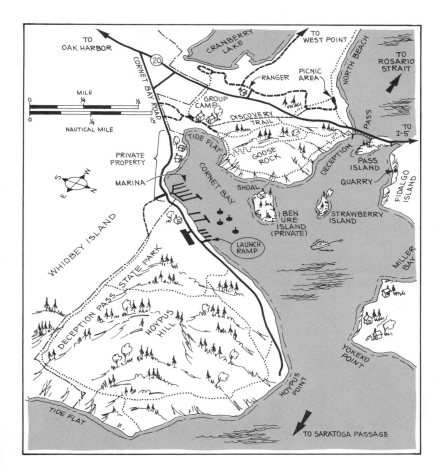

ated near the spot where Ben Ure's wife maintained her navigational aid.

Boaters unfamiliar with the area should not attempt to enter Cornet Bay on the west side of Ben Ure Island as a shoal extends westward from the island.

GOOSE ROCK AND GROUP CAMP

The state park's group camp, with rustic cabins, kitchen, and dining hall (available for use by reservation), provides a base of operations for visiting environmental-education groups. Camp facilities, located at the head of Cornet Bay, are reached via the turnoff road to the group camp, ½ mile east of the Highway 20/Cornet Bay Road intersection.

Low tide bares acres of eelgrass-coated mudflat in the bay, a marked contrast to the wave-scrubbed beaches on the west side of the park. Muck about and examine the variety of tiny marine life that inhabits the intertidal zone. The ½-mile section of property to the east, between the group camp and state park dock, is privately owned, so do not trespass.

Towering nearly 500 feet above Cornet Bay, Goose Rock is a small echo of Mt. Erie to the north, with its glacier-scoured northern slope reflecting the south-bound course of an ancient icefield, and its near-vertical south face, to the lee of the glacier, exhibiting little evidence of such wearing. Trails on the rock interweave, merge, and sometimes end abruptly. Most lead to spectacular views. Trailheads are at the group camp or North Beach parking lot. A wide choice of side paths and alternate destinations makes for an interesting variety of trips and scenery. Total distance for an average loop hike is about 3½ miles.

HOYPUS POINT

The park road continues northeast from Cornet Bay along the shore to Hoypus Point, passing a gated side road and a gravel pit, starting points for a 3½-mile hike that loops around Hoypus Hill.

The road drive is scenic enough, with views through a fringe of trees

Skagit Bay and Mt. Erie

of boating traffic in the channel; however walking the beach provides a more pleasant activity, with unobstructed views of Mt. Erie due north and Mt. Baker rising above Similk Bay to the northwest. The beach is passable during all but the highest tide. When high water forces the route inland, the low bank can easily be climbed and the road walked for a distance. Hoypus Point, at road's end, is reached in slightly over a mile.

From 1912 until the Deception Pass bridge was completed in 1935, a ferry operated between here and Dewey Beach, linking Whidbey and Fidalgo Islands. A concrete bulkhead and pilings, remnants of the old ferry landing, can still be seen at the road end at Hoypus Point. Old newspaper accounts tell of the crowded ferry conditions on Sundays (even then!), when carloads of tourists would make springtime excursions to the park to picnic and to view the pink masses of wild rhododendrons. Although the ferry has long since ceased operating, the flowers are still a spring attraction.

Beyond the point the walking is even better, with a broader beach and views across the channel to Skagit, Kiket, and Hope Islands. In about a mile the park boundary is reached; the tideflat continues on for yet another mile to Ala Spit. The trip from Cornet Bay to the park boundary and back is about 4 miles.

HOPE AND SKAGIT ISLANDS

Island Areas: Hope Island—166 acres; Skagit Island—21 acres
Access: Boat
Facilities: Mooring buoys, picnic tables, fireplaces, pit toilet, *no water*
Attractions: Fishing, canoeing, crabbing, clam digging, scuba diving, beachcombing

Stretched across the middle of the channel between Whidbey and Fidalgo Islands, Hope Island heralds the end of Skagit Bay and the beginning of Deception Pass waters. Hope and its smaller neighbor, Skagit Island, are undeveloped parts of the state park.

The meager indentation of Lang Bay is on the north side of Hope Island. Four mooring buoys are stretched along the shore to the east. Ashore, a few picnic tables with fireplaces can be found in clearings above the beach; drinking water is not available. A trail that cuts across the island can be followed from the campground to the south shore. During moderate to low tides the beach can be walked for a mile or more from Lang Bay around the east end of the island to a magnificent sand and driftwood beach on the south. Incoming tide can trap unwary hikers on any of three beaches.

Less than a mile to the north, Skagit Island is a much smaller version of Hope Island, duplicating its open, grassy bluffs on the southwest side and thick forest on the remainder. A 6-foot rocky bank circles the island,

Hope Island moorage

except on the northwest side where a shoal reaches out to Kiket Island.
Two buoys off the northeast shore provide a place to hang a boat while
dinghy-exploring nearby shallow waters, or while waiting to go through
the pass. Shore adventurers can hike the trail that rings the island along the
top of the embankment. On the northeast end of the island are two primitive campsites. Raccoons, porcupines, crows, and other scavangers often
scatter trash; to minimize the problem burn food scraps and papers in fireplaces and take other garbage home with you.

The waters around the islands west to Hoypus Point and north to the
shallows of Similk Bay offer splendid small-boat excursions; however the
tidal current is quite strong in some areas and a paddle-propelled or un-
derpowered craft may find itself going in a different direction than intended. Use care, watch for tide rips, and stay well away from large,
moving boats.

Skagit Island is said to have been a hideout for smugglers and all sorts
of ruffians on the run from justice at the turn of the century. Its strategic
location, at the bend of the channel with views into Deception Pass and up-
channel into Skagit Bay, made any stealthy approach by law boats quite
difficult.

Hope Island beach

Bowman and Rosario Bays

Access: Land, boat
Facilities: 24 campsites (on Bowman Bay), picnic tables, fireplaces, drinking water, picnic shelters, kitchens, restrooms, showers, boat launch (ramp), dock with float, fishing pier, underwater park, children's playground
Attractions: Boating, paddling, fishing, scuba diving, hiking, tidepools

Yet another facet of this diverse park: here rounded bays facing away from the swirling current of the pass enable sea life to grow in profusion on rocks and beaches. Offshore, salmon runs attract fleets of commercial and sport fishermen.

BOWMAN (RESERVATION) BAY

Nautical charts still designate this as Reservation Bay, a holdover from World War I when a military reservation was located here. Local residents, agreeing with the U.S. Geological Survey, prefer the name of Bow-

117

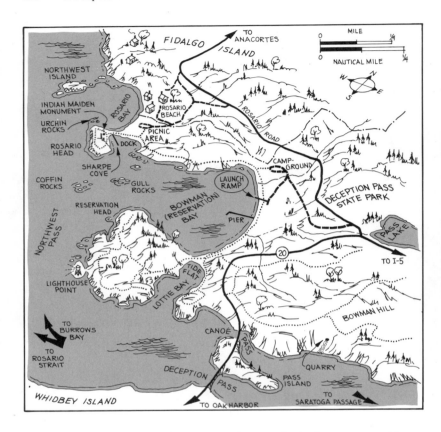

man Bay, honoring the Fidalgo Island pioneer who had a summer cabin on the shore.

Bowman Bay is reached by car by following the signs at the intersection of Highway 20 at the west end of Pass Lake. The road, which may be closed in winter, drops sharply downhill to a large open flat at the head of the bay. The campground is located in timber on the northern edge of the bay. A gravel ramp between the campground and a long pier is the only launching facility for boats in this section of the park.

The bay offers some anchorages for boaters, although numerous rocks foul the entrance and care must be used on entering. The bay is open to swells from Rosario Strait, and an overnight stay may be uncomfortable. The long stationary pier in the bay is the remains of a defunct fish hatchery. While it is a fine place from which to fish, it is unsatisfactory for mooring boats since the vertical pilings are widely spread and the dock level is so high above the water that disembarking is impossible except at the ladder on the north side.

Although much smaller than Bowman Bay, Sharpe Cove to the north,

Sharpe Cove

tucked behind Rosario Head, is usually a better spot for a layover. The park maintains a small dock with a float on the cove, and there is space for several good anchorages.

RESERVATION HEAD

The path south along the shore of Bowman Bay leads to hiking trails that traverse Reservation Head and a smaller, unnamed headland lying east of Lottie Bay. Climbing high on exposed, grassy bluffs, the trails offer views into Deception Pass, across to Cranberry Lake, and out to the inviting blue-green islands of the San Juans. Shallow Lottie Bay separates the two cliffy headlands. Long ago Bowman and Lottie Bays were joined as a continuous waterway; over the years wave action built the sand neck linking Reservation Head to Fidalgo Island that created the two bays.

At extreme low tide Lottie Bay is nearly drained, and the interesting sea life on its muddy bottom exposed. The shoreline can be followed past tiny, rock-walled coves clear around to the neck connecting Lighthouse Point, where a trail can be hiked back to Bowman Bay. Use care not to become trapped on the rocks by the incoming tide. An average loop stroll from the Bowman Bay parking lot around either headland is about 2 miles.

ROSARIO BAY

The state park shares this choice bay with a university marine research facility and a number of private homes. To reach the beach, at Pass Lake turn north from Highway 20 onto Rosario Road (Highway 525). In about a mile signs direct motorists to Rosario Beach. Follow the road to the state park property, avoiding private side roads.

The spacious picnic area with tables and fireplaces faces on Rosario Bay and Sharpe Cove. Restrooms have outside showers for rinsing saltwater from swimmers and scuba divers.

Trails from the picnic area lead upward to the modest heights of Rosario Head or around Sharpe Cove and on to Bowman Bay. Lanky firs along the trail extend horizontally out over the water, supported by but a few roots. Possibly the next storm will see their demise, or perhaps they will still be stubbornly clinging there when your grandchildren hike the trail.

The underwater park is legendary among divers and marine biologists for its extravaganza of sea life. Beneath the water is a rococo world of flamboyant anemone, sea pens, nudibranchs, sponges, and one of the largest concentrations of purple and green sea urchins to be found on the inland waters. The rocks lying just off Rosario Head are well named as Urchin

Scuba divers at Rosario Beach; Northwest Island on right

Rocks. The bay itself is suitable for snorkelers and divers with beginning skill; greater experience is needed to venture out of the bay into deeper, swifter water. At low tide pools form in the rocks and give land-bound sightseers a glimpse of what lies beneath the water. This is a marine preserve; the taking or destruction of any marine life is prohibited.

The territory from Deception Pass eastward belonged to the Indians of the Samish tribe, who harvested the vast runs of salmon that swarmed through the channels. The pass obviously impressed early natives as much as it does people today, for it is mentioned in several of their legends. One tells of an Indian princess named Ko-kwal-alwoot, who lived at Deception Pass and who became the bride of the king of the fishes, going to live with him in his underwater kingdom. Her long, flowing hair, turned green from its long exposure to water, can still be seen drifting in the current, although some people know it only as seaweed.

A monument representing this legend has been placed near the beach on Rosario Head. The 24-foot cedar log, carved in the traditional style of the Samish Indians, shows Ko-kwal-alwoot on one side as an Indian maiden and on the other as the sea spirit she became.

NORTHWEST ISLAND

Northwest Island, ½ mile northwest of the Rosario Beach picnic area, is yet another of the park's small undeveloped islands. The grassy, 1-acre rock is visited mainly by gulls and scuba divers. Although it lies temp-

Starfish

tingly close, divers are advised to take a boat to the island rather than attempt to swim the distance, as the tidal current is very strong.

Pass Lake Area

Access: Land
Facilities: Boat launch (ramp on Pass Lake), picnic tables
Attractions: Boating, paddling, fishing, hiking

Water holds its own special fascination, whether as ocean swells surging through narrow rocky channels, as placid waves lapping on sandy beaches, or in brackish marshes choked with cattails. Here the state park offers 100 acres of crystal-clear water for trout fishing or stillwater canoeing.

Pass Lake lies at the junction of Highway 20 and Rosario Road (Highway 525). A gravel public boat ramp and parking lot adjoin the intersection. Some pull-offs where the road parallels the lakeshore provide spots to put in portable boats or to park and have a waterfront picnic.

The trout-stocked lake is open to fly fishing during fishing season; gasoline motors are not permitted. Canoeists will find idyllic paddling the length of the lake and along the brushy shoreline. Deer, muskrat, skunk, fox, and other small wild animals may be seen on shore, especially at dusk. In winter migratory ducks stop to rest on the lake, floating together in convivial rafts.

Bowman Hill, south of the lake, is a densely wooded, undeveloped section of the park. About 2 miles of unimproved trails loop over and around the hill, leading to stunning panoramas from bald viewpoints. The

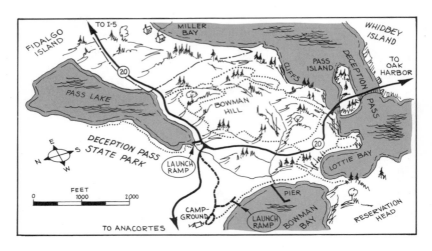

trails are recommended only for hikers experienced in route finding. The south slope of Bowman Hill is extremely cliffy; hikers are warned to stay well away from the edge. Trails begin at the pullout just north of the bridge.

Cranberry Lake Vicinity

Access: Land
Facilities: 230 campsites (at Cranberry Lake), bicycle campground, picnic tables, fireplaces, drinking water, picnic shelters, kitchens, restrooms, bathhouse, showers, swimming beach, boat launch (ramp on Cranberry Lake), fishing dock, playground
Attractions: Boating, paddling, fishing, hiking, beachcombing, swimming

The Cranberry Lake entrance to the park is on the west side of the road, slightly less than ¾ mile south of the Deception Pass bridge on Highway 20. At the entrance two intersections direct visitors first north to the North Beach picnic area, then west to the campground and West Point or south to the Cranberry Lake picnic area. At the second intersection are a large display board giving information on the park and the trailhead for a ¼-mile nature walk.

This is one of the best bicycling areas in the park, with smooth and level roads first wending through cool forest then edging the lake shore. Tent sites for late-arriving bicyclists are guaranteed at Cranberry Lake Campground, even if the campground is filled with car campers.

NORTH BEACH

Whether seen from the forest trail that traverses it or from the water's edge, North Beach is one of the most popular areas in the park. The trailhead can be found on the outside loop of the lower Cranberry Lake Campground, or by heading east on any of several well-beaten paths from the West Point parking lot.

The nearly mile-long curve of the beach is broken by three rocky headlands. The most prominent of these, Gun Point, was the location of 3-inch rapid-fire cannons that guarded the pass during WW II. At low tide the beach is easily walked from West Point to the base of the vertical cliffs below the Deception Pass Bridge. Higher tides force the route inland at times for scrambles over the rocky bluffs or a retreat to the trail higher up in the forest. From the North Beach picnic area the trail continues east beneath the bridge and on to Goose Rock. East of Gun Point hikers enjoy ant's eye views of the bridge and, at slack tide, the parade of boats through the pass.

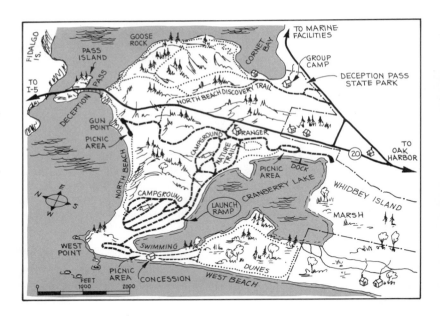

CRANBERRY LAKE

Had the ancient glacier that carved Deception Pass tried a little harder and dug a mere 50 feet deeper, Cornet Bay would have reached through to Rosario Strait, Goose Rock would have been an island, and Cranberry Lake never would have come into being. As it was, a neck of land remained, joining Goose Rock to the glacial outfall of Whidbey Island and forming the Cranberry Lake area merely as a shallow saltwater inlet of the sea. Over the centuries wind and waves sweeping in from the Strait of Juan de Fuca built a sand bar that eventually joined to the rocks of West Point, forming a lagoon similar to those found in other places on the island. However, instead of the brackish sea water entrapped in other lagoons, here an underground spring filled the shallow depression and changed the environment from salt-to freshwater marsh, with cattails, willows, skunk cabbage, lily pads, muskrat, beaver, river otter, and trout.

The lake is only about 10 to 20 feet deep throughout, with its deepest point a 40-foot "hole" near the north shore. It continues to be filled in with sediment; the closing-in of the lake margins is quite evident in photos taken over a period of years. In perhaps just a few hundred years the lake will be completely filled in and overgrown with vegetation.

The lake, which is stocked with trout, is inviting for either fishing or quiet-water paddling; boats with gasoline motors are not permitted. Mus-

North Beach from Deception Pass bridge

keg bogs on the southwest can only be reached by water; there the observant may spot beaver and muskrat lodges at the edge of the marsh. A boat-launch ramp is on the north shore of the lake just below the campground. Lightweight boats can be put in from the picnic area by carrying them the short distance from the parking lot to the water.

WEST POINT AND WEST BEACH

Contained in this small area is probably the greatest diversity of environment within the park—forest, lake, cattail bogs, rocky headland, ocean surf, and one of the finest sand beaches and dunelands on Puget Sound, all enhanced by views back to Mt. Erie and out across the Strait of Juan de Fuca to snowy Olympic peaks.

On hot summer days visitors can bathe in the supervised swimming area on the northwest beach of the bathwater-warm lake or dash across the sand bar for a bracing dip in the frigid ocean. Picnic tables along the beach face on either the lake or the sound. Prospective clam diggers will find slim pickings on West Beach—waves sweeping in from the strait constantly shift the sand, making it an impossible environment for sea life. The beauty of the shore lies in its pristine, unbroken sweep, and in the dunes that back it. A blacktop path leads into the dunes, which are now anchored by vegetation. Several picnic tables are along the path; a small wooden balcony provides an overview of the marsh.

In winter, when storm winds howl in from the ocean, sending waves crashing against the rocks at West Point, hardy souls who savor the excitement of marine pyrotechnics enjoy a visit to West Beach. Such storms are literally breathtaking; at times they are so severe it is impossible to stand against the force of the wind. Post-storm beachcombing may yield driftwood, agates, interesting flotsam, and seafoam to play in.

DECEPTION ISLAND

Lying less than ½ mile northwest of West Point, rugged Deception Island is the farthest outpost of the state park. Eastern approaches to the island are shallow and rock-riddled and the current can be strong; boaters should use great care. Immediately to the west the underwater shelf drops off quickly, making for excellent fishing and scuba diving just offshore.

Small boats may be beached on any of several rocky coves; the largest bay on the northwest side of the island is probably the easiest. Due to its difficult access and limited use, the island has not been developed by the park and has no onshore amenities.

Beach at Joseph Whidbey State Park

6. WHIDBEY ISLAND

Early sea captains, seeking shelter from Puget Sound storms, found refuge for their vessels and crews behind Whidbey Island. They were so fond of this long, sheltering arm that upon retirement many of them, along with their men, settled on the friendly island. Thomas Coupe, the most well known of these seamen, had the town of Coupeville named after him.

The island was given its name by British sea captain George Vancouver during his voyage of discovery. In May of 1792 Vancouver, along with his lieutenant, Peter Puget, explored the southern channels of Puget Sound. The examination of the South Sound completed, Vancouver turned

his attention to the maze of waterways lying to the north. On May 31st Vancouver anchored in Possession Sound, just off Gedney Island, and dispatched Ship's Master Joseph Whidbey to explore the two branches of the waterway leading to the north. After a brief examination of the waterway to the east, Whidbey explored the western one along the shores of a long island, as far north as Deception Pass. Vancouver named these two channels Port Susan and Port Gardner. The name of Port Susan remains today, but Port Gardner later came to be known as Saratoga Passage; only the small bay by Everett is now Port Gardner.

As he continued his exploration up Admiralty Inlet, Vancouver discovered that Deception Pass, which he had thought to be a bay, was a passageway that connected to the long channnel that Whidbey had explored earlier, and therefore the land mass was an island. He named the island in honor of Whidbey.

Vancouver and Whidbey had noted the friendy, peaceful nature of the Skagit Indians living on the island. Although these natives warred with their enemies, the Haida Indians from Canada, their early contacts with

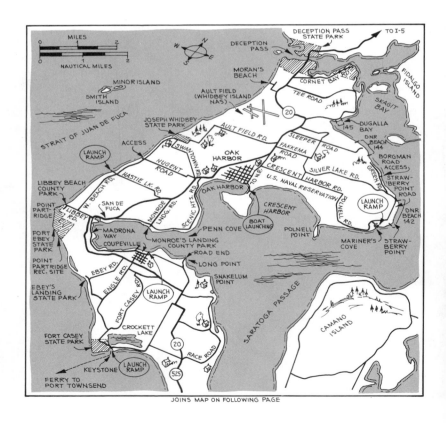

JOINS MAP ON FOLLOWING PAGE

white settlers were usually amicable. One of the Skagit chiefs, Snatelum, invited a French Catholic missionary from Fort Nisqually to visit the island. In 1840 Father Blanchet visited the island, conducted a mass baptism, and established a mission.

Thomas Glasgow is credited with being the first white man to settle on Whidbey Island. He traveled to the island by canoe in 1848 and selected a homestead site on a windswept prairie near the west shore of the island.

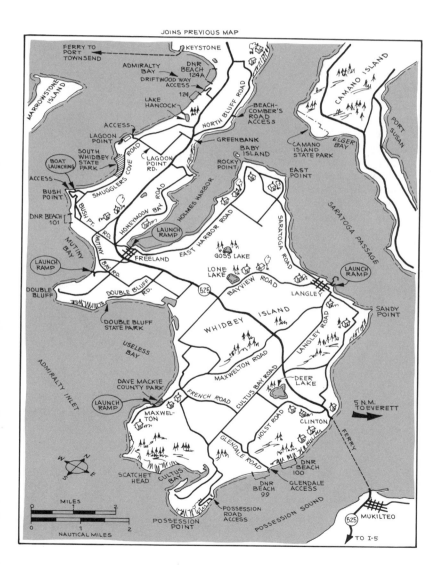

The Indians were beginning to have second thoughts about intrusions by the white men, and the threatening attitude of the natives caused Mr. Glasgow to depart suddenly, leaving his crops of wheat and potatoes behind. In October of 1850 Colonel Issac N. Ebey filed the first land claim on the island—on exactly the same fertile prairie that Glasgow had left.

The central section of Whidbey Island is markedly historic, with pioneer relics around nearly every bend of the road. Eight separate vicinities are included in Ebey's Landing National Historical Reserve, commemorating over 100 years of rural settlement and coastal defense.

The northern part of the island has a distinctive Dutch flavor, with Dutch names on some streets and businesses, a Holland festival in the spring, and even a replica of a windmill in the Oak Harbor city park. Back in 1894 a Whidbey Island land company made a concerted effort to attract Dutch settlers to the island, touting the rich farmland and temperate climate, quite similar to their homeland. Over 200 Hollanders came to Whidbey Island, some who had previously immigrated to the Midwest, and others who came directly from the Old Country. Most settled on the northern end. The farming skills of these industrious people turned much of the rich soil, and even some of the poorer, into productive farmland.

A second industry, the military, has also left its mark on the island. Admiralty Head was the site of Fort Casey, one of the World War I forts that guarded Puget Sound. Although the Army post at Fort Casey is closed and the site is currently a state park, the military influence is now felt in the form of the huge U.S. Navy air base on the north end of the island. Military planes are so commonplace that a jet fighter screaming overhead attracts less attention than the presence of a soaring bald eagle. Navy personnel, civilian employees, and their families account for nearly half of Whidbey Island's population. Quite a number of these like the sea captains of yore, have settled permanently on the island after being mustered out of the service.

This 45-mile-long ribbon of an island averages a mere 3 miles in width. From some vantage points it is possible to see at one time both bodies of water that flank it—Saratoga Passage on the east and the Strait of Juan de Fuca or Admiralty Inlet on the west. Whidbey holds the honor of being the longest island in the United States; for many years New York's Long Island was considered to be the longest, but in 1985 the U.S. Supreme Court, ruling in a boundary dispute case, determined that Long Island is actually a peninsula.

The western edge of the island is frequently buffeted by winds and heavy seas sweeping in from the strait. Boaters will find no protection along the long, smooth windward shoreline or in its few broad, open bays. Whidbey's leeward eastern shore is deeply indented by several snug coves, providing welcome protection in foul weather. Much of the island's population and its few small towns are concentrated along this eastern side.

Access to Whidbey Island is by bridge at Deception Pass at the north end of the island, or, at the southern end, by ferry from Mukilteo to

Trail to beach at Point Partridge Recreation Site

Smith Island

Clinton. To reach the ferry leave I-5 at Exit 189 and follow signs for 2.6 miles to the terminal at Mukilteo. One main thoroughfare traverses the length of Whidbey Island—state Highway 20 from the northern end becomes 525 in the southern part of the island. Midway, at Keystone, a second ferry gives access to and from the Olympic Peninsula via Port Townsend.

Strait of Juan de Fuca

SMITH AND MINOR ISLANDS

The extreme eastern end of the Strait of Juan de Fuca is marked by the navigational lights on Smith and Minor Islands, which serve as an important landmark for boats traveling between Puget Sound and the San Juan Islands. The two islands lie 4 nautical miles off the northwest shore of Whidbey Island. At low tide Smith joins the much smaller Minor Island. West of Smith Island a large kelp bed that extends for 1½ miles and a rock that bares at extreme low tides are boating hazards. Smith and Minor Islands are designated as a National Wildlife Refuge in order to protect nesting seabirds. Minor Island is a major breeding site for harbor seals.

In the mid-1800s Smith Island, along with points on Cape Flattery, New Dungeness, and Admiralty Head, were noted as critical navigational points and were selected as sites for Coast Guard lights. Construction on the Smith Island light began in 1857, and it was first lit in October of 1858. The beacon was manned continuously until it was automated in 1976. Life on this remote rock was hardly exciting. Generally two men, with their families, were assigned to Smith Island. When not tending the lights they raised food in their garden or hunted the rabbits that overran the island. When seas were calm they could row their small boat eight miles to the closest civilization—Richardson, the tiny general store on the southern tip of Lopez Island.

Battering by wind and waves from the strait has caused extreme erosion of the island, sometimes as much as five feet in a single year. In 1860 the island was about 50 acres in size; today it is less than 15. The light was originally located on a frame building, but erosion endangered the old structure, necessitating the relocation of the light on a tower farther inland. Some of the buildings are now so badly undercut by erosion they are collapsing into the sea.

JOSEPH WHIDBEY STATE PARK

Park Area: 112 acres; 3100 feet of shoreline
Access: Land, boat
Facilities: Picnic tables, fireplaces, picnic shelter, pit toilets, *no water*
Attractions: Beachcombing, boating, picnicking

One of the most glorious beaches on Whidbey Island lies just south of the Naval Air Station. Here the state has acquired from the Navy a section of land that they are holding for future development as a park. At present the park is a day-use picnic area with a dozen or so picnic tables and paths leading down to the beach. Some picnic tables are in the open on a low windswept bluff, while others are sequestered in the trees.

Waves from the Strait of Juan de Fuca toss driftwood onto the long sandy beach. Smith and Minor Islands can be seen directly offshore, 4 miles away. The northern boundary of the park is marked by the posted signs of the military reservation; beach homes of Swantown delineate the southern end. A second access to the park is on the south, right next to the first residence. Here are a graveled parking space for a few cars and a trail that leads directly to the beach.

To reach Joseph Whidbey State Park, take Highway 20 south out of Oak Harbor. Just outside of town at a major intersection turn right onto Swantown Road and follow it for 3 miles to its intersection with West Beach Road; the park entrance is immediately to the right. If traveling from the north, just after passing the Navy base turn west off Highway 20 onto Ault Field Road and follow the road to the park.

POINT PARTRIDGE LAUNCH RAMP

At the intersection of West Beach Road and Hastie Lake Road, 3.7 miles south of Joseph Whidbey State Park, is a small parking lot sandwiched between private homes. Near the south end of this parking lot is a single-lane concrete boat-launch ramp. The graveled lot has space for half a dozen boats with trailers.

Launching at any of the ramps on this side of the island can be difficult. The access may be choked by sand, logs, or debris; winds off the strait frequently cause additional problems.

LIBBEY BEACH COUNTY PARK (ISLAND COUNTY)

Park Area: 3 acres; 300 feet of shoreline
Access: Land, boat
Facilities: Picnic tables, fireplaces, picnic shelter, pit toilets, *no water*
Attractions: Beachcombing, picnicking, boating

A very small county park just north of Point Partridge gives access to some wild and wonderful beach walks below the steep eroded cliffs on the west side of the island. To reach it, turn off Highway 20 onto Libbey Road and follow it 1¼ miles to its end at the loop road in the park. Picnic tables are away from the beach and do not provide a view of the water. A former launch ramp at the site is badly eroded, attesting to the hard life launch ramps have on this side of the island.

Beach walks south around the point lead to connecting trails from Fort Ebey State Park, ½ mile away, or Point Partridge Recreation Area, 2 miles distant. To the north lie 6 magnificent miles of public tidelands beneath sandy bluffs that soar to a height of 200 feet. Use care not to become trapped by incoming tides.

FORT EBEY STATE PARK

Park Area: 228 acres; 9000 feet of shoreline
Access: Land
Facilities: 50 campsites, bicycle campground, picnic tables, fireplaces, drinking water, restrooms, hiking trails
Attractions: Historical display, hiking, beachcombing, viewpoints, fishing (freshwater)

Standing on the heights above the Strait of Juan de Fuca it is easy to see why the Army chose this site for a fort to protect the inland waters. From here there is a sweeping panorama out to Point Wilson and Port Townsend, south down Admiralty Inlet, and north to Vancouver Island and the San Juans. This park does not have as fine a display of old military equipment as does Fort Casey, to the south, but there's enough to keep inquisitive youngsters busy for a day, and the campground is much nicer.

Fort Ebey State Park is reached from Highway 20 by driving west on Libbey Road. One mile from Highway 20 turn south onto Valley Drive and

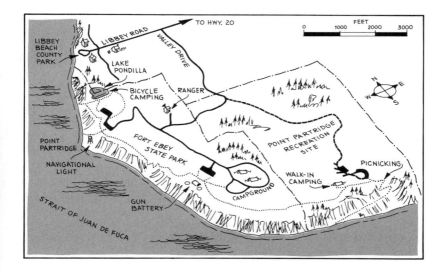

follow the signs to the park. Near the ranger's residence the road splits at a T. At the end of the road to the north, trails near the restrooms lead southward along the top of the bluff to the gun emplacement or steeply down the grassy bluff to the beach. The beach is sandy and gently sloping, with a high-tide decoration of silvered drift logs.

A short trail from the north parking lot goes to Lake Pondilla, which has a bicycle camping area on its shores. Drinking water is available near the north end of the trail, but campers must hike the short distance back up the hill to use the restrooms. Bass fishing is rumored to be good in the 3½-acre pond.

The southern section of the park, at the other end of the road T, has the gun battery and the campground. This coast artillery fort was established in 1942, a world war later than Fort Casey. Fort Ebey was manned during World War II, but was surplused soon after the war ended. The smaller, more modern Navy guns placed here were designed as back-up for the large guns on the new gun emplacements built farther out on the Strait of Juan de Fuca at Point Flattery, Point Angeles, and Striped Peak west of Port Angeles.

There are no guns remaining, but youngsters will enjoy climbing a metal ladder down a concrete shaft to a fire-control center overlooking the strait. From here observers directed the fire of the two 6-inch guns located in the batteries. Trails from the emplacements continue southward to the Point Partridge Recreation Site, ¾ mile away.

Campsites with picnic tables and fireplaces are along two forested loops at the end of the road. Rhododendron bushes scattered throughout the timber promise a blaze of beauty in the spring.

View south from Point Partridge to Perego's Lake

POINT PARTRIDGE RECREATION SITE

Park Area: 23 acres; 9000 feet of shoreline
Access: Land
Facilities: 11 primitive campsites; picnic tables, fireplaces, pit toilets, hiking trails, *no water*
Attractions: Viewpoints, hiking, picnicking

A primitive DNR camping and picnicking area adjoins the south boundary of Fort Ebey State Park. The road to the Point Partridge site is reached just before entering the state park. Follow the road south for 1 mile to the parking lot at road's end. Four campsites border the parking lot; some additional ones are down a short trail. These are all primitive sites—pit toilets, pack out your litter, and no water available.

Picnic tables are along the trail to the beach. Each table is on a terraced log-edged platform, giving picnickers their own "balcony view." Just past the picnic area the trail breaks out onto a grassy wind-swept slope 150 feet above the water. Wide views encompass Perego's Lake, a saltwater lagoon at the end of a sweeping crescent of beach. Across Admiralty Inlet are Marrowstone Island and Port Townsend, and north of it Protection Island and Discovery Bay. The trail cuts diagonally down the headland; a sturdy chain-link fence prevents hikers from slipping off the path.

This side of the island is frequently buffeted by strong winds off the strait, and beach walkers may face brisk, bone-chilling weather, even in the summer. When weather or high tide precludes beachcombing, settle for a hike atop the bluff on the trail that connects the DNR campground with Fort Ebey State Park.

Skagit Bay and North Saratoga Passage

DNR BEACHES 142, 144, AND 145

Three sections of Department of Natural Resources public tidelands are located along the northeast shore of Whidbey Island. At the very tip of Strawberry Point is DNR Beach 142, a 4800-foot strip of tidelands accessible only by boat. Good clamming here during low tides, and good beach walking beneath towering bluffs anytime tides permit.

Farther north, as the bluffs begin to temper near Dugalla Bay, DNR Beach 144 offers 4800 feet of shoreline as well as several acres of state-owned uplands. This beach is also accessible by land. To reach it, turn off Highway 20 onto Sleeper Road and follow it to its end. Hike down the bluff to the beach.

Near the head of Dugalla Bay, along the north shore, DNR Beach 145 is an 800-foot-wide chunk of tideflat. Although the uplands are private, the beach is easily reached from the dike at the end of the bay.

STRAWBERRY POINT BOAT LAUNCH

An obscure, unmarked, but nevertheless public boat ramp on Strawberry Point gives access to Skagit Bay and several nice DNR beaches. To reach the ramp from Oak Harbor, head north out of town on the road that follows the boundary of the Navy base, 70th N.E. Turn east onto Crescent Harbor Road, following the blacktop road along the north edge of the reservation. As the road turns south it becomes Polnell Road. In 8 miles, at the point where Polnell Road becomes Strawberry Road, Mariner's Cove, a real estate subdivision, is reached. Turn right at either Ferry Road or N. Beach Drive into Mariner's Cove, then turn left onto the road that circles the north side of the development.

As the shore is reached a short gravel loop road leads to the unmarked launch ramp, sandwiched between two private homes. Parking in the vicinity is minimal. All surrounding property, as well as the dredged lagoon housing a small yacht club, is private. Boaters can explore the shoreline north along Strawberry Point and on to Dugalla Bay.

OAK HARBOR

Effects of the nearby Naval air base are strongly felt in Whidbey Island's largest town, Oak Harbor. The town does not have the "quaint"

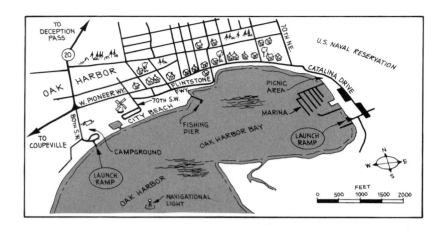

aura that Langley and Coupeville have—most of the stores are modern, and the main highway is lined with fast-food restaurants, car dealerships, and service stations. Despite the jets screaming overhead, however, life here is still relatively sedate, with both townfolk and tourists on hand to take part in its "Holland Happening" festival the last week of April and its "Old Fashioned Fourth of July."

Instead of cluttering the waterfront with high-priced restaurants and privileged businesses, Oak Harbor has devoted most of its shoreline to parks, ranging from the tidy little picnic area overlooking the marina to the multi-use City Beach Park on the west end of the shore. These parks provide a nice setting for visitors approaching the city by water.

OAK HARBOR MARINA

Facilities: Complete boat and crew facilities, boat launch (ramp and hoist), boat rentals and charters, boat pumpout station, tidal grid, picnic tables, children's play equipment, shopping (nearby)

Oak Harbor offers the best marine facilities on Saratoga Passage. In fact, the city-operated marina ranks with the best to be found anywhere on Washington's inland waters. The harbor itself is a 1½-mile-long curving arm tucked behind Maylor Point. Navigational markers on the dogleg channel leading into the marina should be followed scrupulously; shoals lie immediately outside the dredged channel, and several rocks lurk just off the end of the point.

Behind a unique new floating breakwater protecting the marina are transient moorage slips for more than 36 boats. Part of the breakwater's wave-cancelling design includes a series of 18-foot-square concrete floats on the outboard side of the walkway. For the slips behind, these make an excellent "front porch" for picnicking or sunbathing. A key card, obtained at the marina office, is necessary to operate the main gate and restroom doors after hours.

A very nice little park on shore has picnic tables, a barbeque pit, and a view of downtown Oak Harbor. The boat-launching area is immediately to the south. Here a former Navy seaplane ramp has been converted into a four-lane ramp, with an ajoining float for loading. An additional pier with float has overnight space for a dozen boats.

The Oak Harbor marina is about ½ mile from downtown stores; bicycles are provided for visitors who do not want to walk the distance, or taxi service is available. The town offers a full range of services and boating supplies.

OAK HARBOR CITY PARKS

Park Area: 30 acres; 2100 feet of shoreline
Access: Land, boat
Facilities: RV campground, picnic tables, fireplaces, drinking water, restrooms, tennis courts, basketball court, children's play equipment, wading pool, swimming beach, boat launch (ramp), fishing pier with float
Attractions: Fishing, paddling, swimming

Oak Harbor Marina

The shoreline on the west side of the city is devoted to City Beach, a large, multi-use park. The park has two entrances. One leads to the day-use area, the second road, farther west, to the RV campground. A single-lane concrete boat-launch ramp is on a loop at the end of this second road, just past the campground. Ample parking for cars and trailers is nearby. Since the park faces on a long tideflat, the ramp may not be usable during moderate to low tides.

Centerpiece of the park is a full-sized replica of a windmill, paying homage to the city's Dutch heritage. Near it are a swimming beach (lifeguard on duty in the summer), wading pool, and a wide assortment of play paraphernalia. Views from the park are down the length of Saratoga Passage.

A second park is east of City Beach, at the end of Flintstone Freeway, the street that parallels the shore. It is comprised of a small grassy waterfront area with picnic tables, a fishing pier, and fish-cleaning stations. The pier has a short float with space for about four boats. Since water surrounding the pier is shoal, it is recommended only for shallow-draft boats, and even they should approach with care.

PENN COVE

The eastern shore of Whidbey Island bends around two major bays—Holmes Harbor on the south and Penn Cove on the north. Penn

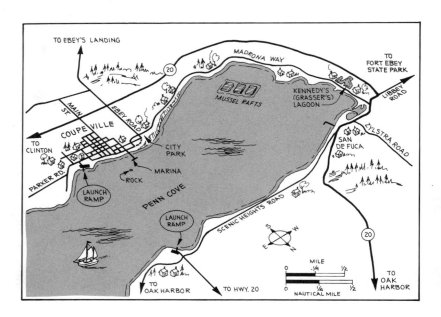

Cove runs westerly from Saratoga Passage for 3½ miles. A ½-mile-long sandspit extends north from Snakelum Point, the southernmost point at the entrance to the cove. Boaters entering the bay from the south should stay well outside the buoy marking the end of the spit.

At the turn of the century a syndicate had plans to dig canals through the island at points where the land was constricted to a mere mile in width. One canal would have gone from Penn Cove through to West Beach, in the vicinity of Libbey Road. The second canal would have been built from the northeast shore of Holmes Harbor through to Lake Hancock. It was reasoned that shipping traffic would take advantage of the canals as a shortcut between the Strait of Juan de Fuca and the growing port of Everett. The canals, of course, were never dug, and one can only imagine what Whidbey Island would be today if the plans had come into being.

The island is still wrestling with commercialism—the latest venture is mussel-raising farms on Penn Cove. Seed mussels are attached to ropes suspended from floats or rafts, where they grow in the nutrient-filled water. After two years the bivalves are harvested and shipped to restaurants and lucky gourmets throughout the U.S. This type of venture would seem in keeping with traditional Whidbey Island enterprises, but there are those waterfront residents who object to the rafts and floats in their "front yards." Boaters are concerned the farms will restrict their activities on the bay, but so far this does not seem to be a problem. Most of the floats lie along the side of the cove, between Coupeville and the head of the bay, and do not present a hazard.

A scenic drive or bicycle route follows the shoreline of Penn Cove, with views of the cove, Saratoga Passage, and Skagit Bay. Follow the shore south out of Oak Harbor on Scenic Heights Road, which becomes Penn Cove Road. Join Highway 20 briefly at San de Fuca, then in ½ mile turn left onto Madrona Way and follow it into Coupeville. As the road nears Coupeville the broad view is lost, and there are only brief glimpses through the trees of Penn Cove and the mussel floats.

MONROE'S LANDING COUNTY PARK (ISLAND COUNTY)

Park Area: .5 acre
Access: Land, boat
Facilities: Boat launch (ramp), *no water*

This undeveloped park on the north shore of Penn Cove gives access to some of the cove's shoreline. Monroe's Landing County Park is 2 miles east of San de Fuca at the intersection of Penn Cove Road and Monroe Landing Road. All that is to be found here is a large parking lot, a single-lane concrete launch ramp, and some pretty beach. A dirt road that goes east into the seagrass deadends at nothing—better to walk it and enjoy the scenery.

Coupeville city dock

Monroe's Landing is one of the eight sites in Ebey's Landing National Historical Reserve. This was one of the stops made by Ship's Master Joseph Whidbey while conducting explorations for George Vancouver in 1792. Whidbey found a large village of Indians here; an Indian longhouse was located near here as late as 1892.

COUPEVILLE

Coupeville is in many ways the essence of Whidbey Island—at times salty, at times rural, but at all times conscious of its pioneer heritage. The town is one of the sites in Ebey's Landing National Historical Preserve. It was one of the earliest towns on the island; numerous homes around the town bear signs telling the date they were built and their original owner. One of these residences is that of Thomas Coupe, the sea captain who founded the town.

By land Coupeville is reached by turning off Highway 20 at the signed intersection and following the road ½ mile into town. It can also be reached via the scenic route from Oak Harbor.

All of the interesting old store-front buildings are along either side of Front Street. Many of these stores now house antique shops, arts and crafts galleries, and other businesses catering to tourists. A guide for a historical walking tour of the town is available from local merchants. On Alexander St., near the intersection with Front, is a historical display featuring one of the old blockhouses, several Indian war canoes, and a wooden cross dating from the time of the first missionaries on the island. Across the street is the Island County Historical Museum; open 12−4 p.m. daily in the summer, and 12−4 p.m. Saturdays and Sundays from fall through spring.

After exploring the town, take time for a picnic in the city park located immediately west of the Port of Coupeville wharf. The park, on a high grassy bluff, has picnic tables, restrooms, children's play equipment, and wide views out over Penn Cove. There is no access to the shore down the steep embankment; walk a blocked-off road down the hill for beach access near the wharf.

PORT OF COUPEVILLE MARINA AND LAUNCH RAMP

Facilities: Complete boat and crew facilities (no marine repair), mooring buoys, boat and bicycle rentals, boat launch (ramp), boat pumpout station, shopping (nearby)

Focal point of the town is the long Port of Coupeville wharf that stretches into the bay. A short float off the pier has space for about eight boats; fuel and marine services are available at the barn-like building on the end of the wharf. Several mooring buoys have been placed in the bay for the use of visitors, and there is enough space for others to find good anchorage within dinghy distance of the float. Boaters should be wary of a large submerged rock that lies 300 yards northeast of the wharf.

A public launch ramp is located on the east side of town. Here there are two single-lane concrete launch ramps, with a finger pier between them. A sign on the float warns that it is aground at low water. The ramp to the west is in the best condition; the one on the right may be unusable during low tide. The large parking lot has space for a number of cars with trailers; a restroom beside the parking lot is a recent addition. At the entrance to the parking lot is a sewage disposal dump.

Admiralty Inlet

EBEY'S LANDING STATE PARK AND NATIONAL HISTORICAL RESERVE

State Park Area: 45.8 acres; 6120 feet of shoreline
Access: Land, boat
Facilities: Hiking trail, *no water*
Attractions: Historical display, hiking, beachcombing

Colonel Isaac Ebey certainly didn't intend to make history in quite the way he did—by being decapitated by some surly Canadian Indians. Ebey

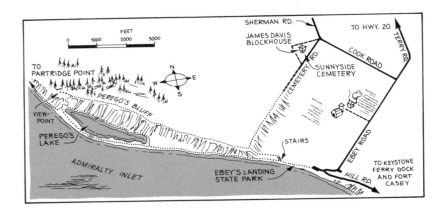

was already assured a place in Washington history as the first permanent settler on Whidbey Island and as a political leader. As it was, this very leadership quality brought him to the attention of the Indians who, in August of 1857, were looking for some kind of white "chief" on whom they could avenge the untimely demise of one of their chiefs.

The beach section of the late Colonel Ebey's homestead is now a state park; the upland portion of the farm as well as the cemetery where he is buried are included in Ebey's Landing National Historical Reserve. The purpose of this reserve is to "preserve and protect a rural community that provides an unbroken historic record from the 19th century exploration and settlement in Puget Sound to the present time." Eight areas are included in the historical reserve: Coupeville, Fort Casey State Park, Ebey's Prairie, Grasser's Hill (in the San de Fuca vicinity), Fort Ebey, Crockett Lake, Monroe's Landing, and Smith Prairie (south of Snakelum Point).

Ebey's Prairie and the state park can be reached by land by turning south off Highway 20 onto Ebey Road and following the signed route. The road travels through the finest farmland on all of Whidbey Island—a green and gold prairie that has seen human habitation for around 12,000 years. Land at Ebey's Prairie is owned by the National Park Service, but it is leased for agriculture, assuring that its traditional use will remain unchanged.

Sunnyside Cemetery lies on a slight hill above the prairie and offers a panoramic view of the plain. To reach it, turn north off Ebey Road onto Cook Road and proceed ½ mile to the intersection of Cook, Cemetery, and Sherman Roads. For headstone history stroll through the cemetery; Colonel Ebey is buried here, as well as a number of early pioneers. The James Davis blockhouse, dating from the 1855 Indian uprising, is also located here.

Ebey Road continues on toward the beach; at the end of a sharp turn is a parking lot. At present the state park is undeveloped except for this parking lot and a historical billboard. A trail gradually ascends the 200-foot

Beach at Ebey's Landing State Park

wind-blown bluff, with glorious views out over Admiralty Inlet and down to the tawny beach below. It then descends to the north end of Perego's Lake, a brackish saltwater lagoon named for an eccentric recluse who once lived on the bluff above. From here continue on by trail to Partridge Point or walk the beach back to the parking lot. The trip around the end of the lagoon and back is about 3½ miles.

FORT CASEY STATE PARK

Park Area: 411.4 acres; 10,810 feet of shoreline (including Keystone Spit)
Access: Land, boat
Facilities: 35 campsites, picnic tables, fireplaces, restrooms, showers, drinking water, museum, lighthouse, hiking trails, boat launch (ramp), underwater park
Attractions: Historical displays, fishing, scuba diving, hiking

The kids will have so much fun they will never suspect they are getting a history lesson! Here are dozens of darkened corridors to explore, masses of concrete parapets to scramble over, and acres of bluff and beach to roam. Don't miss the searchlight emplacements below the rim of the bluff and the switchboard building to the east that controlled electrical power to the emplacements; take along a flashlight to aid your investigations. Use care in exploring the fortifications. Don't allow youngsters to become rowdy, and keep a tight hand on the younger ones. Falls from the bunkers and bluffs have caused serious injuries and even fatalities.

Fortification was not the initial governmental use of Admiralty Head. A lighthouse reservation was acquired here in 1858, and the first light, which stood west of the present emplacements, was shown in 1861. When Admiralty Head was chosen as one of three sites for primary defense of Puget Sound, the lighthouse was moved to its present position. In the 1920s it was determined to be obsolete, and the light was removed in 1927. During WW II the lighthouse building was used as a training center and kennel for the dogs of the military K-9 Corps, much to its detriment. It was finally converted to a museum when the fort became a state park.

The first gun emplacements at Fort Casey were completed in 1899. Over the following years more batteries were added, until by 1907 the fort complement included ten batteries with nineteen guns ranging in size from 3-inch to 10-inch, sixteen 12-inch mortars, and a garrison of over 200 men. Most lethal of the armaments were the seven 10-inch guns mounted on disappearing carriages that withdrew behind a thick protective wall after each round was fired. The batteries at Fort Casey, along with those at Fort Worden near Port Townsend and Fort Flagler on Marrowstone Island, formed a "Triangle of Fire" designed to guard Puget Sound and the vital Navy shipyards at Bremerton.

In 1917, when the U.S. entered the World War, the fort was placed on

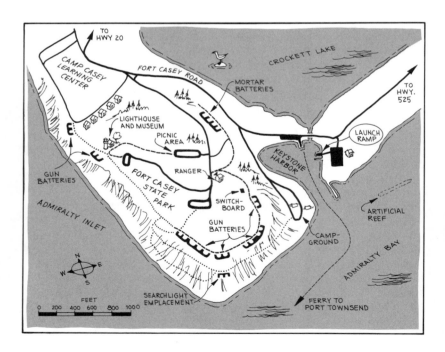

Battery Trevor at Fort Casey State Park

24-hour alert and activities expanded to provide training for harbor defense companies headed for Europe. At the end of the war the fort was placed on caretaker status, and then used as a training center by the National Guard, ROTC, and Citizen's Military Training Corps. Some of the guns had been removed during the war for use on the European front. By 1933 all the remaining original armaments were taken to be melted down; however a few new anti-aircraft batteries were placed in recognition of this new style of warfare.

With the outbreak of WW II the fort again served as a training site, and for five years after the war was a satellite camp for engineering troops stationed at Fort Worden. The property was eventually surplused, and in 1956 was acquired by Washington State Parks.

Fort Casey's emplacements, which are the best preserved in the state, include four guns in place; the two 3-inch rapid-fire and two 10-inch disappearing carriage guns were procured from Fort Wint in the Philippines in 1968 for display here. Several billboards explain the history of coastal fortification. The museum in the lighthouse (open 10 a.m. to 6 p.m., Wednesday through Sunday) exhibits some of the ammunition used in the guns and other informative displays. The lighthouse tower can be climbed for views of the huge water highway that the fort guarded.

After curiosity with the Army fortification is satisfied, there are still a

147

beach and several miles of trails to wander. Footpaths lace the bluff below and around the gun batteries. Reach the shore from the campground or from the northernmost battery; this can be the start for a 5-mile beach walk beneath the wildest bluffs on the island, all the way north to Point Partridge.

The picnic area is in trees on the hillside above the emplacements. The old wooden barracks, passed on the way into the park, are now used as housing for school and scout groups that schedule educational camps here. On the east side of the park, below the bluff, is the overnight camping area. The rather cramped campsites lie on a beach formed by material dredged from the Keystone channel. Due to the popularity of the park, the 35 sites are usually claimed by mid-day in the summer. A trail leads from the end of the campground up the bluff to the emplacements, or the road can be walked to the upper portion of the park.

On the east shore of Keystone Harbor, behind a piling breakwater, are the two concrete ramps of the state park boat launch, separated by a loading float. This is one of the best launch ramps on the island, with a good drop-off and excellent protection by breakwater and rock jetty. Launching can be difficult during the comings and goings of the Keystone–Port Townsend ferry.

The state park's offerings do not end at the water line. Keystone's rock jetty and pilings of the old Army quartermaster dock immediately to the east are now an underwater state park. This marine habitat is the most popular diving spot on Whidbey Island for both snorkeling and scuba diving. Underwater is a kaleidoscope of sea life—lacy white sea anemones, brilliant purple plume worms, swarms of kelp greenlings, shy octopus hiding in dark niches, rockfish, and large ling cod. Since this is a protected sanctuary many of the fish are quite tame and can easily be approached.

To reach Fort Casey State Park from the north turn south off Highway 20 onto Engle Road at the pedestrian overpass in Coupeville and follow signs to the Keystone Ferry. From the south, turn west at the point where Highway 525 joins Highway 20 and follow signs.

KEYSTONE

Keystone has several of its own attractions, as well as being the terminal for the Port Townsend ferry. Crockett Lake, the 250-acre marsh formed by the sandbar at Keystone, is a prime birdwatching area, especially during migratory season. Look for hawks and passerines around the edges of the lake and herons and transient waterfowl in the water.

The saltwater side of the sandbar is good for birdwatching too, as well as beachcombing. A small public access is at the road intersection at the east end of Crockett Lake. Next to the white Navy spotting tower is parking space for a couple of cars.

Keystone ferry landing

In 1988 Washington State Parks acquired all of Keystone Spit, running for 1.4 miles west of the ferry landing between Crockett Lake and the sound. The two beaches, one freshwater and one saltwater, are open to day use for picnicking, bird watching, kite flying, or whatever else strikes your fancy.

Two public DNR beaches lie beneath steep cliffs on Admiralty Bay south of Keystone. Beach 124A is a 4200-foot strip south of the Admiral's Cove subdivision. Beach 124, which is 2400 feet long, lies a mile farther south. Neither of these beaches have land access; they must be reached by boat. The public beach is below the mean high water level.

SOUTH WHIDBEY STATE PARK

Park Area: 85 acres; 4500 feet of shoreline
Access: Land, boat
Facilities: 54 campsites, group camp, picnic tables, fireplaces, picnic shelter, restrooms, showers, drinking water, trails
Attractions: Fishing, clam digging, beachcombing, hiking, swimming

Here are both greenly forested uplands and open, wave-washed beach, in what is probably the prettiest park on all of Whidbey Island. The forest is wonderful old Douglas fir, with a thick layer of undergrowth. Trails are edged by ferns, red elderberry, salmonberry, and a goodly

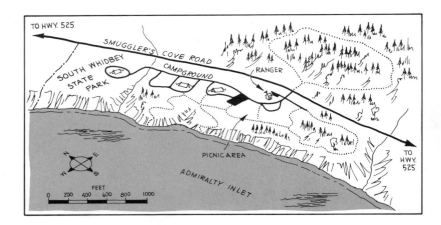

amount of stinging nettles (don't stray off the trail!). The shore is gently sloping sand, giving way to cobbles and rocks at the low-tide level. At high tide the strip of exposed beach is quite narrow. A northerly breeze sweeping down from the strait cools the shoreline much of the time.

Trails lead from the campground and parking area down the high bank to the beach. Another trail loops through the dense forest in the southern section of the park, giving quiet-stepping hikers a chance to spot deer, raccoon, pileated woodpeckers, and other little critters. A recently acquired section of the park lies on the east side of Smuggler's Cove Road. This 255-acre tract includes a stand of old-growth forest, with some giant Douglas firs and red cedars over 250 years old. A 1½-mile loop trail starts immediately across the road from the park entrance.

To reach the park from the north, turn off Highway 525 just south of Lake Hancock onto Smuggler's Cove Road and follow it for 4½ miles to the park. From the south, 9 miles from Clinton turn west off Highway 525 onto Bush Point Road which eventually joins Smuggler's Cove Road and goes north to the park, a distance of 6 miles from the highway intersection.

The state park can be visited by boat, but since the shore is unprotected, anchoring offshore is difficult except during calm weather.

BUSH POINT

Bush Point has a mixture of small attractions. On the north side of the point is a commercial marina, the only such facility on this side of Whidbey Island. The resort has boat rentals, fuel, a restaurant, sling launching, and the usual marine amenities, although they have no moorage. Two

Beach at South Whidbey State Park

nearby street ends provide public access to the water. Immediately next to the marina is the Main St. road end. Farther south, at the end of Admiralty Ave. is a second public access, marked by two white pillars.

Either of these street ends can be used as boat put-ins to reach DNR Beach 101, a public beach 1 mile to the south. This 1650-foot section of beach lies beneath bluffs just north of Mutiny Bay. Use care in small boats as the tide can be very strong in this area.

MUTINY BAY LAUNCH RAMP

Why Mutiny Bay? No one knows. Someday perhaps an inventive sea captain will spin a yarn to explain the name. Although the name is intriguing, the bay isn't much—just a slight indention in the shoreline, as bays along this side of Whidbey Island are inclined to be.

The one public area on Mutiny Bay is the launch ramp at the end of Robinson Road. To reach it, drive east out of Freeland on the Bush Point Road, and turn south at the intersection of Mutiny Bay Road. In 2 miles turn right onto Robinson Road, which is signed to the boat launch. On the right side of the road is a gravel and grass lot with parking space for a dozen cars with trailers. The single-lane concrete ramp is straight ahead, between private homes. This ramp, like others on this side of the island, is subject to considerable wave action, and the access may be choked by sand or debris.

DOUBLE BLUFF STATE PARK

Access: Land, boat
Facilities: None
Attractions: Beachcombing, swimming, paddling, clam digging

The beach area on Useless Bay along the shore north of Double Bluff is owned by the state parks, but is undeveloped except for the blacktopped parking lot at the end of the road. One could certainly argue that Nature has done all the development necessary on this shore, and any further refinement by man would be sacrilegious. It is just the place for the serious beach fanatic, with acres of sand for wandering at low tide, piles of driftwood providing private little niches for an afternoon of daydreaming, rustling beach grass, the plaintive cries of seabirds, and water in the shallow bay warmed for dabbling bare toes.

To reach the park by land, 9¼ miles from Clinton turn south off Highway 525 onto Double Bluff Road and follow it for 2 miles to its end. To the east of the road are rows of homes snuggled against the beach; to the west lies the park. A long row of weathered logs forms a bulkhead at the high-water mark. A sandbar in the long, shallow tideflat traps shallow ponds of water at low tide for toddlers to delight in. At the far end of the beach is a

Heron at Double Bluff State Park

glacial till bluff, at 367 feet one of the tallest and sheerest precipices on the island. The beach can be walked west all the way around the point to the homes of Mutiny Bay.

Sailors call this Useless Bay because its widespread arms offer scant protection against wind and waves and the shallow bottom reaches out to trap unwary keels. For kayakers though, when the weather is calm the bay offers interesting exploration along its shores and south around the corner to Cultus Bay. Here are two bays, side by side, with identical names (albeit in different languages)—"Cultus" is the Chinook jargon word meaning "useless." Most of Cultus Bay dries at low tide, except for a dredged basin, and becomes useless, even for canoes.

DAVE MACKIE COUNTY PARK (ISLAND COUNTY)

Park Area: 4 acres; 400 feet of shoreline
Access: Land, boat
Facilities: Picnic tables, fireplaces, restrooms, drinking water, children's play area, baseball field, boat launch (ramp), groceries and fuel (across street)
Attractions: Boating, paddling, swimming, clam digging

With its baseball diamond and bleachers, Dave Mackie County Park is obviously a facility meant for the use of residents, not necessarily tourists, but residents (who know a nice beach when they see one) probably won't object to an outlander or two dropping by to share it.

The park is at Maxwelton on the extreme south end of Useless Bay. To drive to it, turn south off Highway 525 onto Maxwelton Road and follow it for 5 miles to the community. Maxwelton is a collection of homes strung along the beach on either side of the road. The only commercial business is the combination grocery store/gas station across the street from the county park.

Dave Mackie Park lies on a low grassy bank above the bay; a boulder bulkhead lines the high-water level. Two roads go into the park—the one on the south leads to the one-lane concrete boat-launch ramp. Mooring buoys offshore are private. Since the ramp faces on a long tideflat, launching is possible only at moderate to high tide, and with boats that are small enough to be at least partially carried or dragged. There is no loading float.

Water flowing over the gently sloping bottom warms to temperatures bearable for wading and swimming. Picnic tables along the bank offer lunchtime views of the beach and boating activity as well as impressive views across Useless Bay to the rapidly-rising cliffs at Double Bluff.

South Saratoga Passage and Possession Sound

HOLMES HARBOR

The largest cove on Whidbey Island, Holmes Harbor, runs southward off Saratoga Passage, penetrating the shoreline for over 5 miles. There are

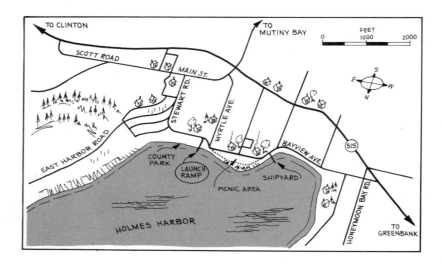

no public docks or moorages on the bay; the only public facilities are the launch ramp and park at Freeland, the small town at the head of the bay. Holmes Harbor is large enough that boaters can spend a full day here—fishermen trying the traditional "hot spots," sailors enjoying long tacks across the mile-wide bay, and pleasure cruisers drifting along the scenic shoreline.

Good anchorages can be found in the bay along the northwest shore by Greenbank. The head of the bay offers good anchorages in a mud bottom at 17 fathoms; however there is little protection here from either northerly or southerly blows since the land at the head of the bay is very low.

FREELAND COUNTY PARK (ISLAND COUNTY)

Park Area: 7 acres; 1500 feet of shoreline
Access: Land, boat
Facilities: Picnic tables, fireplaces, children's play area, restrooms, drinking water, trail, boat launch (ramp)
Attractions: Beachcombing, picnicking, hiking

After its 5-mile flow southward, Holmes Harbor peters out in a mudflat at the village of Freeland. The small county park at the head of the bay has a launch ramp, a single-lane concrete affair, next to the park restroom. Do not mistakenly try to use the ramp to the west by the shipyard; that one is private. Launching or landing at moderate to low tide or with large trailered boats may be difficult, due to the gentle slope of the tideflat.

The park itself has a nice beach and a few picnic tables with fireplaces. On a slight knoll to the west are a picnic shelter and a woodland trail that can be jogged or sauntered, depending on whether your interest is fitness or relaxation.

The Freeland shopping center, which sits on the hillside ½ mile above the harbor, has grocery, marine supply, and other stores, service stations, a laundromat, and a cafe. Freeland, one of several utopian cooperative communities founded on Puget Sound around the turn of the century, was established in 1900 by a group of defectors from Equality, a socialist colony south of Bellingham on Samish Bay.

LANGLEY

The town of Langley is in itself a good reason to visit Whidbey Island. The term "quaint" might well have been coined just to describe this small village by the sea. Although local merchants do like to capitalize on it, the town's particular aura is authentic—most of the weathered little store-front shops have been soaking up history along with the salt air for nearly 100 years. For shopping addicts the town is pure heaven, with marvelous little art galleries, crafts shops, antique stores, bookstores, and, when you need a rest, numerous purveyors of refreshments.

Langley was a product of the railroad hysteria that infected so much of Puget Sound during the late 1800s. Jacob Anthes, a Whidbey Island settler, reasoned that the arrival of the railroad on Puget Sound would mean increased steamer traffic as the fleet of boats carried goods up Saratoga Passage and the Swinomish Channel to Bellingham and points north. These steamers would need cordwood to keep their boilers fired. Anthes convinced a Seattle judge, J. W. Langley, to join him in purchasing land on the south end of Whidbey Island and establishing a town that would provide firewood for the steamers and be a trading post for island residents.

The town flourished for a time, but in 1894 the Great Northern Railway completed its line to Bellingham, and steamer traffic on Saratoga Passage virtually stopped. The result was devastating—settlers went bankrupt and left the island, and Langley became a near ghost town. As Whidbey Island has become increasingly settled and developed over the years, Langley has benefited, but it has never reached the boom proportions that Anthes and Judge Langley anticipated.

To reach Langley from the Clinton–Mukilteo ferry terminal, follow Highway 525 out of town. In 3 miles turn north on Langley Road and follow it for 3 more miles into town. At the eastern edge of town is the high school; the main brick building of the school houses a museum operated by the South Whidbey Historical Society. Museum hours are 12–4 p.m. Saturday, Sunday, and holidays during the summer, Sundays only, fall through spring.

LANGLEY MARINA

Facilities: Guest moorage, gas, groceries, ice, bait, tackle, marine supplies and repairs, boat launch (ramp and hoist), fishing pier

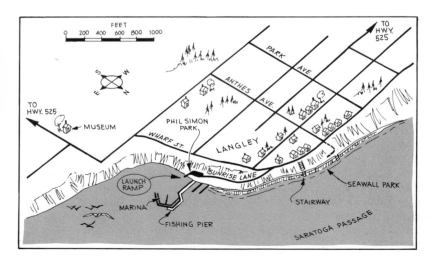

Seawall Park at Langley

Langley faces directly on Saratoga Passage without the benefit of any kind of natural land protection. The marina on Wharf Street at the east end of the town once had a meager little guest float that bobbed and rolled with every swell off the channel. Finally the old wharf and the guest float were removed, and in 1986 were replaced with a dandy little yacht basin behind a sturdy breakwater. Here there are 18 slips for transient boats as well as additional permanent berths. The moorages are quite short and narrow, and may be difficult to get into for boats over thirty feet. A long fishing pier with cleaning stations and rod holders follows the outside of the breakwater.

On shore, immediately east of the yacht basin, is Phil Simon Park, which has a single-lane concrete boat-launching ramp and a boarding float. Parking space for several cars with trailers is adjacent. The commercial marina to the west has fuel, sling launching, and marine supplies and repairs.

If approaching the marina by land from the east, it is not possible to take a right turn onto Wharf St.; drivers must continue on, circle around in town, and enter the street from the west. Boaters arriving at the yacht basin will find the town's shopping district is just a block up the hill.

SEAWALL PARK

Park area: 1 acre; 1000 feet of shoreline
Access: Land, boat
Facilities: Picnic tables
Attractions: Beach walking, viewpoint

The two-block-long business district of Langley sits above the water on a 100-foot embankment. The town has made the most of its beachfront by turning it into a pretty little park. Seawall Park, as it is called, is a 30-foot-wide grassy strip between a concrete bulkhead and the blackberry-covered embankment. Picnic tables in the park provide views of boat traffic in Saratoga Passage and of the impressive bluffs of Camano Head, immediately across the channel. Bas-relief Northwest Indian designs decorate the bulkhead, and two sets of concrete steps breach the wall, giving access to the gravel beach below. From above, the park can be reached by a long set of stairs at an overlook near the east end of the shopping district, or by a steep blacktopped path at the intersection of 1st St. and Anthes Ave.

COLUMBIA BEACH (CLINTON)

Facilities: Fishing pier, float, stores, restaurants, fuel (service station)

To most people arriving at Whidbey Island via the Mukilteo ferry, Clinton is just a blur as they leave the ferry and whiz by headed for points north. Slow down a bit and you will find the town has several points of interest.

Immediately north of the ferry landing is the Clinton Recreational Pier, a combination fishing pier and boat dock. The elevated platform is a nice place to observe ferry and boating activity or watch other people catching fish. The concrete float below has space for 4 or 5 small boats. Parking is at the top of the hill in the ferry parking lot.

The town of Clinton has a few stores; more are scattered along Highway 525. About a mile out of town on the east side of the road is a gravel pullout; on Saturday mornings in the summer local farmers gather here to sell their garden-fresh produce.

Fishing at the Clinton ferry landing

POSSESSION POINT

Two public beaches on the extreme south end of Whidbey Island can be reached by hand-carried boats put in the water at Clinton or at the Glendale road end. The nearest boat launches are at Mukilteo, 3 miles away across Possession Sound, or at Dave Mackie County Park, 5 miles away around the end of the island.

DNR Beach 100 is a 2550-foot-long strip beneath bluffs ½ mile north of Glendale. Beach 99 is 1160 feet of tidelands just north of the beach homes at Possession Point. The public lands are only the area below mean high water. Dungeness and red rock crabs can be caught in the area.

An artificial reef has been placed just off Possession Point as an aid to fishing in the area. It is shown by buoys and lies west of the lighted bell buoy that marks shoals at the south end of the point.

Whidbey Island Road Ends

Nearly a dozen road ends give access to beaches and water around the island. Typically these are 50-foot-wide strips of shoreline flanked by a host of "Private Property, No Trespassing!" signs; parking nearby is usually minimal. All of them provide a place to put in a hand-carried boat for exploration of nearby shores. None of these road ends warrant the space it would take to fully describe getting there; they are listed below with a brief hint as to their location. Armed with these hints and a good map, anyone determined to enjoy a bit of personal beach for the day should be able to find one. Public use of adjoining shoreline is dependent entirely on the goodwill of the property owners and the good manners of the visitors.

Moran's Beach. Facing on the Strait of Juan de Fuca immediately south of the Naval Air Station. Turn off Highway 20 at Banta Road. Public area is at the end of Powell Road.

West Beach Road. Facing on the Strait of Juan de Fuca. South of Swantown the road parallels the shore; park near an overgrown house foundation at the intersection of Nugent Road for beach walks southward below towering bluffs.

Driftwood Way. On Admiralty Bay. Turn off Highway 525 onto Ledgewood Beach Drive. The north end of Driftwood Way ends at the water.

Lagoon Point. On Admiralty Inlet just north of South Whidbey Island State Park. Turn off Smuggler's Cove Road onto Lagoon Point Road. Public area is on the north side of the lagoon. The boat-launch ramp at the lagoon is private. A second public access on the south side of the lagoon is at the end of Salmon Street.

Dugalla Bay. On Skagit Bay where Dugalla Bay Road crosses a dike. Along the north shore of the bay is DNR Beach 145, an 800-foot-wide strip of tidelands accessible at low tide.

Borgman Road. On Skagit Bay between Dugalla Bay and Strawberry Point. Where Strawberry Road becomes Silver Lake Road, turn north on Green Road.

Long Point. On the south shore of Penn Cove. Turn off Parker Road onto Portal Place.

Beachcomber's Road. From Highway 20 just north of Greenbank turn on North Bluff Road.

Glendale. On Possession Sound south of Clinton. Follow the Glendale Road to its end.

Possession Road. On the east side of Possession Point. Turn off Highway 20 onto Cultus Bay Road.

7. ADMIRALTY INLET

At Admiralty Inlet the waters of Puget Sound and Hood Canal flow together for the final 20-mile leg of the journey to the Strait of Juan de Fuca. It was here, at Foulweather Bluff, on May 10th of 1792, that George Vancouver paused, contemplating whether either of these two channels led to the hoped-for Northwest Passage across the top of the continent. It was

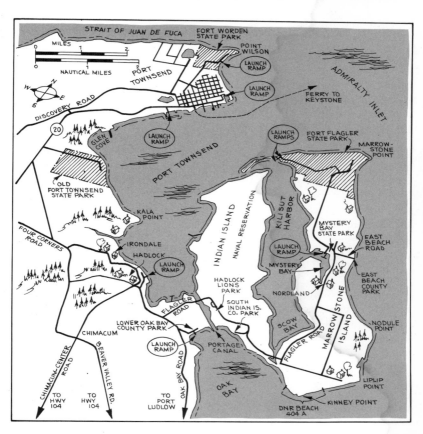

161

Sailing on Oak Bay

here also that Vancouver discovered the joys of Northwest weather, and named the bluff accordingly.

Admiralty Inlet flows between Whidbey Island and the northeast edge of the Olympic Peninsula. The 3½-mile-wide channel is unobstructed throughout; the only hazards are severe tide rips off Foulweather Bluff that occur when the merging ebbs from Hood Canal and Puget Sound meet with a strong north or northwest wind. In calm weather, boats cutting close to the bluff should watch for rocks that lie 100 yards north of the highest part of the promontory.

Oak Bay and Portage (Port Townsend) Canal

To Puget Sound boaters used to expansive channels, the narrow chute of Portage Canal is an interesting diversion, as well as a quick route between Hood Canal and Port Townsend. The channel is known locally as Portage Canal, although some nautical charts show it as Port Townsend Canal. The south end of the ¾-mile-long channel opens out into Oak Bay; public parks lie along both sides of this end of the canal.

The dredged canal has a controlling depth of 14 feet, and the fixed bridge that crosses to Indian Island has a vertical clearance of 58 feet. Both ends are marked with lights. Tides can run up to 3 knots in the channel; tide rips that form at either end, depending on the direction of the current, can cause small boats some concern. Liplip Point, at the southeast end of Marrowstone Island, is a Chinook Indian word meaning "boiling water" — take warning.

In early days the two islands were joined to the Quimper Peninsula by a neck of land known as the Chimacum Portage. Pressure from commercial shippers in Port Townsend for a protected short cut up the sound resulted in the dredging of the canal between the Quimper Peninsula and Indian Island in 1913. Island residents were forced to use private boats, and later a ferry, to reach the mainland. It wasn't until 1952 that a bridge finally linked the islands to the mainland.

LOWER OAK BAY COUNTY PARK
(JEFFERSON COUNTY)

Park Area: 31 acres; 1840 feet of shoreline
Access: Land, boat
Facilities: 68 campsites, picnic tables, fireplaces, restrooms, *no water,* boat launch (ramp)
Attractions: Fishing, clam digging, crabbing, boating, swimming, scuba diving, beachcombing, paddling

Lower Oak Bay County Park

Lower Oak Bay Park is the first of a row of public beaches along the south entrance to Port Townsend Canal. The park, which is on the west shore, encompasses a rock jetty and a gravel and sand beach that extends all the way north to the bridge. Informal campsites are stretched along the southern arm of the beach between Oak Bay and a saltwater lagoon. The campground is best suited for RVs, since there is no water.

The road leading to the park is ½ mile south of the turnoff for the Indian and Marrowstone Islands bridge. Turn off Oak Bay Road onto Portage Way, which is signed to the park. The park is reached in ¼ mile. The single-lane boat-launch ramp is usable, but it is not in the best of condition. The area is excellent for fishing and clam digging.

Geoducks can be dug here at extreme low tide. Once the siphon neck is spotted above the sand begin excavating, but be prepared to move a small mountain of mud since the body of the clam may be as much as 4 feet down. It cannot move away, although it may seem to as it retracts its enormous siphon. Do not pull on the neck—it will break off and you will lose your prize and the clam will die. The best allies when going for a geoduck are a number of energetic children who love to dig in the mud.

HADLOCK LIONS PARK
(LLOYD L. GOOD MEMORIAL PARK)

Park Area: 2.5 acres
Access: Land
Facilities: Picnic tables, picnic shelter, fireplace
Attractions: Clam digging, beach walking

This park on a grassy hillside is a convenient spot for watching activity in Portage Canal and Oak Bay. Facilities are few, but the view is grand. The park entrance is to the right of Flagler Road, shortly after crossing the Portage Canal bridge onto Indian Island.

At the top of the slope, 50 feet above the water, are the parking lot and a picnic shelter next to an old orchard. After polishing off the fried chicken and potato salad, wander down to the beach, where the Lions Park joins county park property, and enjoy walks south to the jetty at the end of the canal or clear around the corner to the picnic area at the county park, over a mile away.

SOUTH INDIAN ISLAND COUNTY PARK
(JEFFERSON COUNTY)

Park Area: 54 acres; 11,350 feet of shoreline
Access: Land, boat
Facilities: Picnic tables, fireplace, latrines
Attractions: Fishing, paddling, clam digging, crabbing, swimming, scuba
    diving, beachcombing

Rock jetty at South Indian Island County Park

This park is a companion to Lower Oak Bay Park, which it faces across the bay. It has minimum facilities; its great attractions lie in its beautiful saltmarsh and its 2-mile-long stretch of smooth, gravelly beach.

To reach the park, turn east off Oak Bay Road on the road signed to Fort Flagler, which crosses the bridge over Portage Canal. About 1 mile from the bridge (½ mile beyond Hadlock Lions Park) is a side road to the south signed to Jefferson County Park. A single-lane gravel road drops steeply down to the water.

A few picnic tables are scattered about a grassy area near the lagoon. Beach walks go north all the way to the bridge, with an interesting side trip out onto the rock jetty; beyond the bridge Navy property begins. South, the shore can be walked to the sand spit that joins Indian and Marrowstone Islands. At low tide dig for clams and geoducks in the beaches facing on Oak Bay.

At Kinney Point, on the extreme south end of Marrowstone Island, is DNR beach 404A. The public area includes a 3900-foot section of beach that wraps around the point and adjacent uplands; however there is no access to the property from above; it can only be reached by boat—or by walking politely across private beaches east of the county park, if landowners will tolerate it. If approaching the point by boat, be wary of tide rips.

Indian and Marrowstone Islands

To drive to an island may seem to be a contradiction in terms, but people around Puget Sound are used to such a paradox. Here are not one, but two nice little islands that are easily reached by road. Unfortunately Indian Island is an off-limits Naval ammunition storage depot, so it can only be enjoyed from a distance or from the two parks on its south end that front on Oak Bay and Portage Canal.

Marrowstone Island is primarily devoted to family homes, small farms, and the large state park that encompasses its northern end. Some beach homes along Kilisut Harbor are owned by summer residents and retirees. The main concentration of homes is mid-island at the community of Nordland, where the only business is a combination gas station and grocery store.

For many years Marrowstone Island was famous for its annual production of thousands of premium turkeys, a business that began in 1924 and boomed until the 1940s, when the rising cost of feed made it unprofitable. When Fort Flagler was reactivated during World War II and the Army planned to commence with practice firings of their guns, alarmed farmers informed the commanding officer that the fort would have to put its war on hold until incubating turkey eggs hatched since the vibrations would disturb the delicate embryos. Thereafter the Army notified the farmers far in advance of practices so the turkey eggs could be incubated accordingly.

The western shore of Marrowstone Island is well protected by its neighboring island and the Olympic Peninsula. The windward shore is frequently buffeted by heavy weather from Admiralty Inlet. Severe tide rips can occur off Marrowstone Point and at Kinney Point at the south end of the island, especially when the wind and tide are moving in opposite directions. Boats heading out of Port Townsend Bay can run into trouble when they round Marrowstone Point and are suddenly confronted by southerly winds howling down the sound.

EAST BEACH COUNTY PARK (JEFFERSON COUNTY)

Park Area: 1 acre; 100 feet of shoreline
Access: Land, boat
Facilities: Picnic shelter with tables, fireplaces, restrooms
Attractions: Boating, fishing, clam digging

A small county park in mid-Marrowstone Island provides a nice access to the Admiralty Inlet shores. Since most of the mobs head north to Fort Flagler, there is a good chance of finding privacy here, along with gorgeous views across to Whidbey Island and the Cascades.

From land, drive north on Flagler Road, and ½ mile north of Nordland turn east on East Beach Road. The park is reached in a little over

¼ mile. A pretty stone and log shelter that contains picnic tables and fireplaces provides protection from winds off Admiralty Inlet.

The park is on the only stretch of low-bank waterfront on the east side of the island. The wide gravelly beach holds some promise of clams at low tide, or at least a good time romping in the waves.

KILISUT HARBOR

Indian and Marrowstone Islands are separated by a long waterway that is almost a channel, rather than a harbor. Before the digging of Portage Canal, boats sometimes avoided heavy weather in Admiralty Inlet by traveling up Kilisut Harbor and at high tide crossing the sand spit that ran between Indian and Marrowstone Islands. Today the islands are joined together at the south by a dirt causeway over which Flagler Road runs.

A ¾-mile-long sandspit reaches out from Marrowstone Island to guard the northern end of the harbor. Entrance to the winding channel is at the far west end of the spit, by Indian Island. Follow navigational markers carefully; the S-curved channel is dredged to a depth of 5 feet at mean low water, and in some places shoal water lies immediately outside the marked channel. Use care approaching the harbor entrance from the north and consult navigational charts, as a submerged pile lies north of the west end of

Mystery Bay State Park, Kilisut Harbor

the sand spit. Once the channel is cleared inside Kilisut Harbor, good anchorages can be found in 4 to 6 fathoms of water. Stay well away from the shores of Indian Island.

The 5-mile-long inlet was originally known as Scow Bay, and the pair of islands were the Scow Peninsula. Today it has its more lyrical Klallam Indian name meaning "protected waters"; only the far southern end of the harbor is called Scow Bay.

Kilisut Harbor and the waters surrounding Indian and Marrowstone Islands are ideal for small boat exploration, with numerous put-ins for dinghies, kayaks, and canoes. A circumnavigation of Indian Island is about a 12-mile trip, with a variety of adventures ranging from the quiet water of the harbor to the busy highway of Portage Canal. Boats can easily be carried across the causeway and sandbar at the south end of Kilisut Harbor. Plan the trip so the direction of the tide is favorable in the canal, and watch for tide rips. Do not go on shore at Indian Island except at the parks on its south end.

MYSTERY BAY STATE PARK

Park Area: 10 acres; 685 feet of shoreline
Access: Land, boat
Facilities: Picnic tables, fireplaces, latrines, fishing pier with float, mooring buoys, boat launch (ramp), *no water*
Attractions: Paddling, fishing, picnicking, crabbing, clam digging

Halfway down Kilisut Harbor, past a scattering of beach homes, Mystery Bay indents the Marrowstone shoreline. The small recreation area on the north shore, near the entrance to the curving bay, is an outpost of Fort Flagler State Park. The onshore portion of the park is day-use only, but the boating facilities invite overnight moorage. The pier that extends from shore has a 550-foot float at its end; additional tie-ups are on 7 mooring buoys, and there is plenty of space to spare for dropping a hook. The only hazards in the bay are two submerged concrete blocks that lie 20–30 feet off the east end of the float.

The park's single-lane boat-launch ramp is west of the pier. Picnic tables on shore have a nice view of the Olympic Mountains rising behind Indian Island and of bird life in the bay. The Navy manages Indian Island as a wildlife refuge, and herons, cormorants, and a wide variety of ducks and shorebirds are commonly seen along the beaches.

If nautical legs are aching to be stretched, take a ¾-mile stroll across the island to East Beach County Park. Walk south from the park on Fort Flagler Road, and then east on East Beach Road. Quiet walkers may be rewarded by seeing deer—if not, cows and other local wildlife are assured. The windswept beach of the park is a marked contrast to the calm shores of Kilisut Harbor.

FORT FLAGLER STATE PARK

Park Area: 783 acres; 19,100 feet of shoreline
Access: Land, boat
Facilities: 118 campsites, group camp, picnic tables, fireplaces, picnic shelters, drinking water, restrooms, showers, trailer dump station, hiking trails, nature trail, groceries (limited), snack bar, boat launch (ramp), dock with float, mooring buoys, fishing pier, underwater park
Attractions: Boating, paddling, fishing, clam digging, crabbing, beach-combing, hiking, swimming, scuba diving, historical displays

Mile upon mile of goodies—so much that one could hardly appreciate it all in a weekend. Here are beaches, bluffs, woodlands, and the most spectacular sand spit to be found on the inland waters, all flavored with the intrigue of a historic old fort.

To reach the park by land, turn off Highway 104 (which crosses the

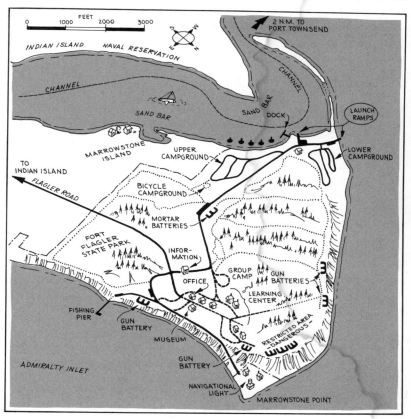

Battery Downs at Fort Flagler State Park

Hood Canal Bridge) on any major road headed north and signed to Port
Townsend. Watch for signs pointing east to Marrowstone Island and Fort
Flagler State Park. Once on Flagler Road you can't miss it.

By water the state park is 2 n.m. from Port Townsend and 11 n.m.
from Port Ludlow (via the Portage Canal). Navigational comments on entering the channel leading into the harbor are included with the discussion
on Kilisut Harbor, above.

Park facilities are on the east and west edges of the park, with a network of roads and hiking trails connecting them. The ranger's residence
and buildings of the old fort are on the east, inside the park entrance.
Building 9, across from the headquarters, houses an interpretive exhibit
that is open for viewing when personnel are available.

Camping and boating areas are on the west. The upper campground is
on a wooded bluff above the water, the lower one is situated on an open,
windswept flat near the beach. The docking float on a T-shaped pier has
space for about 10 boats. Mooring buoys stretched along the shore to the
south provide tie-ups for an additional seven boats, with some anchoring
space nearby. One of the single-lane boat-launch ramps faces on Port
Townsend Bay, while the second one is on Kilisut Harbor.

Scow Bay Spit, a ¾-mile-long curving sandbar, nearly blocks the
entrance to the harbor. At high tide, water covers a low spot midway along
the spit—do not attempt to shortcut through this gap in a boat, as it is very

shallow. At moderate to low tides the full length of the sandbar is exposed for beach roaming or clam digging. A row of old pilings offshore to the north were used during WW II for holding four antisubmarine nets that stretched across to Port Townsend.

From the fort residence campus, a hard turn to the right leads downhill past a gun emplacement to a parking lot. A trail continues down to a 500-foot-long wharf originally used by the Corps of Engineers during construction of the fort but now serving as a fishing pier. A forest of pastel sea anemones coats the old pilings of the wharf. The underwater park lying on either side of the wharf is marked by buoys; fishing line near the pier can pose a hazard to scuba divers. Since this is a sanctuary, spearfishing is prohibited.

Battery Wansboro, the gun emplacements on the hillside above, is the only one of the Fort Flagler batteries to have guns in place. The original guns were removed long ago; the two 3-inch guns that are here now were placed after the fort became a park. Battery Gratten, at the northeast corner of the park, is down a short trail behind the buildings of the Environmental Learning Center. When passing through this section of the park, notice the buildings—this was the original Officer's Row, but those houses were torn down and replaced with WW II barracks.

The Marrowstone Point lighthouse is reached by a steep, narrow road that goes north from the east side of the residential campus. The automated lighthouse is not open to the public, but at moderate to low tides the shore here opens the way to beachcombing—west for 1½ miles to the park campground, or south for ¾ mile to the fishing pier. Buildings near the lighthouse are occupied by the U.S. Fish and Wildlife Service research laboratory.

Walks can be extended beyond the beaches to include bluff-top routes or forested trails. A complete circuit of the perimeter of the park, following beach, road, and trail is about 5 miles; exploring inviting side paths can occupy an entire afternoon. Watch for deer, squirrels, raccoons, and bald eagles. Foxes and coyotes also live here but are shyer and harder to spot. The trail that heads south along the east edge of the park was initially beaten out in the early 1900s by the boots of thirsty soldiers heading for a saloon on the bluff just outside the fort boundary. The saloon hauled its supplies up the steep bluff by means of a winch wrapped around a tree stump and hence was known as "The Stump."

Along the park road to the west, well inland, are the mortar emplacements of Battery Bankhead. Batteries Downes and Caldwell, situated on the north side of the bluff, can be reached by trail from the park campus or the lower campground. These are quite overgrown, and brush hides the view of the water that the guns once commanded. The main batteries, which are farther east, are dangerous and are posted as off limits.

Flagler was one of the forts that, along with Casey and Worden, guarded the entrance to Puget Sound from foreign invasion. The three forts, facing each other across Admiralty Inlet, formed what was to be-

Horse clam at Fort Flagler State Park

come known during WW I as the "Triangle of Fire." Construction began on Marrowstone Island in 1897; the fort was named for Brigadier General D. W. Flagler two years later when it was activated. The first troops to arrive had to make do with tent living until the completion of construction of quarters. Armament was placed over the next few years until by 1905 all ten batteries were completed and armed. At full strength the fort consisted of eighteen guns, ranging from 3-inch to 12-inch, and eight 12-inch mortars, aiming death at any enemy ship that dared to poke its prow into view.

It soon became apparent that the fort was poorly situated. The water supply on the island was not adequate to supply such a large installation, although this was eventually solved by running a pipeline from Port Townsend. More serious was the limited sector of fire—Point Wilson obstructed the view of the Strait of Juan de Fuca, and the guns could not engage targets much south of Marrowstone Point.

Initially Fort Flagler was to be headquarters for the Harbor Defense, but pressure by Port Townsend bigwigs who felt their fair city should host the headquarters caused it to be relocated at Fort Worden. The only noticeable change was the transfer of the Artillery Band.

With the onset of WW I the fort served as a training center for troops, but since there was no threat of naval attack on the sound, the guns were considered unnecessary and many were removed and sent to the European front. At the end of the war the fort languished in a caretaker status until a new global war revitalized it. Antiaircraft guns were installed in WW II to combat the new threat from the skies, and new buildings were constructed to house another generation of trainees.

The final military use of the post was as a base for training an Engineering Amphibious Brigade after WW II. In 1953 the fort was deactivated, and two years later the property was acquired by Washington State for use as a park.

Port Townsend Bay

It is hard to understand why geographers or town founders insist on naming cities after waterways, thus causing an endless amount of confusion. The large inlet here is correctly named Port Townsend, but in order to avoid confusion with the more well known town, we end up referring to it as Port Townsend Bay.

The bay is well protected and without obstructions along its 6-mile length. Some good anchorages can be found at its south end, along the west shore near Hadlock and Irondale.

HADLOCK

Facilities: Boat launch (ramp), float, picnic tables, latrines, *no water*

The small town of Hadlock lies on the bluff above the water at the southwest corner of Port Townsend Bay. Beneath the bluff is a small portion of the community called Lower Hadlock, where there is a public boat-launch ramp. To reach it, turn off Oak Bay Road south of Hadlock onto Lower Hadlock Road, which angles off to the right and goes steeply downhill to the shore. The launch area has recently been improved with a new pier and boarding float, and some nice picnic tables on shore.

South of here, near the entrance to Portage Canal, is the Hadlock Marina, a facility that sat vacant for many years but which is currently undergoing a major rebuilding. At present all moorages at the marina are private.

Although one would never guess it from today's quiet demeanor, Hadlock, along with Irondale to the north, was once a hotbed of industry. When the sawmill at Seabeck burned in 1886, it was relocated at Hadlock. In addition to shipping lumber throughout the Pacific, the mill provided lumber for the construction of Forts Worden, Flagler, and Casey.

As its name suggests, Irondale was a major smelting center, in its prime turning out 300 tons of steel daily. When the local ore proved to be of a poor quality, better ore was imported from Texada Island in B.C.

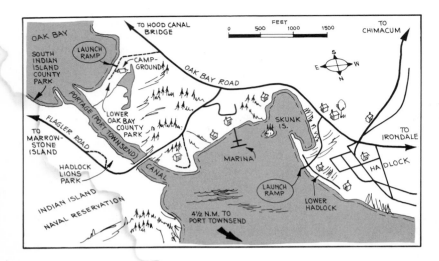

Eventually, bringing ore from Canada or even farther afield proved too costly, and the mill closed. The last fling at industrialism was a wood alcohol plant at Hadlock, but this was short-lived, and the area settled back to a quiet residential existence.

OLD FORT TOWNSEND STATE PARK

Park Area: 377 acres; 3960 feet of shoreline
Access: Land, boat
Facilities: 52 campsites, group camp, picnic tables, fireplaces, kitchen, restrooms, RV pumpout, drinking water, mooring buoys, hiking trails, nature trail, children's play equipment, horseshoe pits, softball field
Attractions: Boating, historical displays, hiking, clam digging, crabbing

After tramping through numerous World War I and II forts throughout Puget Sound, Old Fort Townsend comes as a surprise—this one is a relic from the time of the Indian Wars. The fort was established in 1856 when settlers in the Port Townsend area became uneasy about the growing hostility of Indians after the government's efforts to move them on to reservations. The Indian uprisings had largely been settled by the time the fort was garrisoned, and troops were left with little to do. The discovery of gold in British Columbia's Fraser River country led to a number of desertions by soldiers more interested in the promise of riches than endlessly marching on a parade ground.

The boredom at Fort Townsend was relieved briefly when a company of men from the fort were sent to San Juan Island in 1859 when an altercation over a pig and some potatoes promised some action. The Pig War stand-off between the Americans and British led to more waiting and boredom.

As the Civil War was proving to be a more serious problem, demanding the full attention of the government and its army, all the troops remaining at Fort Townsend were withdrawn in 1861, and the post was manned by local volunteers. Although the military commanders thought the fort was poorly located as a defensive position and should be abandoned, when the San Juan boundary dispute (precipitated by the pig incident) was finally settled, the troops stationed on San Juan Island were relocated to Fort Townsend.

The fort was actively manned for another 20 years, although there was no particular threat from either natives or foreign nations and there were few American citizens in the area who needed protecting. One general declared that, "Instead of the garrison protecting Port Townsend, the town is guarding Fort Townsend." In 1895 a kerosene lamp caught the barracks on fire and, perhaps fortuitously, it burned to the ground. This proved a good excuse for the army to decommission the fort and ship out the troops.

In 1907 the site was briefly considered for the placement of eight 12-inch mortars that would be aimed west toward Discovery Bay. The mortars were to be fired across the Quimper Peninsula into the bay to discourage the enemy from a backside attack on Fort Worden. The plan was dropped when it was proved that Fort Worden was capable of defending itself from the rear. The Fort Townsend site was used briefly by the Navy during World War II as an enemy munitions defusing station, and in 1958 it gave up all claim to a military existence when the land was purchased for a state park.

Old Fort Townsend State Park is located 4 miles south of Port Townsend, east of Highway 20. The intersection of the road to the park is well signed.

The only military building remaining at Fort Townsend is the tall, brick, WW II-era Navy Explosives Laboratory located near the park entrance. Near the upper parking area is a self-guided historical walk past the buildings and facilities of the early fort.

The park sits on a bluff 200 feet above the water, with a commanding view though the trees of Port Townsend Bay and Indian and Marrowstone Islands. Beautiful old-growth Douglas fir and cedar surrounds the upper campgrounds; in spring rhododendrons in the camp area and along the entrance road bring a splash of blazing pink to the somber green forest. A smaller, lower campground with RV hookups is on an open, level area near the ranger's residence.

The road snakes downhill, ending in a loop near the edge of the bluff. From here a trail along the old service road continues steeply down to the water. Pilings in the water along the north edge of the park are from the fort's old wharf. There no longer is a dock here, but four mooring buoys are provided for visiting boaters. A nature trail that climbs a forested gulley

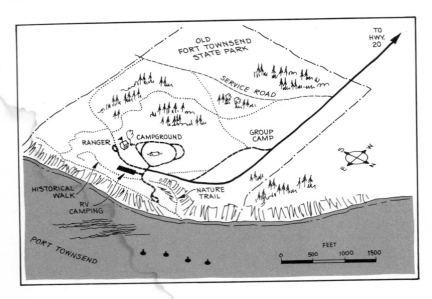

provides a nice alternative return route to the upper parking area. Other trails follow the top of the bluff or wander into the hinterland, back to the group camp.

Port Townsend

Port Townsend has made a graceful transition into a tourist-oriented town without sacrificing its integrity. This is no Victorian Disneyland, but a real city, with genuine old buildings filled with antiques. The antique ambience is complemented by a cultural one, with shops selling work by the finest Northwest artists, photographers, and craftsmen. Whatever one's interest, there is something to lure them here.

Port Townsend lies at the north end of the Quimper Peninsula. It can be reached by driving west 3½ miles from Hood Canal bridge and turning north on Beaver Valley Road, which is signed to Port Townsend. The Keystone ferry, which docks at the new ferry terminal on the south side of town, provides access to the town from Whidbey Island.

Annual events in the town include jogging and bicycling races, a sand castle building competition, a wooden boat show, a salmon fishing derby, an old-fashioned county fair, a quilt show, both modern and folk dance festivals, a boating regatta, plays, music festivals ranging from Bach to Bluegrass to Basie, and prose and poetry readings by nationally known writers. Many of the events are sponsored by Centrum, a performing arts foundation located on the grounds of Fort Worden. Upon request the

Chamber of Commerce will send prospective visitors a list of events scheduled for the year.

Even if one does not come to Port Townsend to take in a special event, there is still plenty to fascinate. The town, the best example of a Victorian seacoast town north of San Francisco, has been designated as a National Historical District. Stores in beautifully restored old commercial buildings along Water St. offer hours of wonderful browsing and buying—heavy on the nautical and the Victorian. Food purveyors have everything from homemade ice cream cones to gourmet dinners. A little park along the waterfront, at the former site of the ferry terminal, is a nice spot to enjoy that cone. The numerous antique stores provide a history lesson in themselves, but for an added dash of nostalgia, drop in at the Jefferson County Historical Museum, located in City Hall.

Port Townsend's real jewels are its beautiful old Victorian homes, built when the town seemed destined to be a major center of commerce on Puget Sound. The Chamber of Commerce provides a map describing seventy points of historical interest, including some three dozen private homes built before the turn of the century. Twice yearly—the first

Port Townsend Boat Haven

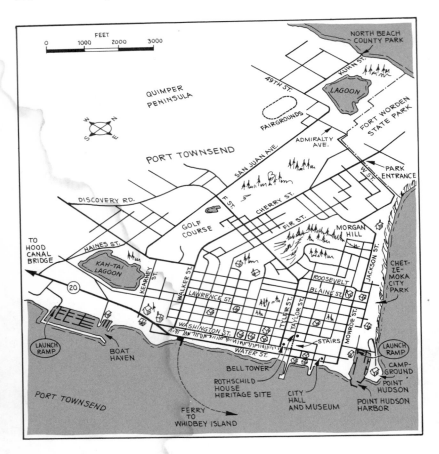

weekend in May and the third weekend in September— many of these residences are open for viewing during the city's Historic Homes Tours.
Some of the homes operate as bed-and-breakfast inns and can be enjoyed
by persons staying there.

Port Townsend is probably the state's most spectacular example of
dreams gone awry. The fine, deep harbor was noted (first) by Captain
George Vancouver, who gave it its name. Sixty years later, in 1851, it was
settled by Alfred Plummer and Charles Bachelder. They and other pioneers
were sure that with its strategic location at the entrance to the sound it
would become a major point of commerce for boats eager to trade for the
furs, lumber, and other riches of the Northwest. The wharfs built here soon
attracted ships, and when the customs house was transferred to Port
Townsend from Olympia in 1854, the city's future seemed assured. Ships
from every port in the world stopped here, and the town boosted itself as
the "Key City" or "New York of the West." Rock ballast unloaded from

ships was used to build the growing number of commercial buildings along Water Street.

Along with its rapid growth came an unsavory reputation. Public drunkenness, prostitution, and brawling were flagrant, and shanghaiing of sailors was a common practice. Since it was unsafe to walk on Water St., the respected families of the town developed a retail district at the top of the hill, where proper ladies could shop in safety. One journalist called Port Townsend "the town that liquor built": Yankee traders without scruples frequently used liquor in trade with Indians, it was the item greatest in demand by sailors fresh off ships, and it was part of all the other nefarious activities in the town.

Port Townsend continued to boom through the 1880s. What was needed to assure its continued growth and prosperity and keep it abreast with the cities rapidly developing along the eastern shore of the sound, was a railroad to link it to markets in the east. In 1887 enterprising citizens solicited funds to lay their own railroad tracks to link with the transcontinental line of the Northern Pacific that had recently been built to Tacoma. The company ran into financial difficulties, compounded by the depression of 1893, and went into receivership. Several other new business ventures, including a drydock and a nailworks, went bankrupt at this same time, throwing the town into a financial tailspin from which it never recovered. Almost overnight the town virtually shut down, going from a city with a population of over 7000 to less than 2000.

But some Port Townsend residents hung in there. The presence of the Army at Fort Worden brought some economic relief, and in 1927 the building of the pulp and paper mill south of town finally brought a steady payroll to the area. The current era of tourism began in the late 1950s with the first renovation of the Victorian homes and the inception of an artistic and cultural movement. The carefully cultivated promotion of the town's many assets may well be the key to its survival.

PORT TOWNSEND MARINAS

Facilities: Complete boat and crew facilities, laundry, U.S. Customs, boat launch (hoist and ramp), boat rental and charter, restaurants, picnic tables, campsites, shopping (nearby)

Two marinas bracket the Port Townsend waterfront. On the south side of town is the larger and more modern of the two facilities, Port Townsend Boat Haven, operated by the Port of Port Townsend; at the north end is Point Hudson Harbor, which is leased to a private company. Both have transient moorage and full facilities for visiting boaters. Pleasure boats will find Customs inspections at either of the harbors.

A rock jetty protects the 375 moorages at Boat Haven. The entrance, on the northeast, is clearly marked. Just inside the breakwater is a small basin for commercial boats, the U.S. Coast Guard installation (where the

Point Bennett is tied up), and a fuel dock. Once past these, the harbormaster's office and registration dock are immediately on the right. If the office is closed, there is a system for self-registration.

Numerous marine-oriented businesses are located within the basin area. Sling launching is available for trailered boats. A launch ramp is at the southwest corner of the harbor. The highway between the marina and downtown Port Townsend has recently been filled with a continuous row of new stores—groceries, gas stations, restaurants, and all types of services. The older section of town is about a ½-mile walk from the marina. Bus service is available.

Point Hudson Harbor is closer to downtown attractions, although the facilities are not as large or as nice as those at the Boat Haven. The dredged basin lies behind a piling jetty immediately south of the point. A float with numerous finger piers is on the northeast side; a long dock on the southwest has a fuel pump and additional tie-ups. If the harbor is full, rafting is permitted on this long float. At the southwest corner of the basin a single-lane ramp provides launching for trailered boats.

Behind the harbormaster's office on the northeast shore is a commercially operated RV campground that also has some tent-camping space. A small park along the shore facing on Admiralty Inlet has an old Indian longboat on display and some picnic tables. From here except at high tide, the beach can be walked all the way north to Point Wilson.

ROTHSCHILD HOUSE HERITAGE SITE

Two of the historic Port Townsend homes are open year-round for touring: the Commanding Officer's Quarters at Fort Worden, and the Rothschild House at the corner of Franklin and Taylor (near downtown).

The Rothschild House, which is administered by Washington State Parks, is a simple two-story, four-bedroom home, authentically furnished. It is not as opulent as some of the other Victorian homes owned by locally wealthier families, but it does portray an elegant way of life typical of the time.

To reach the house from the business district, climb the stairs that ascend the bluff at the end of Taylor St. To the left is the old bell tower once used to summon volunteer firemen. The Rothschild House is straight ahead one block.

CHETZEMOKA CITY PARK

Park Area: 10 acres; 750 feet of waterfront
Access: Land, boat
Facilities: Picnic tables, fireplaces, restrooms, drinking water, bandstand, children's play equipment
Attractions: Beachcombing, swimming

Kitchen in the Rothschild House, Port Townsend

This small city park pays tribute to the Klallam Indian chief who proved to be a good friend to early Port Townsend settlers. Chetzemoka was derisively called the "Duke of York" by pioneers unable or unwilling to deal with the guttural Klallam tongue. He was portrayed as a buffoon and alcoholic by Theodore Winthrop, who wrote of him in his 1862 book, *Canoe and Saddle*. In truth, Chetzemoka got bad press at the time, as it was the whites who regularly supplied the poison for which the Indians had a genetic weakness. The Indian chief's wisdom in seeing the inevitability of white settlement and his actions as a mediator served both the settlers and his own people very well. During the Indian Wars he was instrumental in discouraging an attack on the whites, an action that surely would have resulted in the loss of many Indian lives.

The city park is on a slight bluff facing Admiralty Inlet within walking distance of downtown Port Townsend. It can be reached by walking the beach north from Point Hudson for about ¼ mile, or by following Monroe St. northwest and turning right on Blaine St., which in one block deadends at the park.

With its covered bandstand and formal rose garden, the area is reminiscent of an old-fashioned park, and one expects to see straw-hatted dandies strolling with their ladies under the blossom-covered arches. The manicured lawn rolls down to a path that leads to the beach. At high tide the shore is narrow, but low tide exposes a wide expanse of sandy beach.

NORTH BEACH COUNTY PARK (JEFFERSON COUNTY)

Park Area: 1 acre; 310 feet of shoreline
Access: Land, boat
Facilities: Picnic tables, kitchen, fireplaces, latrines, *no water*
Attractions: Swimming, beachcombing

At North Beach the steep bluffs on this side of the peninsula briefly dip down to the shore. This small county park provides a handy starting point for beach walks east beneath the 200-foot bluffs of Fort Worden all the way to Point Wilson, 1½ miles away, or even to Port Townsend another 2 miles distance. The way is passable at all times except high tide, so before beginning extended walks check the tide table.

To reach the park, drive west out of Port Townsend on any road to its intersection with San Juan Ave. Follow this street north; at the edge of a swamp/lake it turns west and becomes 49th St. In one block turn north on Kuhn St. and follow it to its end at the park.

Park facilities are rather meager—a few picnic tables and two latrines—but the beach is glorious. The sand slopes gradually into the frothy waters of the straits. Swim if you like, or build sand castles, or just let the nearly constant wind off the channel fill your nostrils with brine. The concrete boat ramp that was once here is badly broken up and nearly covered with sand.

Early Indians landed their canoes here and portaged south across the swampy flat to Kah-tai Lagoon by Port Townsend Bay to avoid tide rips off Point Wilson.

FORT WORDEN STATE PARK

Park Area: 434 acres; 11,020 feet of shoreline
Access: Land, boat
Facilities: 53 campsites, picnic tables, water, kitchens, fireplaces, restrooms, showers, drinking water, laundry, vacation housing, boat launch (ramp), fishing pier, float, mooring buoys, museum, marine science center, underwater marine park, hiking trails, tennis courts, playfields, children's play equipment
Attractions: Boating, fishing, scuba diving, educational and historical displays, hiking, beachcombing

Among the state's many outstanding parks, Fort Worden must rank as one of the grandest. Although it lacks the primeval forest environment (there are plenty of parks elsewhere to provide that), it packs a wealth of activities within its boundaries. It is located just north of Port Townsend; the 2-mile route from the city center to the park entrance is well marked by signs.

The bristling guns of Fort Worden were intended, along with those at

Forts Casey and Flagler, to guard the entrance to Puget Sound. Construction on the fort began in 1898 and, as the fortifications neared completion in 1902, the first soldiers were assigned. On the day scheduled for their arrival the citizens of Port Townsend turned out en masse, complete with a brass band, to welcome them. With dismay and drooping pennants the gentry watched the troop-laden steamer *Majestic* chug by, unaware of the planned celebration, headed for the pier at the fort instead of landing at the town's Union Wharf.

Some small parcels of land within the designated area of the fort had previously been claimed by Port Townsend settlers. The land was needed for fort buildings, and there was also a concern that nonmilitary residents so close to the fort might pose a security risk. When negotiation for the property began there was considerable disagreement between the government and the property owners as to its value. The commandant of the fort took matters into his own hands by beginning the first practice firings of the mortar batteries. As plaster walls cracked from the concussion and pictures and bric-a-brac came crashing down, real estate values fell with them and homeowners rushed to sell their property.

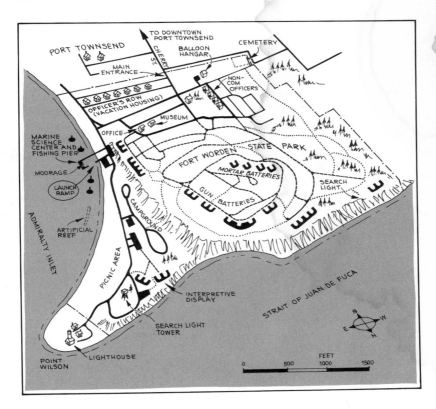

Battery Ash at Fort Worden State Park

With sixteen 12-inch mortars and twenty-five guns ranging from 3-inch to 12-inch, at full strength Fort Casey was the most heavily fortified of the Puget Sound forts. By 1904 underwater cable communications linked Fort Worden to Forts Casey and Flagler, and the following year it was fully garrisoned with four companies of Coast Artillery troops. With the completion of fire-control stations and five 60-inch searchlight emplacements, the fort stood completed by 1912.

In just five years, with the beginning of World War I, the entire character of the fort changed. As additional troops were sent here to be trained for battle on the European front, more barracks were built, and eighteen of the guns were removed for shipment to Europe. At the end of the war the number of troops stationed at Fort Worden decreased drastically. The only new activity was the construction in 1920 of a huge balloon hanger and the addition of two companies of men who experimented, unsuccessfully, with using balloons for gunfire control and observation stations.

The fort saw some activity during World War II as a Harbor Entrance Control Post to monitor radar sites and new underwater sonar and sensing devices; it also served to coordinate all defensive activities on the inland waters. With the end of WW II all the remaining guns were removed and scrapped. The last military use was during the Korean conflict when units of an Army engineering regiment were stationed here prior to being shipped to the Far East.

After the deactivation of the post in 1953 the state of Washington used it as a juvenile diagnostic treatment center, and finally in 1972 it was transferred to the parks commission. Since that time the facilities at Fort Worden have seen ever-increasing use, not only for traditional state park purposes, but also as a site for conferences, retreats, workshops, sports and music camps, and festivals. Today it ranks as the most heavily used of the state parks, with over a million visitors passing through its gates annually.

Twenty-three of the housing units originally used by officers and NCOs are available at very reasonable rates to groups or families for overnight stays. Many have been refurbished with reproductions of Victorian-era furniture. Barracks now serve as dormitories for use by larger groups. The campus exudes the atmosphere of what it once was as a military installation, although the grounds are not quite as carefully manicured as when a crew of as many as 300 enlisted men mowed lawns, swept walks, and groomed beds of bright flowers.

A stop at the state park office, near the entrance, will arm the visitor with maps and a list of current activities. In summer Centrum may be sponsoring a music festival or a play. One park leaflet guides the way on a historical walk around the fort's many buildings. Several miles' worth of strolls are available: to the fort cemetery, to the gun emplacements, to the beach, to the lighthouse—to wherever impulse leads. Next to the park office is a Coast Artillery Museum (open Wednesday–Sunday, 12–5), which has displays of memorabilia from the fort and historical information about the coastal fortifications.

The park road leads past the row of officer's quarters, painted in a rainbow of pastel colors, to Harbor Defense Way, which parallels the east beach. Here are a large wharf and a float with space for about four boats, where overnight moorage is permitted. The two-lane boat-launch ramp is on the north side of the pier, protected by its L-shaped bend. Mooring buoys are spaced along the shore north and south of the wharf, although wind and wave action may make an overnight tie-up uncomfortable.

At the end of the wharf is the building that houses the Port Townsend Marine Science Center, which has hands-on exhibits of marine life and sponsors beach walks, classes, and a number of other marine-oriented activities. Fishing is permitted from the pier; a fish-cleaning station is next to the building.

The offshore waters are designated as an underwater park. Scuba divers explore the pilings of the old wharf and the sandy bottom along the east shore. North of Point Wilson a reef attracts divers expert enough to handle the swift current on this side of the point. The white rock of the reef makes a dramatic contrast with brightly colored sea anemones and fish. Spearfishing is not permitted in the waters of the park.

Two types of beaches are found here: on the east, facing on Admiralty Inlet, is a gradually sloping sandy beach, partially protected by the curving arm of Point Wilson; on the north, the Strait of Juan de Fuca shoreline is a narrower strip, enclosed by rising bluffs and dropping off quickly into the sea. Winds off the straits frequently batter the shore, making walking difficult but often exhilarating. The beaches can be walked south or west of Point Wilson for some distance, depending on the stamina of the walker. Use care on the north shore not to get trapped by incoming tide.

The state park camping area is in an open grassy field west of Harbor Defense Way. None are protected from the wind, which can get quite brisk in this exposed location. An enclosed kitchen shelter is near the beach, and numerous picnic tables are scattered along the shore.

The road continues on to a parking lot near Battery Kinzie. Here can be seen gun emplacements and rooms where munitions were stored. Still in evidence are the overhead metal tracks that were used for transporting munitions. From the top of the battery is a sweeping 300° view of the strait and Admiralty Inlet, blocked only by the hill behind. The rusting metal tower to the east once held a searchlight. Battery Kinzie is the best maintained of the fort's twelve batteries; the others, which are on the hill to the southwest, can be reached by trails from the campground or the residential area.

POINT WILSON LIGHT STATION

The lighthouse at Admiralty Head on Whidbey Island, which began operation in 1861, was one of the earliest to guide boaters on Washington's inland waters. In order to avoid the unmarked shoals at Point Wilson, shippers navigating in the dark or fog kept the light well in sight and stayed to the east side of Admiralty Inlet, following the Whidbey Island shoreline. It wasn't until almost 20 years later that two more lighthouses, at Point No Point and here at Point Wilson, enabled ships to safely follow the shorter route along the western shoreline.

The original lighthouse at Point Wilson was equipped with the most modern Fresnel lens, consisting of an aggregation of seventy-two glass prisms and bull's-eye lenses. The light source, a wick-type lamp that nightly burned three gallons of whale oil, kerosene, or lard, was eventually replaced by a 1000-watt electrical bulb. A 12-inch steam whistle signaled a warning to boats in the fog. The beacon, originally in a tower above the keeper's quarters, was moved to a new building in 1914, and separate housing was built for the personnel.

Until 1939, when the Coast Guard took over lighthouse administration, the U.S. Lighthouse Service operated most stations with civil service personnel. In addition to keeping the light clean, winding the clockworks that rotated it, polishing the brass, trimming the lamp wicks (which prompted the nickname "wickie"), and other maintenance tasks, the keeper was expected to keep a garden and livestock to feed himself and his family. Life at Point Wilson, within a short distance of Port Townsend, was far better than at many of the more remote light stations.

The beacon is now completely automated and is not open to the pub-

Point Wilson Light Station and Admiralty Inlet

lic. If the gate is open, visitors may stroll around the lighthouse area but should not bother the personnel living in the residence as they are caretakers of the property and are not connected with the lighthouse.

8. EASTERN STRAIT OF JUAN DE FUCA

Nearing the end of its northward journey, the waters of Puget Sound pour into the long tongue of the Strait of Juan de Fuca before making the final transition to the open sea. The 100-mile-long strait is a commercial superhighway down which freighters and tankers stream, linking Puget Sound ports with markets throughout the Pacific Rim.

Many pleasure boaters avoid the open stretches of the strait, favoring inland waters or hugging the comforting western shore of Whidbey Island. Stomach-churning swells can be built up by winds sweeping the length of the channel. Fog banks creeping in off the ocean linger in the strait long after they have cleared from inland waters. At such times, when line of sight cannot be relied on, navigational skills are essential to make the 25-mile crossing from Admiralty Inlet to Victoria or the San Juan Islands.

On clear days and when seas are calm, the strait offers sailors steady winds and joyously endless tacks, while cruisers find numerous bays and beaches to explore. Waters of the strait are legendary for salmon and

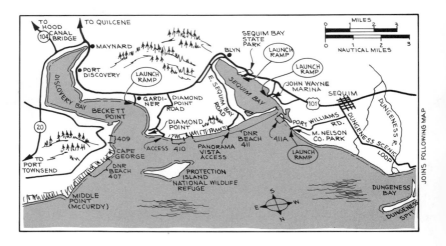

enormous halibut; many of the boats seen in the strait are those of fishermen intent on landing their limit.

The eastern half of the strait, from Port Townsend to Port Angeles, provides boaters somewhat of a transition from the shelter and civilization of the inland waters to the more rigorous demands of the outer reaches of the passage. Two deep inlets, Sequim Bay and Discovery Bay, offer the only well-protected harbors with good anchorages along this south shore. The only town with marine facilities is Port Angeles, which is somewhat sheltered by Ediz Hook and manmade breakwaters.

Protection Island

Not many boaters take note of the rhinoceros auklet, a black, stubby little bird that has been described as flying with the grace of a "winged brick." It is under water that it moves like a ballet dancer, using its wings for propulsion as it pursues herring or smelt and scoops them into its blunt beak. The auklet hunts open waters during the day, and not until twilight does it return to cliff-edge burrows, with fish for its chicks dangling from its heavy, bony bill.

It took a long time before someone noticed that an unusually large number of these birds were living on Protection Island. Studies eventually revealed that an estimated 17,000 pairs, or about ninety-six percent of the rhinoceros auklets in the lower 48 states, nested and raised their young in the sandy cliffs of the 400-acre island. Unfortunately, just at this time bulldozers had begun clearing land for a gargantuan real estate development—and Protection Island itself became desperately in need of protection.

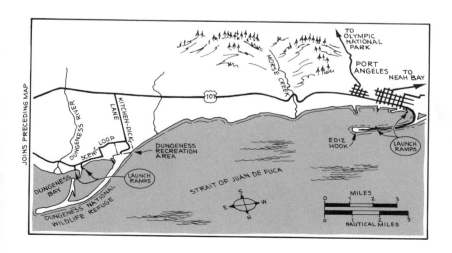

Protection Island from Diamond Point access

The auklet is only one of the numerous species of birds found here. Loss of breeding habitat in other areas along the sound, due to the encroachment of man, has undoubtedly led to the huge concentration of birds on the island. Hillsides, ledges, sandspits, and open fields are used by nearly three-fourths of the sound's nesting population of seabirds, including pelagic cormorants, glaucous-winged gulls, pigeon guillemots, and black oystercatchers.

Huge flocks of tufted puffins once lived on Puget Sound. Indians killed many, using their brilliant parrot-like beaks as rattles and decoration, but the flocks managed to survive until the arrival of the white man brought a serious loss of habitat, a depletion of food sources, and eventually the pollution of their environment. All of the tufted puffins now remaining on Puget Sound—some 35 pairs—are believed to nest on Protection Island.

The island was named by George Vancouver, who noted its protective location at the mouth of Discovery Bay. After that no one paid much attention to it for a long time—the government owned it, but gave it away in 1861; an attempt at farming was unsuccessful; some people tried living there, but gave up due to lack of potable water; and in the late 1940s an unattended beach fire spread and the entire island was burned to a crisp.

The fire-blackened slopes turned green once again, wildflowers bloomed, and life returned to Protection Island. In 1968 some "snake-oil" peddlers bought it and subdivided it into a nauseating network of 1100 postage-stamp-sized lots, including an airstrip and a marina. No matter that there was no drinking water (oh, but there were promises!) and that storm winds on exposed parts of the bluffs were known to blow away livestock and even overturn tractors, over half of the lots were snatched up by persons eager to own an island, and construction began.

Panicked environmentalists, including the Audubon Society and the Nature Conservancy, rallied. Their actions, along with failure to install a suitable water system and the disillusionment of some of the lot owners, brought property sale and construction to a halt. The Nature Conservancy was able to purchase 48 acres of crucial auklet nesting grounds, but the rest of the island was still in danger of eventual settlement. In 1980 Congressman Don Bonker introduced a bill to appropriate $4 million for purchase of land on the island. In August of 1988 Protection Island was officially established as a National Wildlife Refuge. The U.S. Fish and Wildlife Service currently owns 316 acres; the remaining 48 acres of land on the west end is owned and managed by the Washington Department of Wildlife.

The federally owned portion of Protection Island is closed to all public use year-around. Visits to the state-managed lands at the west end are strongly discouraged from March through September when birds are nesting. These intrusions may also disturb harbor seals who, in spring, deliver their pups on sun-warmed sandspits. A 200-yard buffer zone has been established around the island; boaters should stay offshore at least this distance. The Department of Wildlife conducts some organized tours; contact them for information regarding going ashore. Do not take dogs.

Discovery Bay

After his arduous voyage around Africa's Cape of Good Hope and across the Pacific, George Vancouver was pleased to find the sheltered arm of Discovery Bay for a nearly week-long layover to repair his ships and provide the crew some R and R. He wrote glowingly of the beauty of the bay and although the bay is lovely, perhaps all those months at sea with only a scruffy crew to look at affected his enthusiasm.

Discovery Bay hasn't changed a great deal since Vancouver dropped anchor here. Only a few communities and homes along the shore mark the arrival of civilization. The sinuous 8-mile-long inlet provides excellent anchorages at numerous spots along the shore, but nothing in the way of boating facilities except the launch ramp at Gardiner, described below.

The only public shore lands are two sections of DNR beach at Cape George. Beach 409, a 1475-foot strip of tidelands, is about a mile north of Beckett Point; Beach 407, which is just east of the tip of Cape George beneath a sheer 1500-foot cliff, is 5035 feet long. Neither beach has upland access, but they can be reached by boat from Gardiner; only the shorelands below mean high water are public.

DIAMOND POINT

Historically Diamond Point is unique. Although it originally was one of the many military reservation lands along the sound, in 1894 it became a quarantine station, with a hospital and detention area for ship passengers suspected of having been exposed to contagious diseases such as leprosy and elephantiasis. It operated until 1935, when the facility was moved to Port Townsend. A few of the buildings have been remodeled and are now used as private residences. A deteriorating wharf on the south side of the point was once used by ships waiting out the quarantine period.

Diamond Point, alas, has been taken over by the developers and now sports row upon row of summer homes. A small break in the bulkheads along the north shore is a possible spot to launch a car-top boat for access to Protection Island or to two strips of DNR beach to the west. Beach 410, a 2710-foot stretch of tidelands, begins just beyond the beach homes, below a wooded bluff. Beach 411 begins ¼ mile beyond the west end of Beach 410 in the middle of Thompson Spit and continues for nearly 5 glorious miles to the end of Travis Spit by Sequim Bay. A commercial RV and camping park at Diamond Point also provides foot and boat access to Beach 410 for persons registered at the park.

To reach Diamond Point, turn north off Highway 101 about 2 miles west of Gardiner onto Diamond Point Road and follow it to the point. Just below the junction of Beach Drive and Diamond Shore Lane is an opening in the bulkheads and a sign that says "Public Access." Beaches on either side of the access are private. Although this spot once provided access to residents of Protection Island, the island is now a Wildlife Refuge; visits are permitted only at the state-owned lands at the west end of the island, and even there they are discouraged during spring and summer (see p. 191).

GARDINER BOAT LAUNCH RAMP

A more easily located boat-launch site is at Gardiner, farther into Discovery Bay. Turn off Highway 101 onto Gardiner Beach Road and drive directly north to the bay. Just after the road turns left to parallel the shore, the single-lane concrete launch ramp is reached. Parking for a dozen cars is across the road. A small white sign pointing up the hill states, "Restroom ¼ mile."

PANORAMA VISTA ACCESS

DNR Beach 411 can be reached on foot off a road from Sequim Bay. Turn off Highway 101 onto East Sequim Bay Road at either Old Blyn Road or Blyn Crossing. Follow the road around the east side of Sequim Bay to

Panorama Vista Road. Turn right here, then in ¾ mile turn right again onto Buck Loop Road. On the left in another ¼ mile is a gated gravel road; park here and walk down the road 500 yards to the beach.

The public beach, which lies below mean high water and runs for 25,710 feet, extends west to the end of Travis Spit and east to the middle of Thompson Spit near Diamond Point. Some walkable beach is exposed at all times except extreme high water. At the high-tide level is a 6-foot-wide sandy swath with driftwood and beach grass. Below it the shores are gradually sloping cobble. At low water clams and geoducks can be dug; however these shellfish should not be taken from Travis Spit as they are hazardous to eat due to a domestic sewage outfall on nearby Gibson Spit.

The beach can also easily be reached by boat from Sequim Bay or from Marlyn Nelson County Park at Port Williams, north of Gibson Spit.

Sequim Bay

The continuous action of wind and waves from the Strait of Juan de Fuca wears away the soft glacial till bluffs and then deposits the material on several long curving sandspits along the north shore of the Olympic Peninsula. A pair of sandspits at the entrance to Sequim Bay nearly join to form an enormous lagoon.

The tidelands of both Travis Spit, which extends from the east, and Gibson Spit, which lies on the west, are public DNR beaches on which small boats can easily be landed. Land access to Beach 411 on Travis Spit is described above. Beach 411A, on Gibson Spit, can also be reached by walking south along the shore from Port Williams. Keep dogs on a leash (or leave them home) and use special care in walking to avoid disturbing shorebirds and waterfowl nesting in beach grass and driftwood.

Boat access to the inlet is via a dredged channel that starts at the red entrance buoy, runs parallel along the north side of Travis Spit, and then threads along the western shore. Consult a good chart and enter with care, favoring the west side and watching channel markers closely to avoid Middle Ground, a large shoal that lies just inside the entrance; some buoys tow under during strong tides and may not be visible. Once inside there are no navigational hazards, and excellent anchorages can be found throughout the bay in up to 20 fathoms. In addition to the large marina at Pitship Point, a smaller marina midway along the north shore also has fuel and supplies.

Some early maps show the name of the bay as Washington Harbor, but the local settlers preferred the more descriptive Indian name of Sequim, generally thought to mean "quiet water." Today Washington Harbor refers only to the small community at the entrance, where the marine research facilities of Battelle Institute are located.

Stunning displays of nighttime luminescence have been observed in Sequim Bay. When this phenomenon occurs, any disturbance in the water, even the slightest dip of an oar, produces a burst of ghostly radiance. Wake from a churning motor leaves a milky white billow on the black water, and glittery streaks mark the trails of fish swimming just below the surface. Such luminescence is caused by certain dinoflagellates, minute single-celled marine organisms that are part of plankton. Small numbers of these organisms are nearly always present in the water, and many boaters have been startled by nighttime fireworks in their darkened toilets when the heads have been flushed with sea water.

Certain combinations of nutrients, water salinity, and temperature can cause a sudden "bloom," or rapid increase in organisms of a particular kind. Dinoflagellates such as noctiluca ("night light") or a species of Gonyaulax noted for its luminescence may be the ones affected, resulting in a remarkable nighttime display. Several kinds of jellyfish also have this quality, but their luminescence shows as specific points of light when disturbed rather than an overall glow of the water.

PITSHIP POINT (JOHN WAYNE MARINA)

Facilities: Complete boat and crew facilities, laundry, boat launch (ramp), picnic tables, fireplaces, bait, tackle, fishing pier
Attractions: Boating, fishing, clam digging, swimming

On the west shore of Sequim Bay, where a meager little boat launch and a strip of public beach once existed, now stands a sparkling marina—and it's all due to movie actor John Wayne. Wayne brought his converted mine sweeper, the *Wild Goose,* into Sequim Bay on his frequent visits to Puget Sound and was so fond of the area that he purchased property at Pitship Point. The Port of Port Angeles asked him for land for a

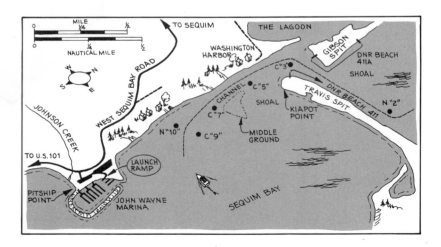

Launch ramp at John Wayne Marina

marina to serve the needs of Sequim and Port Angeles residents, and he generously donated 23 acres adjoining the public lands.

After several years of haggling with government agencies and anguished environmentalists who feared for marine life in the bay and bird life on nearby Protection Island, construction began on the marina in 1983 and was completed the following year. The compromise worked out by developers and environmentalists is, in general, a happy one, but only time will reveal the long-range impact of the marina's presence.

The marina, which is about half the size originally projected, snuggles neatly behind a curving rock breakwater on the north side of the point. Picnic tables are on a grassy knoll north of the marina building, and a walkway leads south across a scenic bridge where Johnson Creek empties into the bay. The beach south of the breakwater remains natural, with a long sandy tideflat for clam digging and puddle dabbling.

The first pier inside the marina breakwater is open for public fishing and crabbing. Next to it are the gas dock and a fine two-lane concrete boat-launch ramp. Floats G and H, the first two piers in the moorage area, are guest slips.

To reach Pitship Point by land, turn off Highway 101 onto Whitefeather Way 1¾ miles west of Sequim Bay State Park and follow signs to the marina. A commercial RV campground is nearby.

SEQUIM BAY STATE PARK

Park Area: 90 acres; 4900 feet of shoreline
Access: Land, boat
Facilities: 89 campsites, group camp, picnic tables, fireplaces, shelters, restrooms, showers, RV pumpout, fishing pier, float, 6 mooring buoys, hiking trails, children's play equipment, tennis courts, softball field, horseshoe pits
Attractions: Boating, fishing, clam digging, crabbing, hiking

A wonderful state park for either boaters or land-bound campers! Visitors arriving by water can tie up to the dock, send the kids ashore to work off energy on hiking trails and the tennis courts (or even to camp for the night), and settle back to enjoy some peace and quiet. Or perhaps even the "old folks" would enjoy a ramble through the woods and along the beach.

At the south edge of the park a long fishing pier has a 50-foot float on the end, where overnight tie-ups are permitted. At mean low water, the float has 6–7 feet of water under it but a piling directly north has only 3 feet at the same time; use care approaching or leaving the dock at low tide. Additional moorage is on six state park buoys spread along the shore. A two-lane launch ramp with a boarding float is down the beach to the north.

The park is situated on a series of wooded terraces on the hillside above the bay. A ravine with a cool trickling stream separates the campsites, on the north, and a picnic area, on the south. Trees obscure the view of the bay from the campground, but there are water vistas, both high and low, from trails that thread along the embankment and shore.

The state park, which lies 4 miles southeast of the town of Sequim on Highway 101, has one drawback—as all but the soundest sleeping campers will discover—both a major highway and a railroad run right through the park.

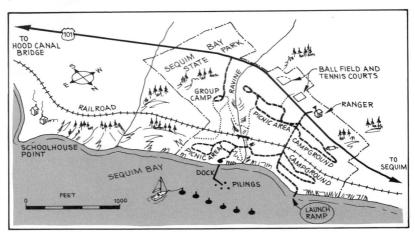

Rustic Bridge at Sequim Bay State Park

MARLYN NELSON COUNTY PARK (CLALLAM COUNTY)

Park Area: 1 acre; 500 feet of shoreline
Access: Land, boat
Facilities: Boat launch (ramp), picnic tables, fireplaces, latrines, *no water*

The influence of the little steamers of the early-day mosquito fleet extended clear out into the Strait of Juan de Fuca; Port Angeles was one stopover point, and Port Williams, near the entrance to Sequim Bay, was another. Cars followed a rough trail from the villages of Sequim and Port Washington to reach the Port Williams dock where passengers and freight were unloaded.

Where once there was a postoffice, a hotel, a dance hall, and residences, there is now only a tiny county park with a boat-launch ramp, some picnic tables, and two fireplaces. The park opens the way to beach walks below 80-foot-high bluffs of vertical glacial till. The beach walk north is halted in ½ mile by the boundaries of a private game farm. South is Gibson Spit, which encloses a salt-marsh lagoon. The ½-mile section of tidelands wrapping around the tip of the spit is designated as DNR Beach 411A. Shellfish taken from either Gibson Spit or Travis Spit may be hazardous to eat due to a nearby domestic sewage outfall.

Dungeness Bay

One of the most spectacular land features on the Strait of Juan de Fuca is Dungeness Spit, the 5-mile-long ribbon of sand at the delta of the Dungeness River. This sand spit, the longest in the U.S., has been built up by action of the wind and water current, which causes silt from the river and eroded material from nearby glacial till bluffs to be deposited in a long curving sandbar.

The spit encloses Dungeness Bay, a broad harbor open on the east. A shoal extending ¾ mile to the northeast from the lighthouse is marked by a lighted bell buoy; however the buoy may tow under during strong currents. Graveyard Spit, a secondary finger of sand, extends from the north, nearly bisecting the bay. Boaters with local knowledge enter the inner lagoon

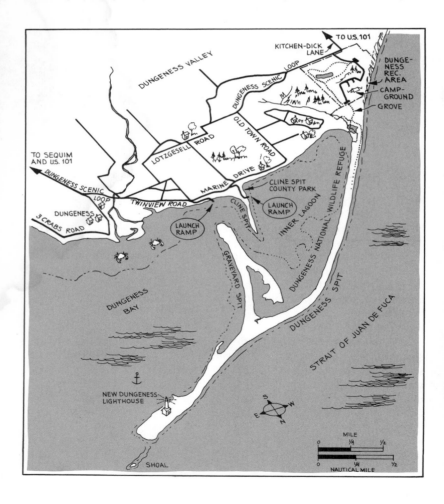

through a winding, unmarked channel, but much of this lagoon holds less than a fathom of water at mean lower low tide, so great care must be used. Anchorages can be found south of the tip of Dungeness Spit in 5 to 9 fathoms of water. The hook affords some protection from swells off the straits, but there is little shelter from strong winds.

Although the spit is called Dungeness, the navigational beacon at its tip is known as the New Dungeness lighthouse. George Vancouver gave the area its name. It reminded him of Dungeness in the British Channel, so he called this New Dungeness. Over the years local usage shortened it to Dungeness, a name that now applies to the spit, the harbor, the river, the community, and also the tasty crustacean that frequents the bay. Only the lighthouse retains the original name.

The New Dungeness lighthouse was the first to be built on the inland waters of Washington. In 1857, when it was built, it stood 100 feet tall, but over the years the masonry weakened, caused perhaps by a structural flaw. When the Canadian army began practice firing of their cannons from their fortifications on Vancouver Island in 1927, the repercussions caused serious cracks in the lighthouse mortar. It became necessary to remove the upper third of the tower, bringing it down to its present height of 63 feet. When this was done the old oil-fired light was scrapped and the electrified Fresnel lens was brought from the decommissioned lighthouse at Admiralty Head. That well-traveled lens is now in the Coast Guard Museum in Seattle.

Graveyard Spit did indeed once serve as a graveyard. A group of Tsimshian Indians from British Columbia who camped here in 1868 were descended upon in the night and massacred by a party of local Klallam Indians. One woman escaped, despite serious wounds, and sought refuge in the lighthouse. The bodies of her companions were buried on the spit.

This is a popular recreation area. The spit itself is a National Wildlife Refuge, and several other public accesses are on the shore, facing on Dungeness Bay. A scenic road north of Highway 101 leads to all these recreation sites. From the town of Sequim head north on Sequim Ave., which is signed as the Dungeness Scenic Loop; the western end of this loop drive rejoins Highway 101 at Kitchen–Dick Lane, 4 miles west of Sequim.

Clam digging and crabbing are permitted at any of the public lands; however all oysters in Dungeness Bay are private property. A private oyster company to the north of the Dungeness Boat Launch, described below, has oysters and shellfish for sale and also advertises U-Pick oysters, the only opportunity on Dungeness Bay to enjoy harvesting these succulent creatures.

DUNGENESS BOAT LAUNCH

As the Dungeness Scenic Loop reaches Dungeness Bay and curves west, it becomes Twinview Road and then Marine Drive. Immediately north of the Twinview–Marine Drive intersection a side road to the right,

Dungeness Spit

paralleling Marine Drive, descends to the beach. At the end of this road is a boat-launch facility operated by the Port of Port Angeles. The two-lane concrete ramp faces on a long tideflat, so launching is difficult at low water. In summer there are a number of floats for loading and tying up. Restrooms are next to a large gravel parking lot.

CLINE SPIT COUNTY PARK (CLALLAM COUNTY)

Park Area: 1 acre; 300 feet of shoreline
Access: Land, boat
Facilities: Boat launch (ramp), restrooms

Clallam County has developed a strip of state park property on Cline Spit, facing on the inner lagoon, as a launch ramp and small public access area. The incline of the one-lane ramp is steeper than the other Dungeness Bay ramp, making it more usable at lower tides; however boats leaving the lagoon must negotiate the circuitous channel around the ends of Cline and Graveyard Spits. This is an ideal put-in for paddle exploration of Dungeness Bay.

To reach the park, turn off Marine Drive onto Cline Spit Road, which drops steeply down to the shore. Signs and chain-link fencing mark the park boundary; the extreme end of the spit is private.

DUNGENESS RECREATION AREA (CLALLAM COUNTY)

Park Area: 216 acres; 2500 feet of shoreline
Access: Land
Facilities: 67 campsites, picnic tables, group shelter, restrooms, drinking water, RV pumpout, hiking trails, horse trails, children's play equipment
Attractions: Hiking, birdwatching, viewpoints, horseback riding

This fine Clallam County park serves as a companion to the Dungeness National Wildlife Refuge, providing camping and upland recreation for people visiting the spit. The park, which lies just off the northwest end of Dungeness Scenic Loop Road, is most easily reached by driving west out of Sequim on Highway 101 for 4 miles, then turning north on Kitchen–Dick Lane, which is signed to the park.

The park is on a 100-foot bluff above the water, with no paths leading directly to the shore, but several cliff-edge picnic areas and a trail that threads between them provide stunning views of the strait and the islands to the north. To the south is an equally stunning panorama of snow-draped Olympic Peaks.

A large section of the park is open grassland with occasional thickets, providing a home for pheasant, bobwhites, California quail, mourning doves, and songbirds such as western meadowlark. A small pond hidden behind a low ridge attracts ducks and sometimes even whistling swans. Hunting is permitted from October to January on Wednesdays, Saturdays, Sundays, and holidays; at other times the area offers excellent birdwatching.

Facilities here rival the best of the state parks. Spacious, level campsites are separated by a nice buffer of shrubbery, and restrooms are modern and clean. Clallam County uses unique fireplaces throughout its parks—old tire rims fitted with grates serve the purpose admirably. The northern boundary of the park abuts the wildlife refuge; trails through a wooded upland lead down to the spit.

DUNGENESS NATIONAL WILDLIFE REFUGE

Park Area: 755 acres; 45,000 feet of shoreline
Access: Land, boat
Facilities: Hiking trails, restrooms, informational displays, *no water*
Attractions: Hiking, beachcombing, birdwatching, clam digging, crabbing, boating, paddling, swimming

Trail at Dungeness Recreation Area

Among birdwatchers Dungeness Spit is legendary, although one doesn't need to be a dedicated ornithologist to appreciate the natural treasures of the refuge. Here is the beach walk to end all beach walks; only the most hardy could explore all the shores in one day—but dawdling is so enjoyable that it doesn't really matter if the end of the spit is reached.

The refuge is reached from the parking lot on the north side of the Dungeness Recreation Area. The grove that the trail passes through before descending to the beach offers a chance to enjoy a contrasting environment. Here fir and spruce provide homes for owls, sparrows, chickadees, bald eagles, raccoons, squirrels, and other wildlife common to coniferous forests. Informational displays along the trail descending to the spit describe the variety of life that can be seen along the spit, in the lagoon, or in offshore waters.

The inner shore of Dungeness Spit peters out gradually into tide flats where clams can be dug and eelgrass-filled shallows where crabs can be trapped. The outer, breaker-washed shore of the spit is smooth and slopes more steeply into the water. Silver piles of nature-sculpted driftwood line the high-tide level. For extended walks, pack a lunch, a canteen of water, and spare clothing. If the weather is severe, stay off the spit, as wave-tossed drift logs can be hazardous. The lighthouse near the end of the spit is open to visitors on weekend and holiday afternoons during the summer.

Nearly every species of waterfowl known to the Washington shores can be found here at some time. A display at the refuge compares the spit to a large hotel—some of the residents are permanent, while others check in and out at various times of the year for short stays. The kinds of birds vary somewhat from the inner shore to the outer shore and as one advances along the spit. Some, such as black brant, prefer brackish waters, while gulls and terns favor the outer shore where currents bring small fish to the surface. Shyer species stay at the outer end of the spit, where fewer hikers stray. Harbor seals may also be seen here, sunning on the shore or popping their heads from breakers to stare curiously.

Hunting is not permitted in the refuge; however, in the fall birds may shy because of nearby hunting, and may stay out farther and be more difficult to spot. During the spring nesting season, use special care not to disturb the birds or their nests.

Port Angeles

Although Port Angeles has long been known as a portal to the high peaks of the Olympics, it has rarely been considered as a marine destination. That has begun to change, however, with the opening of its fine new waterfront facilities catering to tourists and pleasure boaters.

The city is still distinctly blue collar, with smokestacks dominating the skyline, mountains of logs lining the waterfront, and boat basins filled with far more fishing boats than pleasure craft. With a population of 17,000, Port Angeles is the largest city on the Olympic Peninsula. Its stores and businesses offer a full range of services and shopping to visitors. Harbor Towne, a shopping mall in a nicely refurbished turn-of-the-century building, is immediately across the street from the waterfront.

Four mountain streams drain from the Olympic foothills through the town. In early days the business district on the waterfront was subject to frequent flooding during high tides. In 1914 dirt was sluiced down from a hill to the east and the waterfront was filled in raising it 10 feet. Existing buildings were raised or their first floors became basements. A number of these lifted structures as well as hollow sidewalks built on pillars can be seen in a walk through town. The basement level of Harbor Towne was once at street level. Raised buildings on pilings can be seen from the alley between Front and 1st from Oak to Cherry, and an elevated sidewalk can be seen by looking south from Railroad Ave. to Front St. between Laurel

City Pier at Port Angeles

and Oak. The Clallam County Historical Museum, housed in the old County Courthouse at 4th and Lincoln, has displays showing further town history.

In spite of its workaday atmosphere, the city has a dramatically scenic setting. The Olympic Mountains rise abruptly at its back door, and its waterfront is guarded by the gently encircling arm of Ediz Hook. This 3½-mile-long sandspit encloses Port Angeles Harbor, a natural bay broad and deep enough for a small fleet of ocean-going vessels. The only obstruction in the bay is the log-booming sites at the northwest end. Small boats must be watchful for logs and deadheads that sometimes drift in the bay, creating a hazard.

Port Angeles Harbor enjoys a colorful flow of commercial boat traffic. Freighters stop here to load logs and lumber products, tankers as well as freighters sometimes anchor in the protected waters of the bay, and the *M. V. Coho*, a 340-foot-long Black Ball ferry that runs from Port Angeles to Victoria, is berthed on the downtown waterfront.

The city of Victoria on Vancouver Island lies directly north across the Strait of Juan de Fuca. Canadian boaters headed for American waters often stop in Port Angeles to check through Customs.

From mid-March through November land-bound travelers can camp at the city's Lincoln Park, a 144-acre wooded tract with a replica of an Indian longhouse and some interesting pioneer cabins as added attractions. The 25 campsites in the park have water and fireplaces but no electricity. They are more suitable for bicyclists and tenters; RV campers may prefer to stay at one of the town's several commercial RV sites. Lincoln Park lies on the west edge of the town next to the county fairgrounds. To reach it from downtown, follow the truck route south and turn west on W. Lauridsen Blvd. In ¾ mile the park is reached. From Highway 101, turn north on Fairmont or Bean, which end at W. Lauridsen Blvd. and the park.

PORT ANGELES MARINA

Facilities: Transient moorage with power and water, diesel, gas, restrooms, pumpout station, marine supplies and repair, boat launch (ramp), groceries, ice, bait, deli, restaurant, tidal grid, boat rental and charter, shopping (nearby)

The Port Angeles Boat Haven, operated by the Port of Port Angeles, lies in a breakwater-protected basin on the west end of the waterfront. Transient moorage is on dock F, which is in the middle on the east side. Restrooms and most facilities are on shore at the east end; the marina office and gas float are at the end of the jetty, opposite this dock.

Two separate boat ramps are found at the marina. The primary launch

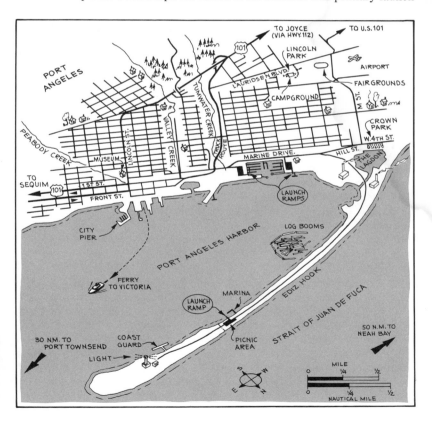

Log booming at Ediz Hook

facility is on the west side of the basin, where there is a two-lane ramp that empties directly into the bay. Floats are placed here in the summer but are removed at other times to protect them from weather. A large parking lot is adjoining. At the northeast corner of the basin, well protected by the land-fill jetty, are a single-lane ramp and loading float. Since maneuvering space and parking on the east side are limited, the ramp is generally used only when weather makes the other ramp unusable.

CITY PIER

Park Area: 4 acres; 300 feet of shoreline
Access: Land, boat
Facilities: Transient moorage, U.S. Customs, picnic tables, drinking water, restrooms, marine research laboratory, viewing tower, fishing pier, waterfront trail
Attractions: Fishing, viewpoint, informational display, boat tour

Focal point of the Port Angeles waterfront is City Pier, a multi-use fa-cility that serves nicely to welcome visiting boaters to the city. During summer, several moorage floats are in the bay, tucked behind the pier; however in winter the floats are removed to protect them from storms that sometimes batter the shore. Five buoys nearby provide additional moorages. At the end of the pier a two-story viewing tower provides a 360° view of harbor activity, the strait, and Hurricane Ridge rising dramatically behind the city.

Large ships such as military research vessels and mine sweepers sometimes moor on the outer side of the pier. The U.S. Coast Guard cutter tied up there usually is open on Sunday afternoons for curious visitors. The center of the pier is occupied by Peninsula College marine lab, which is also open to visitors on weekend afternoons; open-topped aquarium touch tanks display local marine life, and personnel are on hand to answer questions. The wooden causeway edging the waterfront ends at a pocket beach with driftwood and enough sand to keep any toddler happy.

A map display at the pier shows the route of a foot or bicycle scenic waterfront trail beginning here. The trail first follows city streets past the marina, then continues on the Ediz Hook road to the launch ramp near its end. An alternate destination is Crown Park, a small city park on the bluff above the lagoon with a fine view of Ediz Hook.

EDIZ HOOK

Facilities: Boat launch (ramp), transient moorages, restrooms, gas, outboard mix, bait, tackle, snack bar, boat rental and charter, RV parking

Ediz Hook, the 3½-mile-long spit that creates a breakwater for Port Angeles Harbor, is a startling contrast to its sister to the east. While Dungeness Spit has remained largely untrampled, Ediz Hook is a working man's spit—and boy has it been trampled! A road traverses the length of the hook, and logging interests, fishermen, boaters, the Coast Guard, and Puget Sound Pilots all make use of this fragile strip. To ensure its continued stability, the outer beach has been built up with gravel and a revetment of enormous boulders to control erosion.

A large lumber mill covers the base of the hook, spewing smoke and noise. Logging trucks roar along the road, headed for the scaling station midway along the spit. The northwest end of the bay is a booming ground filled with logs awaiting the bite of the saw.

Near the end of the spit is a commercial marina, open April through September. Moorage is available on the numerous floats in place during the summer. Next to the marina is a four-lane public launch ramp; restrooms and parking lot are on the opposite side of the road.

At the marina the road is gated; beyond is the U.S. Coast Guard Station and airstrip. Helicopters stationed here are used in rescues and other Coast Guard work throughout the inland waters. Atop the control tower of the air station is a modern automated beacon that serves as a navigational light.

From the time of earliest settlement, pioneers built bonfires on the end of the spit to guide ships. The lighthouse built here in 1865 was replaced by a new, but still traditional, structure in 1908. That light too gave way to progress when it was replaced in 1945 by the current prosaic Coast Guard beacon.

Despite the bustle of activity on the spit, the outer beach offers opportunities for long walks, exploration, and even some solitude among the scattered driftwood. Look north to Victoria and the San Juan Islands or west to Striped Peak or simply enjoy the play of gulls in wind and wave.

9. WESTERN STRAIT OF JUAN DE FUCA

West of Port Angeles the pulse of the strait quickens. The southern coastline becomes bold, with rock-infested beaches sweeping upward in places to rugged, 1000-foot bluffs. Waves generated by wind sweeping in from the ocean pound against the shores, making approach by boat difficult and at times dangerous.

The few boating facilities along the strait suffer from the severe environment; launch ramps are sometimes washed out or clogged by debris, and floats must be removed off season to prevent their damage by violent storms. The towns of Sekiu and Neah Bay, which have boat basins behind rock breakwaters, are the only harbors of refuge along this section of the strait. The greatest attraction here is for anglers who come from great distances to find exciting action fishing for salmon, halibut, lingcod, or rockfish. Most fishing is done from boats as small as 15-foot kicker boats or from moderately sized trailered craft. Halibut caught here range from young 20-pounders called "chicks" up to an occasional 200-pound

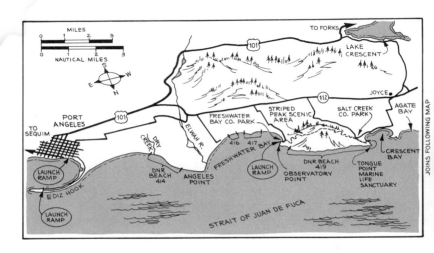

Wave-carved shoreline at Sail River

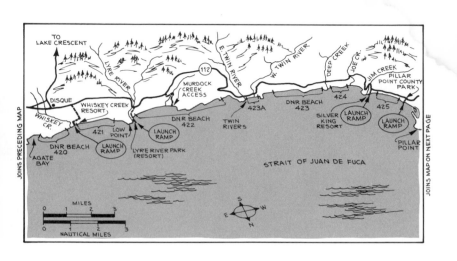

Marina at Sekiu

monster that must be towed to shore behind the boat.

Few pleasure boaters choose this area as a destination; most are in transit to or from ocean voyages. In addition to Neah Bay and Sekiu, a few small bays offer some limited anchorages when seas are calm. When navigating near shore, take care to watch for submerged rocks and reefs. The warmer summer months are often accompanied by dense fog, which usually clears off by mid-morning.

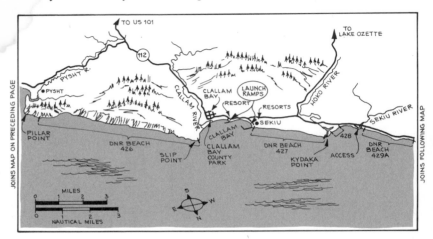

Some forty miles of shorelands at twenty locations along this section of the strait are public. Many of these sites are Department of Natural Resources beaches, where the state-owned land is below the mean high water level; however at several locations the beaches are paralleled by Highway 112, giving easy access. At other places the beaches can be reached via county parks or commercial resorts. At any of the commercial facilities, beach users must obtain permission from the property owner. In some cases the resorts have rental boats and pay launch ramps; even persons with car-top boats can expect to be charged a fee.

Some beaches are rocky and drop off steeply; when approaching by boat extreme care must be used, since a wave or surge can throw a boat against the rocks. Landings on these beaches should be attempted only in calm weather and even then with caution.

Land access to this western section of the strait is from State Highway 112. Follow U.S. 101 west out of Port Angeles, and one mile west of town at a major intersection turn north onto Highway 112. Once it reaches saltwater at Twin Rivers, the two-lane road follows the shoreline much of the way to Neah Bay, turning inland in only a few spots. The twisting road is slow driving, especially if pulling a boat trailer, but the scenery is spectacular. Logging trucks may be encountered on weekdays.

Striped Peak

About 12 miles beyond Port Angeles, 1166-foot Striped Peak is a prominent landmark with its thickly wooded slopes rising abruptly from the water. The area was the site of Fort Hayden, built in the early 1940s at the outbreak of World War II when the government saw the need to modernize its Coastal Defense System. A second fort was planned for Cape

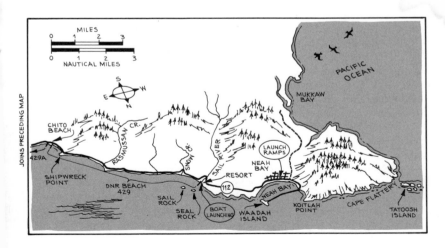

Flattery, near Neah Bay. Land was acquired and excavation completed, but before the concrete was poured the war had moved far into the Pacific and construction on that fort was halted.

The concrete-canopied, heavily shielded bunkers at Fort Hayden were designed to withstand direct hits from offshore guns as well as aircraft bombardment. Two 16-inch guns were installed in the battery at Tongue Point, and a second battery, ½ mile east at the 300-foot level of Striped Peak, held two 6-inch guns. The guns were test-fired only once.

With the advent of missiles and other rapid changes in military technology, the fort became obsolete and the multi-million-dollar guns were cut up for scrap. In 1949 the property was declared surplus and shortly after was acquired by state and county agencies for a magnificent recreation area. Striped Peak Scenic Area, Salt Creek County Park, and Tongue Point Marine Sanctuary encompass a total of some 1700 acres of land and 4 miles of shoreline, with attractions ranging from dense forest to wave-washed rocks to a sublime saltwater estuary.

FRESHWATER BAY COUNTY PARK (CLALLAM COUNTY)

Park Area: 17 acres, 1000 feet of shoreline
Facilities: Boat launch (ramp), latrines, picnic tables, *no water*

Launch ramps are infrequent along the western end of the straits, and well-appointed ones are even more rare. This single-lane launch ramp, maintained by Clallam County, is well-surfaced and has a spacious parking lot adjoining it. The only disadvantage is that it gradually slopes out onto a long tideflat, making it unusable at low water. The picnic area west of the parking lot has a number of tables in a shaded grove.

The 4-mile-wide bay, bounded by Angeles Point on the east and Observatory Point on the west, is quite open, but some anchorages can be found in 6 to 10 fathoms. Bachelor Rock, a 20-foot-high sea stack, lies just off Observatory Point.

The launch ramp is reached by turning north off Highway 112 onto Freshwater Bay Road 9 miles west of Port Angeles. In less than 2 miles the road turns west and becomes Lawrence Road. Turn north on Park Road in a short half mile and follow it to the ramp. The beach immediately north of the ramp is private.

At the road end a sign points north up a dirt road to the Striped Peak Scenic Area. This narrow twisting road can be followed for 2 miles to an expansive viewpoint at the top of the mountain.

Boats launched at Freshwater Bay have easy access to three DNR beaches to the east. Beach 417, which is 2800 feet long, and Beach 416, a 1345-foot strip, are 1–2 miles east, slightly past Colville Creek. Beach 414 lies 5 miles from the launch ramp on the east side of Angeles Point; the eastern edge of this 5580-foot section of tidelands begins just east of a riprap bulkhead at the Port Angeles city limits. The public land of all three beaches is the area lying below mean high water. At low tide the gravelly shores may yield some horse and butter clams.

STRIPED PEAK SCENIC AREA

Park Area: 1500 acres
Access: Land
Facilities: Viewpoint, hiking trail, *no water*

This large section of DNR property abuts the eastern boundary of Salt Creek County Park. The viewpoint can be reached by driving a dirt road from the Freshwater Bay launch ramp, described above, but for hikers a better access is from Salt Creek County Park. To reach it, follow Highway 112 west from Port Angeles 12 miles to Camp Hayden Road, which is prominently signed to Salt Creek and Tongue Point recreation areas. Turn

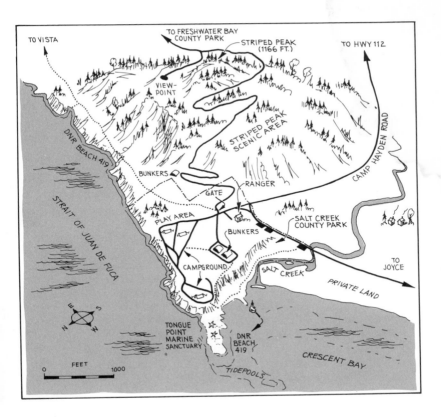

north and follow the road 3½ miles to the entrance of the county park.

Just past the entrance information booth is a small grassy parking lot by a gated road. A sign here indicates a hiking trail that leads to a cove in 1.1 mile and a vista in 2.4 miles. This trail circles the north side of Striped Peak, reaching first a sheltered little cove, then continuing on around the peak to join the road coming up from the east side. The final ¾ mile to the summit viewpoint is hiked along the road. The mountain top affords a 360° view north across the straits to Victoria, east to Port Angeles, Ediz Hook, and Mt. Baker, south to snow-crested Olympic mountains, and west down the misty strait.

The gated road at the county park can also be walked to reach the viewpoint. This route has an added attraction—a glimpse of one of the old bunkers from Fort Hayden. The concrete battery, which is just off the end of the first sharp switchback, is not maintained and is heavily overgrown. Two 6-inch guns, that sat on concrete pads on either side of the battery were covered with thick armor plate. Use care in the area as broken bottles and trash make it hazardous.

SALT CREEK COUNTY PARK (CLALLAM COUNTY) AND TONGUE POINT MARINE LIFE SANCTUARY

Park Area: 196 acres; 5000 feet of shoreline
Access: Land, boat
Facilities: 87 campsites, picnic tables, fireplaces, kitchen shelter, restrooms, drinking water, children's play equipment, softball field, horseshoe pits, RV dump station, informational and historical displays, hiking trails
Attractions: Fishing, hiking, beachcombing, scuba diving, swimming, paddling, tidepooling

A treasure of a park, with stunningly beautiful scenery, acres of tidepools to explore, and a sheltered sandy beach for summer lazing. Directions to the park are the same as for Striped Peak Scenic Area.

Inside the park entrance a road to the west leads to the WW II bunkers built when this area was Fort Hayden. The construction here is unique to Puget Sound forts, most of which were built before the First World War. The concrete canopy was necessary to protect it from airplane attacks as well as bombardment from the large guns ships carried. Enormous 16-inch guns, 45 feet long, and measuring 5 feet thick at the breech, were mounted on revolving turntables inside the bunkers.

Camping at Salt Creek County Park is in two areas. At the east, near the park entrance, is a large grassy field with RV sites in the open; on a road that loops around a small peninsula to the west are tenting sites in light timber. None of the campsites have hookups. Short trails from the camp areas descend to the beach.

Salt Creek County Park

The rocky shoreline east of Tongue Point, along the north edge of the park, drops off abruptly. East of the boundary of the park the public shoreline, designated as DNR Beach 419, continues nearly all the way to Observatory Point. The rock and gravel shore is difficult for casual walking, but with some effort at low tide interesting rock formations and marine life can be seen. At high tide the beach is impassable.

This is a favorite area for scuba divers who explore the submerged rocks and sand channels. Kelp beds, strong currents, and heavy surge conditions are hazards; only expert divers should dive here, and then only on calm days during slack tide.

Tongue Point is a layer of erosion-resistant volcanic basalt that juts out on the east side of Crescent Bay. At low tide a ¼-mile-long tidal shelf is revealed, filled with a dazzling array of marine plants and animals in a jewel-like mixture of reds, pinks, and purples. A single tidepool may contain as many as a hundred different species including limpets, hermit crabs, sculpin, nudibranchs, and sea urchins. A good book on seashore life will help identify the many creatures you may see. This is a marine sanctuary—do not remove or destroy any of the life.

Tongue Point shelters the sandy estuary of Salt Creek, on the east side of Crescent Bay. The estuary can be reached by trails from the campground, or by a road that goes west from the park entrance for ¼ mile to a day-use area. Moderate to low tides expose a broad sandy beach punctuated by a remarkable little wooded island of rock that stands as a lonely sentinel on the beach.

The park boundary is down the middle of Salt Creek; land west of here, including the beaches of Crescent Bay, is private; a private resort is on the west end of the bay. Crescent Bay is suitable only for anchoring small boats. Entry to the bay with large boats is hazardous without local knowledge, as rocks lie off Tongue Point and the unnamed point that marks the west end of the bay.

Whiskey Creek

Continuing west, public shore accesses become more primitive, offering only basic amenities for the hardy anglers who venture out on the waters of the strait. At Whiskey Creek a commercial resort has cabins, campsites, and a launch ramp protected by a short rock breakwater. To reach it turn north off Highway 112, 2¼ miles west of the town of Joyce, onto Schmitt Road, which is signed to the Whiskey Creek Recreation Area. Follow signs 1½ miles to the beach. Off season the resort may be closed and the road gated ¾ mile from its end.

Whiskey Creek Resort provides the only land access to DNR Beaches 420 and 421. Since this is a commercial facility, persons wanting to walk the beaches should be guests of the resort or obtain permission from the property owner. DNR Beach 420, which lies east of Whiskey Creek, is 8750 feet long; Beach 421, west of Whiskey Creek, is 8010 feet long. The public beach, which is below the mean high water level, is gradually slop-

Launch ramp at Whiskey Creek

ing gravel and hard clay, with ample room for beach walking at low tide. Boat landing can be dangerous under severe wave or surge conditions.

Lyre River

East of Whiskey Creek a commercial resort at Lyre River caters more to family camping. Lyre River Park provides tenting and RV facilities, restrooms with showers and laundry, a store with ice, groceries, and fishing tackle, and a boat-launch ramp. The resort is on the eastern edge of DNR Beach 422; however access to the beach at this point, as well as use of the launch ramp, is restricted to guests of the resort.

The turnoff to Lyre River Park is on Highway 112, 5 miles west of the town of Joyce. At the sign indicating the Lyre River Recreation Area, turn north onto West Lyre River Road, and follow it 1 mile to its end at the resort. Do not be confused by a sign on the road ¾ mile to the east on East Lyre River Road pointing to a DNR campground. While that public forest camp is very pretty, it is on the bank of the river, and has no saltwater access.

MURDOCK CREEK ACCESS

DNR Beach 422 can be reached from a logging road 1 mile west of the West Lyre River Road intersection. Turn off Highway 112 onto an unmarked dirt road; there may be a sign at the intersection saying "Twin River Oil and Gas." The narrow, steep, and twisting road has few spots to turn around or to pass oncoming cars. At a branch in the road, in ½ mile, bear right; 1 mile from the highway a dirt parking area in timber by the beach is reached. There is space for camping; however there are no restrooms or drinking water.

The shale intertidal shelf extends for about ¼ mile, exposing a fascinating assortment of marine life at low tide. Small pools are filled with a variety of chitons, barnacles, starfish, and "Chinese hat"-shaped limpets. Note how different the forms of life found here are than those found on the protected shores of Puget Sound. The beach can be walked east for a mile to Lyre River or west for 4 miles to the point just east of Twin Rivers. Landing boats should be attempted only when seas are calm.

Twin Rivers

Highway 112 finally touches the shores of the Strait of Juan de Fuca at Twin Rivers, 27 miles west of Port Angeles. Suddenly a wealth of sand and shale beaches are revealed, only a jump from the bumper—but don't jump too soon, as the uplands of the first beach encountered are owned by a private camping club that objects to any trespassers. Two side roads lead to the private beach; a third road spur (the last to be reached before the bridge over West Twin River) leads to a narrow public access to DNR Beach 423A, where car-top boats can be put in. This access is heavily used in good weather, and parking nearby may be difficult. It is also possible to reach the beach from the bank on either side of the bridge, a short distance away, although boat launching is not possible there.

Beach 423A, which is a 3415-foot section lying below the mean high water level, extends from East Twin River west to a landfill jetty owned by a quarry. Some clams may be dug in the sandy beach. Beyond the quarry property, where the road pulls away from the shore, Beach 423 begins. This section of beach, 15,365 feet in length, is easily accessed from its west end, where the highway returns to the shore by Deep Creek. Some limited parking is available along the road.

Beach 424, 5925 feet in length, which begins west of the delta of Deep Creek, has no upland access—it must be reached by boat. The closest boat launch is at Silver King Resort, ½ mile away. Unfortunately boat landing at this or any of the other beaches along the strait can be hazardous. It should be attempted only during calm seas and even then with great care.

Pillar Point

Pillar Point is rated as one of the fishing "hot spots" along the Strait of Juan de Fuca. In spring and summer king and silver salmon are caught just offshore, and when winter storms permit this is a top area for blackmouth. A county park at Pillar Point and a commercial resort at Jim Creek offer both camping and boat launching facilities.

Pillar Point is a distinctive, 700-foot-high knob with a prominent pillar-shaped sea stack lying off its eastern tip. The point encloses an open shallow bay at the drainage of the Pysht River. Some anchorages can be found in 10 fathoms of water southeast of the point. The surrounding land gives protection from westerly swells; however there is little shelter from winter storms. Numerous rocks lie offshore east of the county park.

JIM CREEK

Silver King Resort, at Jim Creek, offers the only protected moorage for small boats along this section of the strait. A sign on Highway 112, 3½ miles west of Twin Rivers, points north to the Jim Creek Recreation Area. Off season, if the resort is closed, the road may be gated at the highway. The gravel road twists downhill for ½ mile to the resort.

A dredged basin, with floats in summer, is protected by two curving rock jetties; however it is not suitable for boats of any draft. The surfaced, two-lane boat-launch ramp inside the jetty is usable during all but minus tides. The resort offers RV camping with hookups, picnic tables, restrooms with laundry and showers, gas, and a store with some groceries and fishing tackle.

PILLAR POINT COUNTY PARK (CLALLAM COUNTY)

Park Area: 4 acres; 240 feet of shoreline
Access: Land, boat
Facilities: 35 campsites, picnic tables, fireplaces, boat launch (ramp), restrooms, drinking water
Attractions: Boating, fishing, beachcombing, clam digging

This small county park is primarily used by anglers who launch boats here, although its wide tideflat and scenic location make it popular with anyone who loves the shore. Pillar Point County Park is just north of Highway 112, 36 miles west of Port Angeles, and 1½ miles west of Jim Creek; the entrance road is well signed. The camping area, on a slight bluff above the shore, is open only May 15 to September 15, but the park itself is open year-round.

The single-lane boat-launch ramp empties onto a shallow flat and is usable only for cartop or small trailered boats. Some fishermen use waders to reach boats launched at high tide and anchored out.

Two nearby DNR beaches can be reached by boat from Pillar Point. Beach 425, which is 4520 feet long, lies east, midway between the county park and Silver King resort. This beach is a continuation of the long tideflat at the mouth of the Pysht River.

To the west, Beach 426 stretches for 42,750 feet from a cove ½ mile west of Pillar Point all the way to Slip Point at the east side of Clallam Bay. This beach lies beneath an 800-foot bluff, and the rocky shores drop off steeply. Landing boats is possible only in a few small coves, and even there the shore should be approached with caution and only during calm seas.

Sometime between March to April, during the brief annual spawning run of smelt, the area from Pillar Point east to Twin Rivers is a prime spot for catching smelt with large long-handled nets. Smelt dippers work from shore on the incoming tide, scooping the little fish from net to bucket to awaiting frying pan.

Clallam Bay

Clallam Bay is the only protected harbor along the Strait of Juan de Fuca between Port Angeles and Neah Bay. The bay has two small communities along its shore—Clallam Bay and Sekiu. A sandbar at the mouth of the Clallam River fronts the town of Clallam Bay, giving it some shelter

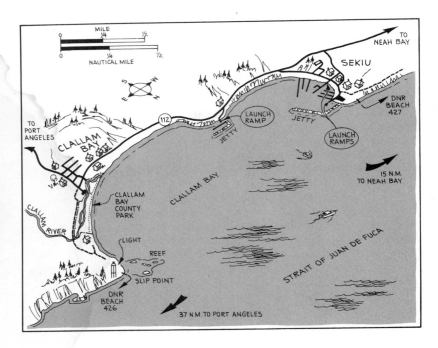

from storms sweeping in off the strait, but also serving to keep boats at a distance. The major boating center is at Sekiu, on the west side of the bay, where a rock jetty forms a well-protected basin for the fleet of small recreational fishing boats that arrive in the summer.

The 2-mile-wide bay has some protected anchorages in 6 to 10 fathoms near the Sekiu jetty. The floats within the jetty are primarily for small boats—some are on dry land at low tide.

By land, Clallam Bay is 50 miles west of Port Angeles on Highway 112. Both the towns of Clallam Bay and Sekiu have service stations, grocery stores, restaurants, and overnight accomodations. Clallam Bay and points west along Highway 112 can also be reached by driving Highway 101 west from Port Angeles to Sappho and turning north on the Burnt Mountain Road; in 9 miles the road joins Highway 112 and continues on to Clallam Bay. This route eliminates some of the narrow twisting road along the shore but is also less scenic.

Extensive DNR public beaches flank either side of the bay. Beach 426, described above, runs east from Slip Point, which is marked by a light at the east side of the bay. Beach 427, 17,890 feet in length, goes west from Sekiu Point all the way to Kydaka Point near the Hoko River. Both of these beaches lie beneath high bluffs and are accessible only by boat. Scuba divers sometimes enter the water at the resort at Sekiu and work

Bridge at Clallam Bay County Park

their way around the point to Beach 427. With permission divers can cross Coast Guard property by the Slip Point light to reach Beach 426.

At low tide Beach 427 has some sandy stretches that hold clams and mussels. The underwater area is rocky, with ledges and caves containing brightly colored rockfish, anenomes, and, in dark corners, octopus and wolf eels. Thick beds of kelp, strong currents, and surge are hazards, making this a dive only for the experienced.

CLALLAM BAY COUNTY PARK (CLALLAM COUNTY)

Park Area: 36 acres; 9850 feet of shoreline
Access: Land, boat
Facilities: Restrooms, picnic tables
Attractions: Beachcombing, boating, fishing, swimming

As it reaches the strait, the Clallam River meanders westward, paralleling the shore before emptying into Clallam Bay. A wide sandy bar that has been built up at the mouth of the river was owned by Washington State Parks, but has been turned over to the county for their management as a jewel of a day-use park.

Here is the ideal spot to spend a sunny afternoon in the sheltering arms of a driftwood snag, or to let the kids dabble toes in the sand and rolling surf. Beach and river shores call for exploration, and the bordering woodland offers promise of a shy squirrel or twittering birds.

Where Highway 112 enters the town of Clallam Bay from the east and takes a left turn, a stub road at the intersection goes straight ahead to the county park's parking lot by a rail fence and some picnic tables. Down a short path to the left an arched bridge crosses the river to the beach.

SEKIU RESORTS

Facilities: Transient moorage, boat launch (ramp), gas, outboard mix, restrooms, showers, laundry, camping, RV sites, cabins, restaurants, groceries, ice, fishing tackle and bait, boat and motor rental, charters

Resorts along the shore at Sekiu cater to the hordes of anglers who arrive during the spring and summer to fish for prized salmon or halibut. Accommodations tend to be plain rather than posh. Reservations are usually necessary during good weather. Some limited charters are available through the resorts; however most fishermen trailer their own boats or rent kicker boats. Not all the resorts and motels have full facilities; some primarily offer overnight accommodations, while others have full boating services.

While a number of the resorts close off season and remove their floats to protect them from storms, a few remain open the year around to take advantage of bottom fishing when an occasional break in winter weather permits.

Sekiu lies just north of Highway 112, 1½ miles west of the town of Clallam Bay. One of the resorts, which has its own rock breakwater, is midway between the two towns.

Sekiu to Neah Bay

Nearing Neah Bay the shoreline becomes even more spectacular, with wave-torn beaches, sea stacks, and imposing offshore rocks. Low tide reveals a boulder-strewn shale shelf with cracks and crevices holding tidepools. Abundant marine life inhabits this shelf—some of it bright and obvious, but much of it blending into the overall purple-brown color scheme. Even flamboyant, bright pastel sea anemones contract into nondescript brown nodules as the tide recedes.

At several places Highway 112 comes close enough to the shore to permit easy access; a few pulloffs provide limited parking. All the beach between the Sekiu River and Sail River, with the exception of a narrow strip at Chito Beach, is public DNR beach below the mean high water

Seal and Sail rocks offshore from Sail River

level. Beach 429A, which is 12,210 feet in length, is east of Chito Beach; Beach 429, 37,440 feet long, is to the west. Chito Beach, a scattering of homes and summer cabins along the highway, has no public access. A commercial RV and camping park may be open in the summer.

Beach 428, at the mouth of the Hoko River, is 2750 feet long. It is located below a housing development; however there is no public access through the residential area; the beach must be reached by boat.

Several exquisite sea stacks are next to the highway near the west end of Beach 429. They are not as large or dramatic as those found out on the coast at La Push and at Shi-Shi Beach, but they are much more accessible and are equally fascinating. The surrounding beaches are prime areas for tidepooling.

Near Snow Creek and Sail River two massive rocks, nearly 100 feet tall, rise ¼ mile offshore. When seen from the southeast, Sail Rock resembles the mainsail of a giant sloop; Seal Rock is an even larger rectangular-shaped monolith lying to the west. The vast numbers of birds that nest here, including cormorants, gulls, and tufted puffins, have found a spot safe from the threat of real estate developers.

SEKIU RIVER ACCESS

A road stub on the east bank of the Sekiu River leads to a sandy spit at the mouth of the river. Watch for the unmarked side road a few hundred feet east of the bridge. A few rough pullouts lead into the timber. Although this is not an acknowledged camping area, people occasionally do camp here. There are a couple of picnic tables but no restrooms or drinking water. Hand-carried boats can be put in at the beach for exploration up the river or east and west along the strait. Boating in the strait during times of waves, surge, or strong current can be hazardous.

SNOW CREEK

At one time the State Department of Fisheries planned to take over a closed resort at Snow Creek, 3½ miles east of Neah Bay, and build a public launch ramp. Plans somehow went awry; all that remains at the site are the delapidated remains of the resort, a rusting hoist, and a nice new restroom (which may or may not be open).

The future may see the completion of launching facilities here, but in the meantime the resort does provide access to DNR Beach 429 and some sensational views of Seal and Sail Rocks, just offshore.

SAIL RIVER

At Sail River, west of Snow Creek 1 mile, the Neah Bay Resort, a commercial facility, has boat-launching and camping space for anglers. The boat-launching hoist is in the shelter of the small bay at the mouth of

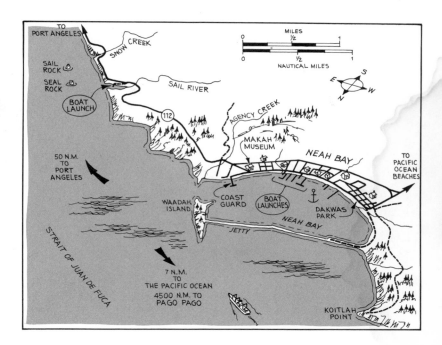

the river, and a float nearby has space for boats up to 18 feet. RV and tent campsites and some rustic cabins are along the east shore. Fuel and rental boats are available here.

The resort gives ready access to reefs around Seal and Sail Rocks that yield large lingcod and rockfish. Beach 429, which begins immediately east of the resort, has miles of beautiful water-eroded rock terraces and tidepools. Access to the public beach through the resort is only for guests or for those who secure permission from the property owners.

Neah Bay

The town of Neah Bay is the center of the Makah Indian Reservation. These Indians, who are more culturally allied with the Nootka Indians of Vancouver Island than those of the inland waters of Puget Sound, at one time occupied all of the coastal land down to Lake Ozette. Archeological evidence shows their presence here for around 3000 years.

The Makahs built large sea-going canoes from which they pursued whales. Using ritualistic preparation and hunting techniques very similar to those of the Eskimos far to the north, they harpooned and killed the whales, then towed the carcasses back to their villages where they were slaughtered and the meat smoked and dried. They were also highly skilled at fishing for salmon and bottom fish, and killing seals.

Cleaning the catch at Neah Bay

Neah Bay was the site of the first attempt by Europeans to settle what is now the state of Washington. In the spring of 1792 a group of Spanish colonists landed here with instructions to build a fort and clear land, in an attempt to establish a claim to the coast north of California. The Spaniards evidently found the coastal climate too bitter for them, even in the summer, and the fur trade not to their liking, as the settlement was abandoned after four months.

Some fifty years later Samuel Hancock, a Yankee pioneer, established a trading post here for storing and shipping oil from whales harpooned by the Indians. At the time of the arrival of white men, the Makah Nation was large, but smallpox, brought in 1853 via a trading ship, ravaged the tribe, reducing it to a mere 150 individuals. Hancock wrote of bodies so numerous that he was unable to bury them and had to drag them to the beach to float off on the tide. The terrible epidemic is described in the book *Exploring Washington* by Harry M. Majors. Today the tribe numbers about 1400 members.

In the Neah Bay Treaty of 1855, initiated by Governor Isaac Stevens, the Makah Indians were assigned 23,000 acres of land at this westernmost tip of the state. The present reservation is about 44 miles square, covering about half the original area. During the last weekend of August, at the annual Makah Day celebration held at Neah Bay, tribes from throughout the Northwest gather to celebrate their heritage with traditional dances and costumes, a salmon bake, games, and canoe races.

The traditional fishing economy has remained one of the mainstays of the Makah tribe, and today Neah Bay is the center of large commercial and sport fishing industries. The deep natural harbor provides moorage for both large and small fishing boats, while ocean-bound yachtsmen often use the bay as a last stop before hitting open water.

Waadah Island, a ½-mile-long wooded knob, lies on the east side of the bay, off Baada Point. A rock breakwater that stretches for 1½ miles between Waadah Island and the shore shelters the inner bay from all but easterly weather. The low jetty does not give complete protection from severe northerlies, but such storms are rare, especially in summer.

A reef and numerous rocks extend from the southwest side of Waadah Island. The entrance channel, marked by buoys, should be followed carefully all the way into the bay, slightly favoring the south side. Anchorages can be found in 20 to 40 feet of water. Floats for pleasure boats are removed off season.

By land Neah Bay can be reached by driving either Highway 112 or U.S. 101 west from Port Angeles. If following 101, turn north at Sappho to join Highway 112. The distance is about 70 miles either route, and much of the way is on narrow twisting roads.

A small shoreside park in Neah Bay provides a place to munch a sandwich and observe waterfront activity. Dakwas Park is marked by a weathered totem pole surrounded by a picket fence. A few picnic tables are next to the water.

NEAH BAY RESORTS

Facilities: Guest moorage, boat launch (ramp and hoist), gas, outboard mix, camping, RV sites, cabins, restrooms, showers, laundry, groceries, ice, bait, fishing tackle, restaurants, boat rental and charters, U.S. Customs

Floats for recreational boats are along the south shore of Neah Bay, on either side of a long pier belonging to a commercial fishing company. Facilities in the town are decidedly utilitarian. A single grocery store offers supplies, but cruising boats should not plan on a major restocking of their ship's stores here, as the selection is limited. Resorts have fishing tackle and bait. There are no marine repair facilities.

Motel and camping accommodations too are rather spartan, appealing primarily to sport fishermen whose main interest is catching a prize salmon.

MAKAH MUSEUM

A splendid museum at Neah Bay displays artifacts from the Makah Indian culture. Many of the items are from the Ozette archeological dig, where part of a coastal village had lain buried in a mudslide for over 500 years. The items are beautifully presented, with photos, drawings, and text explaining their use in everyday Makah life. One display centers around a replica of a longhouse, where visitors can step inside and be transported back to a 15th-century village.

The museum is on the east side of the town, adjacent to Highway 112. It is open 10:00 a.m. to 5:00 p.m. daily during the summer, closed on Mondays and Tuesdays from mid-September to the end of May.

*   *   *

Our journey along Washington's entrance waters is ended. But where next? Ahead lies the battered rock of Tatoosh Island at the entrance to the strait; then a turn hard to port leads to wave-dashed coastal beaches, La Push, and Grays Harbor. To the north the wild coastline of Vancouver Island beckons. Northeast are the harbor of Victoria and the green maze of the Gulf Islands. Or perhaps (oh, blasphemous thought!) to show our stern to the dank and drizzle of the Pacific Northwest and head for the palm-laden shores of Hawaii—or even the South Seas.

Pago Pago, Afoot and Afloat—it does have a nice ring!

APPENDICES

A. *Emergency Phone Numbers and List of Contacts*

All western Washington counties use 9ll as an emergency number. The following phone numbers are listed as additional contacts for nonemergency situations.

All numbers listed are area code 206

SHERIFFS

Clallam County: (Port Angeles) 452-7836
Island County: (Oak Harbor) 678-6116
Jefferson County: (Port Townsend) 385-3831
Skagit County: (Mt. Vernon) 336-3146
Whatcom County: (Bellingham) 911

U.S. COAST GUARD

Anacortes: 293-9555
Coast Guard Patrol Boat: 1-800-592-9911
Neah Bay: 645-2236
Port Angeles: 457-4401
Port Townsend: 385-3070

U.S. CUSTOMS

Anacortes: 293-2331
Neah Bay: 645-2312
Port Angeles: 457-1221
Port Townsend: 385-3777

RADIO CONTACT

Marine VHF: Coast Guard distress or hailing—Channel 16
     Coast Guard liason—Channel 22
Citizens Band: Distress—Channel 9

OTHER CONTACTS

Red Tide Hotline: 1-800-562-5632
Whale Hotline (to report sightings or strandings): 1-800-562-8832

FERRIES

Washington State Ferries Information: (Seattle) 464-6400 or (Toll free) 1-800-542-0810 or 1-800-542-7052
Guemes Island Ferry: 293-6356
Lummi Island Ferry: 676-6730

WASHINGTON STATE PARKS

General information regarding the state parks is available from Washington State Parks and Recreation Commission; 7150 Cleanwater Lane; Olympia, Wa., 98504. Toll-free number for information or reservations (Memorial Day through Labor Day): 1-800-562-0990

The State Parks and Recreation Commission also shares an office with the National Park Service in Seattle at 1222 1st Ave. Information regarding the parks is available there.

OTHER PARKS

Clallam County Parks Department: Courthouse; Port Angeles, 98362; 452-7831, Ext. 291
Dungeness Recreation Area (Clallam County); 638-5847
Jefferson County Parks and Recreation: Lawrence and Tyler; Port Townsend, 98368; 385-2221
Lighthouse Marine Park (Whatcom County): 811 Marine Drive; Point Roberts, 98281; 945-4911
Pillar Point County Park (Clallam County); 928-3201
Salt Creek County Park (Clallam County); 928-3441
Semiahmoo Park (Whatcom County): 9261 Semiahmoo Parkway; Blaine, 98230; 371-5513
Whatcom County Parks Information: 3373 Mount Baker Highway; Bellingham, 98226; 733-2900 or 592-5161
Washington Park (City of Anacortes): Parks and Recreation Dept.; P.O. Box 547; Anacortes, 98221; 293-4541

WILDLIFE REFUGES

Dungeness National Wildlife Refuge Area; 753-9476
Skagit Wildlife Recreation Area; 445-4441

B. Nautical Charts and Maps

Sketch maps in this book are intended for general orientation only. Appropriate nautical charts should be used on all Washington waters. They can be purchased at map stores and many marine-supply centers.

NOAA chart 18423 SC, *Bellingham to Everett Including San Juan Islands*, is a folio of charts, scale 1:80,000, including some detailed insets. It covers most of the water areas in this book. Chart folio 18445 SC, *Puget Sound—Possession Sound to Olympia Including Hood Canal* covers the southern tip of Whidbey Island.

The following charts cover areas not included in the folios:

18421, *Strait of Juan de Fuca to Strait of Georgia* (scale 1:30,000)
18460, *Strait of Juan de Fuca Entrance* (scale 1:100,000)
18465, *Strait of Juan de Fuca—Eastern Part* (scale 1:80,000)
18471, *Approaches to Admiralty Inlet—Dungeness to Oak Bay* (scale 1:40,000)

A book by Totem Publications (Camano Island) *Street and Road Atlas of Whatcom, Island and Skagit Counties*, has detailed street maps that are useful for locating out-of-the-way nooks and crannies.

USGS topographical maps are not necessary for any of the hiking described in this book, but the 7½' series maps are both useful and interesting. All are available at hiking or map stores.

C. Quick Reference to Facilities and Recreation

Some kinds of marine recreation—such as boating, fishing, and beachcombing—are found throughout North Puget Sound. Others, however, are more specific to particular areas. The table on the following pages provides a quick reference to facilities and activities in the major areas covered in this book.

- *Marine Services* include fuel and marine supplies and repair; in some places they may be of a very limited nature.
- *Shopping/Food* generally includes groceries, cafes or restaurants, and a varying range of other types of stores. These too may be of a limited nature.
- *Floats/Buoys* refers to marinas that have transient moorage as well as to public facilities at marine parks.
- *Launch Facilities* may be only a shore access for hand-carried boats. Hoists and slings are always located at commercial marinas. Ramps may be at either commercial or public facilities.
- *Point of Interest* includes historical or educational displays, museums, and self-guided nature trails.

Some facilities listed may be entirely at commercial resorts or marinas; some may close in the off season. For detailed information read the description of specific areas in the text.

H = Hoist; R = Ramp; C = Hand Carry
* = Boat access only; ** = Land access only
( ) = Nearby; [ ] = Freshwater

1. STRAIT OF GEORGIA

	U.S. Customs	Marine Services	Shopping/Food	Floats/Buoys	Launch Facilities	Fishing Pier	Boat Fishing	Shellfish	Paddling	Scuba Diving	Swimming Beach	Camping	Picnicking	Walking/Hiking	Point of Interest
Point Roberts	•	•	•	•	H		•	•	•						•
Lighthouse Marine County Park			•		R		•	•	•		•	•	•		•
Blaine	•	•	•	•	R	•	•		•						•
Semiahmoo Spit	(•)	•	•	•	H		•		•						
Semiahmoo County Park					C		•	•	•		•		•	•	•
Birch Bay			•		C		•	•	•		•		•	•	
Birch Bay State Park					C		•	•	•	•	•	•	•	•	

2. BELLINGHAM BAY

	U.S. Customs	Marine Services	Shopping/Food	Floats/Buoys	Launch Facilities	Fishing Pier	Boat Fishing	Shellfish	Paddling	Scuba Diving	Swimming Beach	Camping	Picnicking	Walking/Hiking	Point of Interest
Gooseberry Point		•	•		H/R		•		•						•
Legoe Bay (Lummi Island)			•		R										
Lummi Island Recreation Site				•					•			•	•		
Bellingham		•	•	•	H/R	•	•		•		•		•	•	•
Larrabee State Park					R		•		•	•	•	•	•	•	
North Beach (Guemes Island)					C				•					•	
Young County Park					C			•	•		•		•	•	
Strawberry Island Recreation Site'									•	•		•	•		
Cypress Head Recreation Site*				•					•	•		•	•	•	
Pelican Beach Recreation Site*				•				•	•	•	•	•	•	•	
Cone Islands State Park*									•	•					

3. FIDALGO ISLAND AND PADILLA BAY

	U.S. Customs	Marine Services	Shopping/Food	Floats/Buoys	Launch Facilities	Fishing Pier	Boat Fishing	Shellfish	Paddling	Scuba Diving	Swimming Beach	Camping	Picnicking	Walking/Hiking	Point of Interest
Saddlebag Island State Park*							•	•	•			•	•	•	
Bay View Launch Ramp					R										
Bay View State Park					C				•		•	•	•		
Breazeale Interpretive Center**														•	•
Swinomish Channel Boat Launch					R								•		
March Point Boat Launch					R	•	•	•				•	•		
Anacortes	•	•	•	•	H				•				•	•	•
Washington Park (Anacortes)					R			•	•	•	•	•	•	•	•
Burrows Bay (Flounder Bay)		•	•	•	H	•	•								
La Conner		•	•	•	H	•			•			•	•	•	•
Pioneer City Park (La Conner)					R							•	•	•	•

4. SKAGIT DELTA AND CAMANO ISLAND

	U.S. Customs	Marine Services	Shopping/Food	Floats/Buoys	Launch Facilities	Fishing Pier	Boat Fishing	Shellfish	Paddling	Scuba Diving	Swimming Beach	Camping	Picnicking	Walking/Hiking	Point of Interest
Skagit Wildlife Recreation Area					R		•	•	•				•	•	•
Leque Island					R									•	
Kayak Point County Park				•	R	•	•		•	•	•	•	•	•	

	U. S. Customs	Marine Services	Shopping/Food	Floats/Buoys	Launch Facilities	Fishing Pier	Boat Fishing	Shellfish	Paddling	Scuba Diving	Swimming Beach	Camping	Picnicking	Walking/Hiking	Point of Interest
Utsalady County Park					R										
Saratoga Passage Beach Accesses					R										
Onamac Point*							•			•					
Camano Island State Park					R		•	•	•	•	•	•	•	•	•
Cavelero Beach County Park					R				•		•		•		
English Boom					C										•

5. DECEPTION PASS STATE PARK

	U. S. Customs	Marine Services	Shopping/Food	Floats/Buoys	Launch Facilities	Fishing Pier	Boat Fishing	Shellfish	Paddling	Scuba Diving	Swimming Beach	Camping	Picnicking	Walking/Hiking	Point of Interest
Cornet Bay	(•)	(•)		•	R/H				•				•	•	
Hope and Skagit Islands*				•			•	•	•			•	•	•	
Bowman and Rosario Bays				•	R	•	•		•	•		•	•	•	
Pass Lake**					[R]		[•]		[•]				•	•	
Cranberry Lake					[R]	[•]			[•]		•	•	•	•	

6. WHIDBEY ISLAND

	U. S. Customs	Marine Services	Shopping/Food	Floats/Buoys	Launch Facilities	Fishing Pier	Boat Fishing	Shellfish	Paddling	Scuba Diving	Swimming Beach	Camping	Picnicking	Walking/Hiking	Point of Interest
Joseph Whidbey State Park					C						•		•		
Point Partridge Launch Ramp					R										
Libby Beach County Park					C								•	•	
Fort Ebey State Park**												•	•	•	•
Point Partridge Recreation Site**												•	•	•	
Strawberry Point Boat Launch					R										
Oak Harbor	•	•		•	S/R	•	•						•		
City Park (Oak Harbor)		(•)			R	•	•				•	•	•		•
Monroe's Landing County Park					R										
Coupeville	•	•		•	R	•			•				•		•
Ebey's Landing State Park														•	•
Fort Casey State Park/Keystone					R					•		•	•	•	
South Whidbey State Park												•	•	•	
Bush Point	•	•			H										
Mutiny Bay Launch Ramp					R										
Double Bluff State Park					C			•	•		•		•	•	
Dave Mackie County Park		(•)			R			•	•		•		•		
Freeland County Park		(•)			R								•	•	
Langley	•	•		•	R	•	•				•		•	•	•
Columbia Beach (Clinton)		•					•								
Whidbey Island Road Ends					C										

7. ADMIRALTY INLET

	U. S. Customs	Marine Services	Shopping/Food	Floats/Buoys	Launch Facilities	Fishing Pier	Boat Fishing	Shellfish	Paddling	Scuba Diving	Swimming Beach	Camping	Picnicking	Walking/Hiking	Point of Interest
Lower Oak Bay County Park					R		•	•	•	•	•		•		
Hadlock Lions Park							•						•		

	U. S. Customs	Marine Services	Shopping/Food	Floats/Buoys	Launch Facilities	Fishing Pier	Boat Fishing	Shellfish	Paddling	Scuba Diving	Swimming Beach	Camping	Picnicking	Walking/Hiking	Point of Interest
South Indian Island County Park					C		•	•	•	•	•		•	•	
East Beach County Park					C			•					•		
Mystery Bay State Park			•		R			•	•				•		
Fort Flagler State Park			•	•	R	•	•	•	•	•	•	•	•	•	•
Hadlock		(•)			R								•		
Old Fort Townsend State Park				•				•				•	•	•	•
Port Townsend	•	•	•	•	H/R		•		•		•	•	•	•	•
Chetzemoka Park (Port Townsend)											•		•	•	
North Beach County Park					C						•		•		
Fort Worden State Park			•	•	R	•	•	•	•	•	•	•	•	•	•

8. EASTERN STRAIT OF JUAN DE FUCA

	U. S. Customs	Marine Services	Shopping/Food	Floats/Buoys	Launch Facilities	Fishing Pier	Boat Fishing	Shellfish	Paddling	Scuba Diving	Swimming Beach	Camping	Picnicking	Walking/Hiking	Point of Interest
Diamond Point					C										
Gardiner Boat Launch Ramp					R										
Panorama Vista Access									•					•	
Pitship Point		•	•	•	R	•	•	•	•		•		•		
Sequim Bay State Park				•	R	•	•	•	•			•	•		
Marlyn Nelson County Park					R								•	•	
Dungeness Boat Launch					R										
Cline Spit County Park					R										
Dungeness Recreation Area**													•	•	•
Dungeness National Wildlife Refug								•	•		•			•	•
Port Angeles	•	•	•	•	R	•	•		•			•	•	•	•

9. WESTERN STRAIT OF JUAN DE FUCA

	U. S. Customs	Marine Services	Shopping/Food	Floats/Buoys	Launch Facilities	Fishing Pier	Boat Fishing	Shellfish	Paddling	Scuba Diving	Swimming Beach	Camping	Picnicking	Walking/Hiking	Point of Interest
Freshwater Bay County Park					R					•			•		
Striped Peak Scenic Area**														•	•
Salt Creek County Park					C				•	•	•	•	•	•	•
Whiskey Creek (Resort)					R		•						•		
Lyre River (Resort)			•		R		•						•	•	
Murdock Creek Access					C								•		
Twin Rivers					C										
Jim Creek (Resort)			•		R		•						•		
Pillar Point County Park					R		•	•					•	•	
Clallam Bay County Park			(•)		C				•				•	•	
Sekiu		•	•	•	R		•			•			•	•	
Sail River (Resort)					H		•						•		
Neah Bay	•	•	•	•	H/R		•						•	•	•

D. Selected References

HISTORY

Eastwood, Harland, Sr. *Fort Whitman on Puget Sound, 1911-1945*. Lopez, Wa.: Twin Anchors Co., 1983.

Elmore, Helen Troy. *This Isle of Guemes*. Guemes Island, Wa.: Community Club of Guemes Island, 1973.

Faber, Jim. *Steamer's Wake*. Seattle, Wa.: Enetai Press, 1985.

Gibbs, Jim A. *Lighthouses of the Pacific*. West Chester, Pa.: Schiffer Publishing, Ltd., 1986.

Gregory, V.J. *Keepers at the Gate*. Port Townsend, Wa.: Port Townsend Publishing Co., 1976.

Hansen, Kenneth C. *The Maiden of Deception Pass, a Spirit in Cedar*. Anacortes, Wa.: Samish Experience Productions, 1983.

Hilson, Stephen E. *Exploring Puget Sound and British Columbia*. Holland, Mich.: Van Winkle Publishing, 1975.

Meany, Edmond S. *Vancouver's Discovery of Puget Sound*. New York: The Macmillan Company, 1907.

Phillips, James W. *Washington State Place Names*. Seattle and London: University of Washington Press, 1971.

Russell, Karen, and Bean, Jeanne. *Marrowstone*. Port Townsend, Wa.: Port Townsend Publishing Co., 1978.

Williamson, Joe, and Gibbs, Joe. *Maritime Memories of Puget Sound*. Seattle: Superior Publishing Co., 1976.

BEACHES AND MARINE LIFE

Kozloff, Eugene N. *Seashore Life of Puget Sound, The Strait of Georgia, and the San Juan Archipelago*. Seattle and London: University of Washington Press, 1973.

McLachlan, Dan H., and Ayres, Jak. *Fieldbook of Pacific Northwest Sea Creatures*. Happy Camp, Ca.: Naturegraph Publications, 1979.

Puget Sound Public Shellfish Sites. Olympia: State of Washington Department of Fisheries, 1979.

Sheely, Terry W. *The Complete Handbook on Washington's Clams/Crabs/Shellfish*. Snohomish, Wa.: Osprey Press, n.d.

Smith, Lynnwood S. *Living Shores of the Pacific Northwest*. Seattle: Pacific Search Books, 1976.

Your Public Beaches: Strait of Juan de Fuca. Olympia: State of Washington Department of Natural Resources, n.d.

Your Public Beaches: North Puget Sound. Olympia: State of Washington Department of Natural Resources, 1978.

NATURE

Angell, Tony, and Balcom, Kenneth C. II. *Marine Birds and Mammals of Puget Sound*. Seattle: Washington Sea Grant Program, 1982.

Wahl, Terence R., and Paulson, Dennis R. *A Guide to Bird Finding in Washington*. Bellingham, Wa.: T. R. Wahl, 1981.

BOATING, PADDLING

Hilson, Stephen E. *Exploring Puget Sound and British Columbia.* Holland, Mi.: Van Winkel Publishing Co., 1975.

Pacific Boating Almanac: Pacific Northwest and Alaska. Ventura, Ca.: Western Marine Enterprises, Inc., published annually.

United States Coast Pilot: 7 (Pacific Coast: California, Oregon, Washington, and Hawaii). Washington, D.C.: U.S. Department of Commerce, published annually.

Washburne, Randel. *Kayak Trips in Puget Sound and the San Juan Islands.* Seattle: Pacific Search Press, 1986.

BICYCLING

Woods, Erin and Bill. *Bicycling the Backroads of Northwest Washington.* 2nd ed. Seattle: The Mountaineers, 1984.

HIKING

Manning, Harvey. *Footsore 3: Walks and Hikes Around Puget Sound.* Seattle: The Mountaineers, 1978.

SCUBA DIVING

Fischnaller, Steve. *Northwest Shore Dives.* Edmonds, Wa.: Bio-Marine Images, 1986.

Pratt-Johnson, Betty. *141 Dives in the Protected Waters of Washington and British Columbia.* Seattle: The Writing Works, 1976.

FISHING

Haw, Frank, and Buckley, Raymond M. *Saltwater Fishing in Washington.* 2nd ed. Seattle: Stan Jones Publishing, Inc., 1981.

Olander, Doug. *Northwest Coastal Fishing Guide.* Seattle: The Writing Works, 1984.

INDEX

About the authors:
Seattle residents, the Muellers have been active in the outdoors around Puget Sound for well over twenty years. Both Marge and Ted are long-time mountain climbers and worked with Mountain Rescue Council; they have also instructed in mountain climbing through the University of Washington. More than a decade ago they added sailing to their round of interests and, with their two children, began wandering the inlets and outlets of the Sound year round.

Researching and writing the *Afoot & Afloat* series took the Muellers more than eight years, and included visits to every beach, bay, island and "point of interest" covered in the text, plus many hours spent in libraries and museums and contacting land management agencies for historical and useful information.

The Muellers' first book, *Northwest Ski Trails,* was also published by The Mountaineers.

Other books from The Mountaineers include:

THE SAN JUAN ISLANDS, Afoot & Afloat. Marge and Ted Mueller

MIDDLE PUGET SOUND, Afoot & Afloat. Marge and Ted Mueller

SOUTH PUGET SOUND, Afoot & Afloat. Marge and Ted Mueller

BIRDING IN THE SAN JUAN ISLANDS: Mark Lewis and Fred Sharpe. Guide to locating the birds in the Islands, understanding their behavior.

FOOTSORE: Walks and Hikes Around Puget Sound. Harvey Manning, Vol. 1 — Seattle, Issaquah Alps. Vol. 2 — Snoqualmie to Skykomish. Vol. 3 — Everett to Bellingham. Vol. 4 — Puyallup, Nisqually, Kitsap.

TRIPS AND TRAILS Series. E. M. Sterling. Camping facilities, short hikes from campgrounds. Vol. 1 — North Cascades. Vol. 2 — Olympics, South Cascades, Mt. Rainier.

For complete, illustrated catalog, write:

The Mountaineers
1011 S.W. Klickitat Way, Suite 107, Seattle, WA 98134